THE UNSEXPECTED STORY

THE UNSEXPECTED STORY

Darren Roberts

THE UNSEXPECTED STORY

COPYRIGHT © 2012 DARREN B. ROBERTS
All rights reserved.

First Edition

Cover illustration by Natalie Shau
Cover design by Gavin Antill
Edited by Kathee Brewer & Erin Zavala

Library of Congress Cataloging-in-Publication Data has been applied for.

ISBN: 978-0-9854032-0-1 (Hardback)
ISBN: 978-0-9854032-1-8 (Paperback)
ISBN: 978-0-9854032-2-5 (eBook)

For more information visit:
darrenroberts.com
theunsexpectedstory.com

THE REAL STORY ABOUT THE BILLION-DOLLAR
ADULT ENTERTAINMENT INDUSTRY

THE UNSEXPECTED STORY

DARREN ROBERTS

Author's Note

The material in this book is the result of dozens of interviews conducted by the author and his publishing team. In some cases, interviews and text were excerpted from other sources, including magazines, newspapers, journals, websites, and other books. You will find a complete list of these sources located on the last few pages of this book. We would like to acknowledge and give proper recognition to all of these sources and to the individuals whom have dedicated so much to preserving our rights to freedom of speech and expression.

Acknowledgments

I would like to thank and give special recognition to the following individuals for their cooperation, encouragement, and support throughout the years.

Paul Fishbein
Peter Acworth, Joanna Angel, Kevin Beechum,
Barrett Blade, Kathee Brewer, Greg Clayman, Scott Coffman,
Susan Colvin, Chris Cuffaro, jessica drake, Greg Dumas,
Scott & Sue Field, Larry Flynt, Teresa Flynt, Teri Hernandez,
Steve Hirsch, Ethan Imboden, David Joseph, Joy King,
Michael Klein, Sunny Leone, Christian Mann, Nick Manning,
Steve Orenstein, Theo Sapoutzis, Lou Sirkin, Lucky Smith,
Stephanie Smith, John Stagliano, Bobbi Starr, and Allison Vivas

Contents

Foreword

When it comes to subjects that inspire strong emotions, few topics compare to the adult entertainment industry. The idea of broadcasted sex, whether in print, in a movie, on a computer screen, or in any other format, may be considered lewd and unacceptable by some while it is readily accepted as a form of entertainment and arousal by others.

But the world of adult entertainment is so much more. While pornography may seem straightforward, sex is actually only the tip of the adult industry iceberg. Much like the bigger portion of an iceberg exists below the waterline, the majority of the adult industry's work and innovation takes place when the cameras are not rolling.

Adult entertainment is a business staffed by countless employees, marketers, executives and other professionals, the majority of whom will never see their names in the credits of a film. Many go to work in offices similar to those found anywhere else in corporate America. They generate tax revenue, create jobs and contribute to the economy. Admittedly sex, or the illusion of sex, may be the most apparent product of this behemoth moneymaking machine, but behind the scenes lays a highly profitable and relevant business plan that has been modeled and copied by mainstream companies across America and around the globe.

For eleven years I served as the chief executive officer of *AVN Media Network*, an industry trade publisher and adult entertainment integrated-media company. To say that I could have predicted I would end up in this role would be a gross exaggeration, especially since I grew up in a conservative, albeit entrepreneurial, environment. They say joy is found not in the destination, but in the journey one takes along the way, and what a journey it has been. I have learned far more about business, ethics, and humanity than most people experience in a lifetime.

When I joined the AVN team in 1996, the company was already thirteen years mature and operating under the leadership of its founder, Paul Fishbein. At that time, the company's key product was *AVN Magazine*, a monthly trade journal dedicated to informing adult retailers about changes in business or breaking news. The publication's ad revenues were healthy, and the company's brand was perfectly positioned for growth within the business-to-business sector. My mission was to design a growth plan that would convert the boutique publishing company into a full-service, integrated-media corporation serving all of the industry's business-to-business needs. During my tenure as CEO, we successfully created more than a dozen vertically integrated specialty magazines, eleven websites and seven trade shows, and developed the AVN Awards Show into a globally recognized brand. This vertical growth allowed the company to increase its revenues by eight hundred percent over the course of a few years.

As a business, the adult entertainment industry has an amazing composition. To say it is multi-faceted would be an understatement. While the word pornography might be synonymous with the industry, the product lines are diverse. Many people might first think about videos or movies; others about the Internet and the millions of websites offering round-the-clock, on-demand entertainment. Still others may think about the "accessories" of the industry: the toys, glossy magazines, and the celebrity personalities who go by single names that are as easy to recognize as Angelina, Madonna, and Britney.

Few businesses can trace their roots through the ages the way adult entertainment can. After all, pornography, while it may be ugly or sinful to some, is a natural form of self-expression for others. The industry's journey, development, and challenges made it what it is and will carry it into the future. Regardless the roadblocks it has faced or the controversy it inspires, there is little doubt the industry will work to maintain a platform that not only makes money, but also stays at the forefront of new media and technological advancements. That's how the industry has garnered success in the past, and that's how it will continue to connect with consumers who are eager to open their wallets in order to fulfill fantasies.

My aim in writing this book is not to provide readers with some tantalizing tale that divulges the salacious secrets of professional erotica. Nor is my goal to condemn or condone the personal beliefs or views about pornography espoused by any group in society. Those books already have been written. Rather, I want to deliver a firsthand account of and an unbiased look at the processes that have built empires while examining the faults and weaknesses that led to cracks in the facade.

The modern adult entertainment industry has evolved over the past thirty years into a multibillion-dollar economic engine comprising of production and distribution, marketing and advertising, technology and promotion, as well as the performers— collectively called "talent"—and what they create. There are many moving parts. While they compose a very specific business model, the components have not always worked together. Combined with outside attacks related to social concerns, changes in media and technology, and other factors, players in the industry have played roles in creating immense fortunes, but just as often have borne witness to their demise.

It's amazing to think this industry once carried a sizeable amount of taboo. During my career I often found myself having to persuade and cajole qualified business professionals into interviewing for lucrative positions after they learned the industry in which *AVN* operates. I also walked into banks, large amounts of cash in hand to open a business account, only to be turned away after revealing the industry in which my company operated.

And *AVN* is just a trade publication! The magazine reported about the business of adult entertainment. We didn't produce explicit material ourselves.

Today, the story is quite different. So different, in fact, that one of the biggest former porn stars is able to see her face on a Times

Square billboard without offending the masses and their better angels. The industry's products are so widespread and the offering so diverse that adult entertainment permeates almost every sector of American life: on-demand video in hotel rooms, on computers at home and at work, in family-owned and -operated neighborhood video stores, at adult stores off highway exit ramps and even within the pages of that old-fashioned media at a local bookstore…the magazine.

This book offers insight into the modern composition and business model of the adult entertainment industry, through my eyes and the eyes of other movers and shakers in the industry. I have been fortunate enough to build relationships with some preeminent professionals who witnessed firsthand the changes the business has undergone, before, during and after my tenure at AVN. I interviewed them for this book. I hope you appreciate their unique opinions, accounts and memories.

My goal is to help you understand how the modern industry has developed and how the business plan has been adapted by organizations that seek to maximize their profits and create megalithic brands.

The old saying is true, to a point: Sex sells. However, nothing sells without a great business plan.

PART ONE

A Timeless Art
Pornography's Progression into Modern Day

A popular adage notes, "A dirty book is rarely dusty." While the author of the quote is unknown, the fact remains that pornography, and people's interest in the art form, are nothing new. Instead, pornography's lure has been handed down from one generation to the next, a form of self-expression that has stood the test of time and is not going anywhere, at least anytime soon.

Pornography, as it is understood today, is the product of an evolutionary process as old as mankind itself. What contemporary society considers pornography is vastly different from what the ancients may have considered arousing or sexually explicit. Societal attitudes about public displays of genitalia and copulation also have changed many times over the years.

A fascination with erotic imagery goes hand-in-hand with being a sexual creature. Despite contemporary critics' claim that only marginal figures and morally corrupt individuals condone pornography, erotic materials actually have held a vital role in the development of society throughout history.

Not to say that every cave drawing of a naked person is a representation of pornography, but there is no denying that the masses always have been hypnotized by sex—not only as a means for procreation and fertility, but also as a component of religious worship and as a form of pleasure and enjoyment. Sex is one of the historical constants in every society, and ultimately, the contemporary adult entertainment industry is a by-product of sex by way of a business endeavor. After all, sex on display is just that; voyeurism.

Of course, the timeline associated with the modern adult industry goes back approximately thirty years, to the early 1980s and the advent of home video. Pornography itself goes back much farther. The earliest known example of pornography—a statue of a couple copulating, discovered in Germany in 2003—is thought to be more than 7,000 years old. Instead of a testament to fertility, the beauty of the female form, or even homage to the phallus, archaeologists speculate the statue's undeniable representation of heterosexual intercourse may have been a chic conversation piece, or even possibly a basis for educating or instructing on personal sexual activity.[1]

Moving forward in time, the Ancient Greeks certainly were not prudes about depicting sexual activity. Greek art overflows with evidence of how intrigued they were with the body. Some of the most enduring sculptures, paintings and religious carvings from ancient Greece depict nudity and sexual activity.

Just as society itself has changed over time, so have opinions about sex and its representation "on paper," so to speak. And the question remains: When did people begin believing sex, and the pornography that developed as a normal offshoot of the activity, was taboo? With so much evidence to support pornography's emergence almost concurrently with man's, when did people begin embracing the idea that depictions of sex and sexuality are deviant, disorderly and perverse?

Pornography in Early America

The roots of current American attitudes about sex and pornography lie in our puritanical roots.   In the early days of American colonialism, the majority of indignation about the "obscene" material finding its way across the ocean from Europe (specifically France) arose in the Massachusetts Bay Colony.   Of course, these were the same people who burned women at the stake based on claims of witchcraft.   More likely the women who met such tragic ends were independent thinkers with intellectual, medicinal, or scientific talent.   Men in early America carried the same fears of independent and empowered women as luddites do today. Only the language has changed: Instead of labeling porn stars as witches, modern critics call them whores.

An early account of the colonial government trying to suppress "sex talk" was printed in the first issue of the colonial newspaper *Publick Occurrences*.   The article related, in some detail, the scandalous behavior in the French Royal Court, taking particular aim at King Louis XIV.   It seems Louis was looking to get it on with his son's wife, and the French being the French, were none too shy their opinions about the whole sordid affair.   The Massachusetts Bay Colony government was not pleased to have this information thrust under the noses of its citizens.   Consequently, the newspaper's first issue was suppressed, becoming one of the earliest victims of censorship in the New World.[2]

Shortly afterward, in 1712, colonial Massachusetts passed a law barring public dissemination of "obscene" writing and pictures.   The new colonial government believed it was responsible for the souls of its citizens and considered obscenity a surefire way to earn a ticket to Hell.

Not all individuals living in colonial times were so prudish regarding sex.   One of America's Founding Fathers (several, if we really wanted to get into it) understood that certain natural "urges" were going to be present in a person, regardless how often an individual attended church.

In 1745, Benjamin Franklin published the pamphlet *Advice to a Young Man*.   The tract, an instructional manual defining how to choose a mistress, stated that when it came to recreational sex, older women were preferable to younger women because "There is no hazard of children, which irregularly produc'd may be attended with much inconvenience." Franklin also wrote "...the sin is less. The debauching [of] a virgin may be her ruin, and make her for life unhappy."   As if that weren't enough, Franklin also insisted older women made better mistresses because "They are so grateful!"[3]

While this may seem humorous compared to contemporary attitudes about sex, Franklin certainly did not shy from the importance of the act, nor its place in the life of a person. He wrote, "I know of no medicine fit to diminish the violent natural inclinations you mention, and if I did, I think I should not communicate it to you... It is the most natural state of man, and therefore, the state in which you are most likely to find solid happiness."[4]

In other words, the Distinguished Gentleman from Philadelphia was saying, "Hey, sex is fun. It's natural. Why not indulge?" Certainly, that mantra has been passed through the centuries, at least by those who feel enlightened about the subject.   It is this contradictory heritage that has fueled the growth of the adult entertainment industry while at the same time demonizing the business.

The Onset of the Peep Show

The modern adult entertainment industry had to start somewhere. Before the mass-production of magazines became affordable and long before videotape was invented, modern adult entertainment got its start in the humble peep show.

Initially used to display rarities at carnivals, circuses and fairs, peep shows as a form of entertainment can be traced back to the 15th century. At their onset they were more likely to appeal to the imagination of children and thus displayed exotic animals or insects instead of nudity or salacious content. Eventually entrepreneurs realized that with a few changes, peep shows would encourage men to open their wallets in order to see something out of the norm. That's when peep shows became synonymous with pornography.

The peep show, or peep box, began as little more than a wooden box with a hole, or multiple holes, cut into it to provide viewing access for one or more people. Considered a form of performance art, peep shows lured with the promise of the unknown. As technology progressed, a telescope-like lens was added to provide a clearer view of the secrets inside the box. The first pornographic peep shows included racy pictures, nude pictures and the like, before graduating to movies, stripping, and then live sex acts.

One of the earliest and most popular peep shows was *"Bedroom Secrets."* Produced during the late 1920s, the British show cost a penny and featured women in various states of undress. Think of it as early reality TV, a kind of *"Big Brother"* that allowed a voyeuristic look at the everyday acts going on behind women's bedroom doors. Typically, a woman would take off her dress and parade around in her bra and panties, sit in a provocative way and draw stockings up her legs, or engage in other not-overtly-sexual activities women often do in the privacy of their boudoirs. While this sort of thing wouldn't tantalize most men looking for a cheap thrill by today's standards, at the time it was quite shocking.

As technology changed in relation to peep shows, the eroticism of the event allowed for greater user interaction. In 1925, The International Mutoscope Reel Company started a new trend when it created one of the first erotic films and described the new medium to the public as "Artistic Figure Studies." Mutoscope was among the first to promote the idea, "Hey, this nudity and sex—it's not naughty. It's *art!*" The Mutoscope productions allowed viewers to stop the movie and view the slides up close...since, you know, it's art and connoisseurs might want to get a better look.

The peep show continued to progress, barely slowing down even during WWII. Apparently, war doesn't get in the way of sex, and as the economy boomed, so did production of the films used in the machines.

No discussion of peep shows would be complete without mentioning the era during which this form of entertainment reached its heyday. Consider Times Square during the 1970s. Long before Rudy Giuliani took all the fun out of this New York City real estate, it was known as a haven for seedy, smutty peep show establishments. Times Square was not the family-friendly tourist destination it is today. Indeed, Times Square offered almost any vice for which a person might lust. Sex, drugs, masturbation? No problem, you could find it in Times Square.

By the 1970s, the peep show had evolved, and it found its penultimate expression in Times Square. Consumers could see anything from a nude girl dancing within a coin-operated Plexiglas booth to live sex shows starring a man and woman, or multiples of both.

Eventually, due to economies of scale and a general relaxing of social customs brought about by the sexual revolution of the 1960s, the single-viewer erotic peep show morphed into erotic theaters in which the audience sat around a glass-enclosed stage. Businesses of this kind are still in operation today in places like Las Vegas, but they do not garner the attention they once did.

The Modern Business of Sex

More innovation has occurred within the past thirty years than took place in the preceding 7,000. As new technology, formats and distribution have changed, so too have the challenges facing producers, giving rise to new and ever-more-creative strategies for connecting with consumers.

Consider this: Although what we think of as the modern adult entertainment industry found its antecedents in photography, print magazines and movies more than a century ago, the majority of explosive growth has happened since pornography became accessible on VHS, then DVD, and finally, beginning in the mid-1990s, the Internet.

Steve Orenstein, president and founder of Wicked Pictures, said of the rapid expansion, "We have seen a shift in the history of the modern industry, and it is this change in accessibility which has both helped and also hurt us."

Product lifecycles in all industries follow a predictable path: Sales explode when the product is new, plateau as it ages, and then decrease as something new comes along to catch consumers' fancy or better meet their needs. The adult entertainment industry's products are no different. For instance, the iconic skin magazine *Penthouse* touted circulation of more than five million readers in the 1980s. In 2002, fewer than ten years after the public advent of the Internet, the magazine's subscriber base dropped to just 650,000.

Steve Hirsch, founder of Vivid Entertainment, reflects on the market of the 1980s, "When I founded Vivid in 1984, the market was small. Although at that time, people were just starting to shoot on video. But even at that time, people were still saying that the market was saturated, even though the market was nowhere near to what it is today. At that time, there were probably only ten real companies out there putting out movies, maybe one a month. Of course, that was at the time when we were only starting to see local video stores carrying adult products."

Moving forward, the Internet had a similar effect on DVDs, a technology the adult entertainment industry embraced when it was introduced in 1998 because of the potential to develop interactive discs and other new features. The DVD's lifecycle was even more abbreviated than that of its predecessor, home video cassettes, which revolutionized adult movie distribution when they were introduced in 1976. Millions of adult DVDs were rented and sold annually until 2006, when a market once considered invincible dropped 15 percent as online video and other subscription services displaced traditional distribution channels by proving even more affordable and convenient.

"The Internet changed everything more than anything else in recent history," said John Stagliano, president and founder of Evil Angel. "We didn't feel the change until the middle part of the first decade of the new millennium; so instead of making 90 percent of my revenue from DVD sales, [Evil Angel] makes 40 percent from that avenue."

Just like any other industry, adult entertainment must modify its product offering and service delivery based upon what customers want. Flexibility plus an open mind equals innovation. As an industry, adult entertainment has learned that lesson over and over again— some individuals and companies more quickly and more successfully than others. One other lesson stands out in adult entertainment's history, as well: Embrace new technology with a vengeance and master it before it masters you.

The way the adult industry conquered Apple's iPad is a stellar example of that philosophy in action. From the beginning, Apple Inc. has been vehemently opposed to allowing X-rated content on any of its platforms. Nevertheless, within twenty-four hours of the iPad's launch in 2010, adult studio Pink Visual launched the first website specifically created to deliver porn to the new Apple product. Apple may be able to control what is available in its AppStore and on iTunes, but it cannot prevent technology wizards within the adult entertainment industry from using the Internet to reach tech-savvy consumers with disposable income.

"I look at where we are with mobile [distribution], and I want to make sure I take into account some of the early lessons learned by large adult companies on the Internet," said Pink Visual President Allison Vivas. "You can't wait [for permission]."

Vivas and Pink Visual are prime examples of the kind of business smarts that have served the adult entertainment industry well over the past thirty years. No longer comprising a seedy underground populated by disreputable characters in trench coats, today's adult entertainment industry is as high-tech as Silicone Valley ever was. Adult entrepreneurs have realized they are at the mercy, and the whim, of consumers—and they had better deliver what consumers want, when they want it and in the format they desire. Because if they don't? Someone else will—or consumers will take matters into their own hands.

The industry has developed a mindset and a business model many mainstream companies envy, and the secret isn't that complicated. In a nutshell: View changes in technology as opportunities, not something to be mistrusted, suppressed or feared.

Creation of the Business Model

The actual business model developed by members of the industry has been copied by mainstream corporations the world over. For instance, Comcast, Time Warner and AT&T all profit because of their affiliation with adult entertainment. Even the old American standard in car manufacturing, General Motors, has reaped a profit from pornography. How? DirecTV, owned by Hughes Technology, once was a subsidiary of GM. (The auto manufacturer sold the asset in 2007.)

This level of economic clout did not happen overnight, nor was it based on lessons easily learned. In fact, while the model followed by the industry has resulted in success, it also has left ruined fortunes and failure in its wake. If anything, the business model's evolution is an example of change management. When considering the industry's march into the current age, bear in mind that as the tools used to produce, distribute and market pornography have become more accessible and cost-effective; the marketplace itself has become more crowded.

As a whole, the industry is littered with ultra-competitive players. In that way, adult entertainment is no different from any other industry. Adult does differ from mainstream, though, in the way the players interact. In most industries, there is benefit to be gained from working together in order to fulfill common goals and protect common interests. In adult, because so many professionals take an intensely personal interest in preserving the industry's maverick reputation, such cooperation is slow to happen or doesn't happen at all.

"Marketing strategies vary, but there has always been this idea in adult of whether or not we can fit one more [competitor] in," stated Vivid's Steve Hirsch. "We had to develop a marketing plan early on."

Competition within the adult entertainment industry is fierce and becoming more so all the time, partly because of the very technology that has driven the industry's success. Despite the longstanding belief that pornography is "recession-proof," the double-whammy of a sea change in technology and a global economic recession hit the adult industry hard. Although the music industry and Hollywood survived "Napsterization," the adult industry continues to struggle with an obstacle neither of its mainstream counterparts faced: Porn is "interchangeable," meaning free products, often produced by amateurs, are acceptable substitutes.   Industry professionals agree the desire for sexually explicit material will never disappear, but a discriminating pornography consumer is much rarer than a discriminating audiophile and "free" is a powerful word.

"The thing that I know after thirty years is that the American public, as well as international consumers, will continue to desire [this material]," said Christian Mann, general manager of Evil Angel and a thirty-two-year veteran of the industry. "But it is also up to [the industry] to make consumers see the value in the product.   Our business is much more similar to that of the music business rather than the mainstream movie business.   [Evil Angel] largely breaks down our product and sells it in individual scenes, which is comparable to how the music industry sells songs."

Even though the industry has struggled to adapt in recent years, it remains committed to finding ways around what most insiders consider a temporary setback. After all, does anyone expect the pack of rebels who pioneered many aspects of e-commerce on which mainstream businesses now rely to roll over and give up? The first online subscription services, affiliate marketing, membership websites, paid video conferencing, user-contributed content destinations (precursors to YouTube), and social media marketing all are attributed to the adult industry.   The players who established these markets and perfected the mechanisms profited from their ability to evolve.   They also were the first to realize they could not continue to make money from boring or generic content.   The realization that consumers have short attention spans is central to modern industry operations.

At the end of the day, adult entertainment is a business in which there is money to be made. Industry insiders know this, mainstream companies try to emulate the successes, and consumers continue to drive the product. The point is, pornography has never been cooler or more accessible—and it's far from finished evolving.

PART TWO

Casting a Wide Net
The Scope of the Adult Entertainment Business

In today's world, product diversity coupled with overall sustainability usually dictates whether an industry or business sinks or swims. Adult entertainment has been around since the beginning of time, literally: Erotic depictions were recorded as early as the Paleolithic period, so in essence, people have been talking about sex since the moment they learned how to carve images on cave walls. However, as an industry, adult entertainment has evolved especially rapidly since the early 1980s.

Pornography, as a term, is defined as any type of media depicting sexual activity or nudity which has the ability to stimulate erotic, as opposed to aesthetic, responses. This is a broad definition, as the concept of pornography has morphed and changed over time. Furthermore, pornography, as a form of art, is subjective. While I would never consider famous nude depictions by Francisco Goya a form of pornography, there are those who would classify the art as shameful, deviant, and in bad taste. Definitions of pornography vary by culture, community, and individual, and they are anything but static.

The modern adult entertainment industry, too, has been defined and re-defined continuously in the past few decades as the face of commerce has changed. Even the term "adult entertainment" has the ability to mean many things. Indeed, there really is no one-size-fits-all product offering. Instead, consumers enjoy a wide array of products, all of them with distinct histories, development processes, and marketing plans. It is not my intention to look at each individual format—books and magazines, videos, toys and Internet-based products—and divulge their history from Day One. Rather, I intend to explore and reveal how each of these different forms became a part of the modern industry, how they have developed followings, expanded and, ultimately, become accepted as part of our culture.

Jessica Drake, contract performer for Wicked Pictures, put everything into perspective: "This business is just so big, and there are so many people involved in making some type of adult content. I don't think there is a divide between many of the divisions, and [as a whole] the business has become accepted as a part of our society."

Books and Magazines:
No Longer Hidden Under the Bed

The history of pornographic books and magazines is part of a larger historical progression of erotic depictions, imagery, and storytelling. This medium, as a whole, can be traced back to the 15th Century. As soon as the printing press was invented, humans figured out a way to provide titillating stories and erotic images to the masses, albeit in secret. Black market trade for this type of material would have been the only way to get it. Most explicit media, along with work by literary greats like Chaucer and Shakespeare, was decried by the powers that be at the time, who labeled purchasers and producers heretics and deviants. Regardless, producers continued to produce and consumers continued to consume, laying the groundwork for the adult entertainment industry that exists today.

Fast forward to the beginning of the 20th Century and to the evolution of halftone printing— a process allowing photographs and illustrations to be reproduced easily in black and white, thereby obviating the need for engravings, woodcuts, or linecuts—ushered in an age of mass-produced and -distributed illustrated magazines. The modern concept of "porn magazine" was born.

The first publicly sold erotic magazine, *Le Frisson*, appeared in France around the turn of the 20th Century. *Le Frisson* contained nude and semi-nude photographs and portraits of burlesque actresses. By modern standards, the publication seems innocent and tame, but at the time it was risqué and shocking.

As this type of magazine developed, publishers looked to attain mainstream acceptance through classification of their products as art magazines, jumping on a cultural movement termed Naturism in order to downplay the sexuality surrounding the images while continuing to promote nudity and sex.

Another popular type of early pornographic magazine was known as Tijuana Bibles. These magazines were little more than comic books containing crude, hand-drawn images, dirty stories, and low-brow sexual humor. Tijuana Bibles originally entered the U.S. market in the 1920s and peaked in popularity in the 1930s, during the Great Depression. The magazines themselves were cheap to produce *en masse*, using low-grade paper and printed on presses otherwise used to create labels for whiskey bottles. Tijuana Bibles fell out of favor as glossy, color magazines aimed at the male demographic entered the market. The first of those was *Playboy*.

The Emergence and Growth of Playboy

Hugh Hefner made quite a splash with the first edition of his magazine in December 1953. People were shocked when Marilyn Monroe appeared as the first centerfold, labeled "Sweetheart of the Month." Compare that to today's climate, in which Playmates like Kendra Wilkinson and Holly Madison are part of pop culture with their own reality TV and Las Vegas stage shows, and mainstream celebrities vie for spreads in the magazine on a monthly basis. Hefner's first edition sold for just 50 cents a copy and boasted a circulation of 50,000 readers. He produced the debut issue on the kitchen table in his apartment after he mortgaged his furniture and raised $8,000 from 45 investors, which included $1,000 from his mother, to buy the photos of Monroe and pay the cost of printing. The magazine didn't include a cover date or an issue number, because Hefner didn't want to commit to a second issue if there was no interest in the first.

The magazine sold out in two weeks.

Hefner made enough money to produce a second issue, and *Playboy* was born.

While Hefner's foray into publishing pictures of nude women was no new thing, the concept of his magazine was. Hefner deliberately created a liberal voice in Post-war America, communicating directly with masculine middle-class males who sought validation of a dream: Sex and sexuality were part of "the good life," normal and a form of recreation.

Playboy arose at a time when American men and women were beginning to play with an expanded, very personal notion of sexuality. Even amidst the outrage from some factions, men were intrigued, and certain women began to consider becoming a centerfold, now termed "Playmate of the Month." With the advent of the Sexual Revolution in the early 1960s, *Playboy's* Chicago Headquarters became The Place to Be, and women like Sophia Loren, Jane Fonda, Sharon Tate, and Elizabeth Taylor were proud to grace the cover of the magazine.

As the 1970s dawned, *Playboy* reached the pinnacle of its empire. In 1972, the magazine touted more than 7.2 million readers and gross annual revenues of more than $20 million. However, a challenge was brewing. Hefner had expanded beyond his initial offering of a glossy magazine, deciding to produce movies and television shows, record music and create sheet music, and develop a gambling and casino division. Unfortunately, many of these ventures diluted Hefner's brand, and the company started losing money.

Partially for a change in scenery and partially to boost his brand with celebrities and the entertainment industry, Hefner relocated his headquarters to Southern California and hired former Knight-Ridder newspaper executive Derick Daniels as president and CEO of Playboy Enterprises. He also began to train Christie Hefner, his eldest daughter, for an eventual takeover of day-to-day operations. While Hugh Hefner had become somewhat ambivalent about the ongoing management of the company, he desperately wanted to boost flagging profits: Playboy Enterprises pre-tax profits grossed only $2 million in 1975 and $5 million in 1976. Hefner believed Daniels possessed the expertise necessary to turn the company around while Hefner continued to lead the artistic end of the business as editor-in-chief.

When Daniels arrived at Playboy in 1976, he discovered a company in disarray. Luckily, he had the full support of Hefner, who agreed to go along with any plan of action Daniels suggested. Daniels decided to reorganize the company, cleaning out and removing unnecessary overhead at all levels and ridding the enterprise of more than 100 employees ranging from lowly second assistants to top-level managers. Additionally, Daniels decided Playboy should cut its losses in sectors not essential to its core brand. He removed the company from its involvement in movies, television, and music and started reassessing the magazine itself, defining the types of advertisers the magazine needed and redeveloping *Playboy's* central message and theme. Daniels also examined where the Playboy gambling operations fit into the brand and decided that focusing on the profitability of certain casinos in specific geographic locations could help offset recent company losses.

As the 1980s dawned, it became apparent that many of Daniels' initiatives had not produced the anticipated results. The company had been forced to sell its gambling business, which resulted in a 50-percent loss in overall income in 1982. Coupled with the $69 million off-shedding experienced in the previous two years under Daniels' control, Hefner decided Daniels had to go. He handed the reins of the family business to his daughter, Christie.

Christie had a considerable task in front of her. Not only did she wish to define herself separately and distinctly from the lifestyle excesses that were promoted by her father, but she also needed to find a way to make the magazine, and the Playboy brand, relevant again. While her father might have built the brand in a time when open sex and nudity in print was shocking, by the time Christie took control that no longer was true. A large portion of her task became to perpetuate and expand the Playboy's reputation as a touchstone in the world of men's entertainment. This was easier said than done in the 1980s, when people weren't shocked or titillated by much.

With the goal of returning *Playboy* to prominence as a Sign of the Times, Christie redirected the magazine to touch upon taboo subjects largely dismissed by the mainstream media: gay rights, AIDS and comparative research, feminism and female empowerment, government corruption, First Amendment rights and free speech. Christie was devoted to making the brand about more than just naked women. She wanted the magazine to be socially conscious and aware of international issues in order to attract a wider audience and more dedicated readership. It was because of Christie Hefner's vision and marketing savvy that the phrase, "Oh, I read *Playboy* for the articles" entered the American lexicon.

Under Christie Hefner, circulation soared to 3.4 million readers, largely because of her dedication to launching a subscription campaign and moving away from relying only on newsstand sales.

Christie also re-envisioned other distribution channels for the brand. At the outset of her tenure, the company re-entered the television space with the Playboy Channel, only to witness lackluster results from the subscription service. Christie realized that the overhead to operate a round-the-clock cable TV channel was not generating the interest, or the subscribers, the company needed in order to justify operating costs. Instead, she analyzed the viewing habits of subscribers to determine when people were most interested in viewing *Playboy*-related programming. She reorganized the channel as a pay-per-view-only operation called *Playboy At Night*, offering on-demand soft-core pornography and Playmate videos. The pay-per-view service, available to more than 4 million U.S. households through cable service providers, realized an increase in revenues and profits almost immediately. Additionally, the service entered the realm of "couples" programming, introducing erotic massage videos for men and women to view together. Suddenly, *Playboy* was inviting female partners into the private sex lives of the magazine's male subscribers.

As the 1990s dawned, *Playboy* found itself with renewed interest from consumers and subscribers, as well as with greater profitability as the brand expanded. Through the direction of Christie Hefner, the company was able to appeal to a wider variety of readers and compete more effectively with other brands, like *Penthouse* and *Hustler*, which focused on raunchier sex, greater nudity, and hardcore pornography. Playboy, as a brand, secured its status as a mainstay in the world of entertainment and became one of the first testaments to crossover between the adult entertainment industry and traditional entertainment avenues. At the beginning of the new millennium, the company rekindled its romance with gambling when the company opened The Playboy Club, a rooftop bar, and a $50,000-per-night Playboy suite at the Palms Casino Resort in Las Vegas. The properties are frequented by celebrities and ultra-rich consumers alike. Additionally, with the introduction of the reality TV show *The Girls Next Door* in 2005, the exploits of "Hef" and his (much) younger girlfriends Holly Madison, Bridget Marquardt, and Kendra Wilkinson, the brand was glamorized and introduced to the E! Network's audience. This made *Playboy* as mainstream, and as accepted, as *American Idol* and *Dancing with the Stars*.

Penthouse: A Magazine of Firsts

In 1965, as Americans were finally getting over the shocking nudity in *Playboy* and making strides toward accepting their individual sexuality amidst the social upheaval that composed the Swinging '60s, a new player entered the magazine field—and that player was determined to push the envelope and shake things up.

Penthouse magazine, founded by Bob Guccione, pushed risqué to the next level with the very first issue, published in 1965 in the United Kingdom. The magazine was the first overtly pornographic publication to show pubic hair and full frontal nudity, eclipsing *Playboy*'s journalistic oeuvre by casting aside any pretense of modesty under the banner of a new kind of "full disclosure."

The magazine began with a loan of $1,170 and a hastily acquired mailing list. Guccione intended to outdo Hefner and create a stir from Day One. His mailing list was un-vetted and therefore definitely not kosher, containing the names of clergy, school-age children, senior citizens and the families of Parliament members. As soon as the first issue went out, outrage erupted, but as they say, there is no such thing as bad publicity. Guccione ate the $264 dollar fine, and the first edition of the magazine sold out in days.

In 1969, the magazine met U.S. censors head on when *Penthouse* launched its first American edition to the overall excitement of male consumers who wanted more explicit material than *Playboy* offered. Furthermore, Guccione's shocking antics propelled *Penthouse*'s reputation. While Hefner obviously was having a great time in Chicago with his bunnies and Hollywood celebrities, Guccione spent lavishly on his infamous "Mansion in Manhattan," wearing hipster pants and silk shirts open to the waist, displaying mounds of gold chains and creating the classic pornographer stereotype. At the same time, he filled his house with philosophers, poets and intellectuals he called friends and bought enough artwork to fill a wing at the Metropolitan Museum of Art.

Amidst the apparent contradiction, Guccione grew his publishing empire, increasing his net worth to $300 million and pushing the limit on what could be shown in a magazine. As social mores changed, *Penthouse* kept up. In the 1970s, the magazine began publishing pictures of simulated sex and male genitalia, skyrocketing sales to 4.7 million copies per month.

Guccione's high profile and his magazine's unrepentant bawdiness made him a target for the anti-pornography campaigns launched by then-U.S. Attorney General Ed Meese in the 1980s. The product also came under fire by The National Federation for Decency (now known as the American Family Association, a hard-line Christian conservative group) and other anti-porn organizations, which launched boycotts of stores that carried pornographic materials. At the same time, Meese convened the powerful Commission on Pornography, which went about naming and publishing a blacklist of known pornographers—including Guccione and *Penthouse*. This puritanical movement resulted in the magazine's removal from about 20,000 retailers nationwide and significantly cut into the company's bottom line.

Guccione and the Penthouse brand spent most of the 1980s fending off and then recovering from the anti-porn attack, made worse by the scandal that erupted upon the revelation that budding adult film star Traci Lords was only 15 years old when she posed for *Penthouse* in 1984. *Penthouse* management successfully argued ignorance of Lords' deception, but the stain of alleged child sexual abuse was slow to fade.

As administrations in the White House changed in the early '90s, Guccione pushed the envelope in new directions while expanding his brand into casinos and video. While some of the controversy served *Penthouse* well, as when the magazine published photos from the *Stolen Honeymoon* sex tape starring Pamela Anderson and then-husband Tommy Lee—the magazine met declining sales and obscenity charges as pictorials pushed the line with female urination, penetration, and other acts. Additionally, Guccione felt the pinch as he struggled to grasp changes in technology, especially with the Internet suddenly throwing open the pages of his magazine…for free.

In 2003, the magazine and its parent company, General Media, filed for bankruptcy protection, and *Penthouse* was put up for sale. Shortly thereafter, in 2004, amidst new information on failed business dealings related to hotels, casinos, and even a nuclear-fusion power plant, Guccione resigned as chairman and CEO of the organization. The magazine eventually was bought, rebranded and is still in circulation today; however, readership failed to rebound.

Bob Guccione died of lung cancer in October 2010.

To date, *Penthouse* still has been unable to regain its former glory: In May 2011, FriendFinder Inc., the organization that came to own *Penthouse* through a series of acquisitions and mergers, issued an initial public offering on the NASDAQ stock exchange, becoming one of only a handful of publicly traded adult entertainment companies worldwide.

Hustler: Giving the Middle Finger to Mainstream America

While other pornographic magazines left behind-the-scenes antics to readers' imaginations, Larry Flynt's *Hustler* adopted a take-no-prisoners approach, leaving no ambiguity about what went on during the magazine's photo shoots.   The first magazine to show hardcore sex acts, penetration, spread-legged female genitalia, and vaginal and anal sex involving sex toys, *Hustler* gave the figurative middle finger to censors.The magazine was actually launched in 1974, following a variety of other Flynt adult entertainment ventures. The first, a go-go bar by the name of The Hustler Club in Dayton, Ohio, opened in 1968. It is this which gave rise to a monthly newsletter for club members, which eventually became a national magazine.

Larry Flynt states, "The newsletter or magazine was originally used to simply promote the clubs that I owned across Ohio.   It started off as a two-page newsletter, and then grew to twenty-four pages and then next thing we knew is that we had a national magazine.   It originally cost us $200 a month and we just put Polaroid pictures in the newsletter.   Inevitably, it took us a while to get our act together. I didn't have a background in publishing at all, and here we were trying to do everything, editing, photography; it was six issues before we made any money, and even then we were operating in Columbus, Ohio, not exactly the talent center of the world. I should have been in New York or L.A."

Hustler's first magazine issue did not live up to Flynt's expectations: He wanted the publication to combine the editorial tone of *Playboy* with *Penthouse's* unerring ability to arouse and offend. Flynt worked to refocus the product, dedicated to providing a raunchier and cruder experience for readers.   Instead of creating another *Playboy* or *Penthouse*, Flynt eschewed tiptoeing around the obvious: If he insulted the sensitivities of the greater public, so be it, but he would put a unique spin on sex, pornography, and what he viewed as societal hypocrisy.

"The magazine came by way of someone telling me, 'you could do what Hefner did, just opposite, he started a magazine and then got into clubs, you start in clubs and get into a magazine," stated Flynt. "I thought about that and said, 'Why not?' The thing was that I had never read any of those magazines, I was only ever interested in the real thing."

Flynt refused to appease censors by addressing social issues the way *Playboy* did in order to become relevant or garner acceptance. He figured if the magazine was about sex, it should be unabashedly, unapologetically, and unrepentantly about sex.

"I bought a *Playboy* and I thought that they were doing it all wrong. You pick up a magazine like this, and no one cares how to make the perfect martini, no one cares about what type of car you drive. Someone who buys [a skin magazine] wants to see pussy and they want jokes," commented Flynt. "With *Hustler*, there was no pretension, we didn't pretend to have any social redeeming value, it was about sex."

And the public responded. *Hustler* evoked strong feelings among Americans. The magazine made no apologies about offending almost every social group with jokes about gang rape, misogyny, homosexuality, and religion, among other topics. Conservative and women's groups repeatedly attacked the publication with obscenity charges. As Flynt's legal troubles grew, so did his readership: The uproar contributed to *Hustler*'s revenues of upwards of $500,000 per issue. After his first trial, during which he was convicted of pandering, obscenity, and organized crime, the magazine's circulation stood at 2.7 million copies monthly.

"I always operated under the notion that we appealed to the guys who had the truck driver mentality," reflected Flynt. "But then one time I was speaking at Harvard and a college professor approached me and said, 'It's not just the truck drivers, college professors read your magazine too. You would find that out if you did a demographic study of your readership.' So we decided to do [a demographic study]. We found that our readership had more degrees and was more highly educated than we thought. Our readership was more intellectual and had higher education levels than that of the readership of *Playboy*."

Regardless of the growth in sales, Flynt encountered legal challenges right and left, one of which almost took his life. While appearing for trial in Lawrenceville, Georgia, in 1978, Flynt was gunned down on the courthouse steps, taking two bullets which almost proved to be fatal. As he recovered, he became less and less interested in the management of his magazine and instead turned his attention to the adversaries who questioned his content. He infused *Hustler* with a new focus by turning his vitriol for those who would judge him into a public forum that mocked the high-handed moralists determined to see him in jail.

In 1984, Flynt set his sights on evangelical leader Jerry Falwell, featuring the televangelist in a *Hustler* article that parodied the outspoken reverend's views during a made-up interview. In the satirical piece, the writer detailed Falwell's personal perversions, including having sex with his mother, as though the words came from the reverend's mouth. Falwell sued. While Flynt beat the libel charges, he was found guilty on the accompanying charges of emotional distress. He didn't allow the split decision to get in his way.

As the 1990s dawned, the *Hustler* brand continued to grow, welcoming the advent of the Internet and gleefully exploring how new media could be used to further the brand and promote *Hustler*'s core moneymaker: hardcore sex. Additionally, *Hustler* stayed true to Flynt's mission of combating moral soap-boxing that took on the proportions of a political plague with the dawning of the Bill Clinton administration. At the height of the Clinton-Monica Lewinsky "I did not have sex with that woman" scandal, Flynt bought a full-page ad in *The Washington Post,* seeking stories and evidence of sexual impropriety among the President's accusers. Flynt's actions toppled Republican House Speaker-elect Bob Livingston, and Flynt subsequently compiled and printed his findings in *The Flynt Report,* thoroughly shaking up Washington D.C. by showing no one was safe from the skeletons in their closets.

"My political work has hurt the magazine. When they started indicting me and prosecuting me, we saw a drop. Even though we always beat [the prosecutors and religious leaders] in the end, they wanted to put me out of business. Falwell, he's crazy, he would preach against me on Sunday mornings, but I wouldn't change what I was going to do," stated Flynt.

Despite his political activism, Flynt never lost sight of *Hustler*'s core business. He quickly grasped how changes in technology and societal viewpoints about sex could further brand expansion, and he pursued that expansion into niches involving bondage, S&M and other fetishes, clearly stepping over the line other glossy magazines toed.

"It's funny because in the beginning, we had these girls showing up to audition and they were these nice, corn-fed girls from Ohio. Even though Hefner always said that he wanted the 'girl next door' for his magazine, it was *Hustler* who really did it," stated Flynt. "Today, the girls are hard. They all have plastic boobs. I try not to publish that sort of girl whenever I can even in light of what [*Hustler's* about]."

As expected, over the years as media has changed, *Hustler's* magazine sales have declined, but the brand's diversity into other market segments such as videos, novelty products, apparel, website subscriptions, casinos, and the launch of the Hustler Hollywood chain of coffee-bar-cum-sex-boutique stores has more than made up for any losses in publishing. As one of the most well-known brands in the world, *Hustler* has not only survived the ages but has progressed into the future of the adult entertainment industry

Flynt stated, "I have told people that I wasn't successful because of what I did, but in spite of what I did. Who would have ever dreamed that a magazine like *Hustler* could come out of a farm in Ohio? Ultimately, *Hustler* is entertainment. We never wanted to be something different than what we were. It was important for me to make sure the magazine was what the readers wanted. We have always stayed true to the vision."

From Movie Screen to Home Theater:
How Video Changed the Industry

As technology changed, the market for pornography did, too. Glossy magazines declined in popularity as adult videos became more accessible to the general public and cheaper to produce than traditional film.

In the 1960s, pornography went to the movies on 35mm film and then on 16mm film. The trend started in California, where about twenty movie theaters catered primarily to heterosexual audiences. By the time the 1970s rolled around, approximately 750 theaters from coast to coast served both straight and gay audiences. Consequently, the Motion Picture Association of America's "X" rating found a foothold. "X" doesn't even exist as a rating today. It was replaced by NC-17 in 1990. "X" and "XXX" are completely voluntary ratings these days (and "XXX" was fabricated by adult producers to indicate their content was ultra-hardcore).

The majority of patrons who frequented adult theaters were male, and the establishments themselves became known as hotbeds of on-premises sexual activity. Rules were not strictly enforced; therefore, patrons often happened upon other theatergoers engaged in masturbation or full-on sex with others. The sexual revolution of the 1960s precipitated shifts in the content of pornographic magazines, which led to shifts in the content of pornographic films, which in turn caused even more changes in magazine content. The self-feeding cycle introduced a "new" pornography to the American public.

Blockbuster Pornography:
Films that Matter

One of the first pornographic films to enter mainstream consciousness was *Boys in the Sand,* a homosexual romp released in 1971. Produced on a budget of only $8,000, *Boys* was directed by Wakefield Poole, known for his commitment to making erotic films that did not demonize or vilify gay sex. The film's notion that physical love between two men could be as fulfilling as heterosexual sex represented a seminal moment not only in pornography, but also in filmmaking as a whole. *Boys* was one of the first pornographic films to embark upon a focused pre-release publicity campaign, going so far as to place advertisements in *The New York Times* and *Variety* magazine. Ticket sales during the first week after the film's release topped $25,000, placing *Boys* on *Variety*'s list of top-grossing films for the week of December 29, 1971.

Poole produced a sequel in 1984, and it also met with success. In 2003, the original film received a coveted GayVN Award for "Best Classic Gay DVD."

The 1972 film *Deep Throat*, starring Linda Lovelace, was produced for about $25,000 and has grossed more than $100 million in sales to date. In addition to cementing Lovelace as the first modern-day porn star, the 61-minute film was the first pornographic movie to garner upper-class interest and entertainment industry acceptance, largely because it had a plot, featured music, and took a humorous approach to the subject matter. Not only a cultural icon in its own right, the film garnered enduring historical significance, somewhat tangentially, when then-FBI Associate Director W. Mark Felt used the moniker "Deep Throat" to conceal his identity as the whistleblower who fed information about the infamous Nixon-era Watergate break-in to reporters Carl Bernstein and Bob Woodward at *The Washington Post.*

Behind the Green Door also was released in 1972. This film was the first hardcore pornographic movie released for mass distribution in the U.S., and it was also the first to reach a mixed-gender audience. The film starred Marilyn Chambers, the proverbial girl next door, whose acting resume prior to *Green Door* boasted only a few Ivory

Soap commercials. Produced for around $60,000, the film had one of the biggest budgets of its time.   Upon nationwide theatrical release, the film's gross topped $1 million, setting a new record. After it was screened at the 1972 Cannes Film Festival and released on home video, *Behind the Green Door* eventually grossed $25 million. It became the second film, after *Deep Throat*, to be inducted into the X-Rated Critics Organization Hall of Fame. *Behind the Green Door: The Sequel*, released in 1986 at the height of the AIDS crisis, became one of the first pornographic feature films to promote safer sex, depicting performers wearing condoms.

In the midst of all of this commercial success, production and distribution companies still understood they were missing out on a large part of the market. Most of middle-class America declined to visit adult movie theaters, at least openly. A radical change in format was coming, and the advent of home video was welcomed by all in the industry.

Increasing Profitability:
Changes in Format Create Industry Growth

The introduction of the videocassette recorder (VCR) largely built the modern pornography industry, helping ease filming, controlling the cost of promotion and distribution, and ultimately leading to much higher profits. While the VCR wasn't designed specifically for the adult entertainment industry, adult embraced the technology with a passion. Low-cost videotape coupled with at-home consumer viewing allowed the industry to expand its product offering and its customer base.

Sony's Betamax entered the market in 1975, but one obvious flaw made the format less than optimal: Betamax tapes could hold only 60 minutes of content—not long enough for a typical movie, mainstream or otherwise. That, coupled with Sony's notorious desire to maintain proprietary control over its technology, probably had more to do with the eventual triumph of the VHS format. Yet the rumor persists that the adult entertainment industry cast the deciding vote, largely because of an alleged prohibition of pornography on Betamax products. There is little confirmed data to back up this claim, so for the moment pornography's role in the format war is little more than a very popular myth.

It was VHS, developed by Japanese electronics giant JVC, that made possible the incredible profits experienced by the adult entertainment industry in the late 1970s and early 1980s. VHS tapes offered significantly more recording time than Betamax, at three hours' capacity, and the VHS playback machines cost significantly less than Sony's rival product to produce and own. For the first time, consumers could purchase their porn via mail order, have it delivered discreetly, and watch in the privacy of their own bedrooms. By the end of the 1970s, adult entertainment video sales accounted for half of all prerecorded tape sales in the U.S.

As the technology changed and became more accessible, so did the public's demand. *Adult Video News* (*AVN*) estimated that 1,250 adult movies were released on VHS tape during 1989 alone; 500 of the films were brand new, not repackaged or cut into compilation sequences. Wholesale revenue from these films is estimated to have equaled $400 million.   On-screen talent like Ron Jeremy, Ginger Lynn, and Christy Cannon, among others, became stars in the San Fernando Valley, where pornography was finding a home. Professionals in the industry had never been happier, the money was rolling in, demand was flourishing, and everyone assumed things would only get better. Sex had never been so good.

The Right Accessories:
Generating Pleasure and Revenue

Any good marketer knows a business without complementary accessories is missing a major piece of the merchandising pie. The incorporation of sex toys into the adult entertainment industry followed much the same marketing-and-promotion path as any other product, except sex toys, prior to modern marketing which found a foothold in the late 1990s, were aimed largely at male consumers. Likewise since the 1990s, a number of porn stars have worked to create brands around their name. For instance, Jenna Jameson's name adorns an entire line of sex toys and accessories, from vibrators and lubricants to whips and ticklers to apparel, costumes and penis extensions. While Jameson's line has been successful, other porn stars have not experienced the same good fortune.

It's amusing to realize that a striptease artist's feather boa once was considered a "sexual enhancement item." But really, much of the modern sex accessory market grew from enhancing desire to enhance the commonplace. Vibrators, for instance, initially were marketed as medical devices to husbands who wanted to keep their wives "young and pretty" and free from "hysteria." The American Medical Association eventually released a report calling hysteria an imaginary condition and condemning the use of vibrators as medical devices.

After the AMA weighed in on the issue, vibrator advertisements disappeared from public view. Enterprising pornographers in the 1930s discovered entertaining ways to incorporate early vibrators into their products, leading proper society to label vibrators "deviant machinery" because they could produce sexual pleasure. The devices became associated with pornography, and when they were advertised (only in the most shocking circumstances) they were labeled "personal massagers." It wasn't until 1965 that the vibrator reemerged into pop culture, using its real name. Partially because of the development of latex, which aided in the production of higher quality devices at lower costs, vibrators once again took their rightful place as hot sex toys, at least in some circles.

But a barrier to complete societal integration of sex toys remained, and that barrier was...women.

Adult Toys, the Industry and Women: Battery-operated Profitability

Until recently, the challenge has been removing the taboo associated with vibrators, dildos and other devices, especially with the fairer sex. Just as theatrical release of pornographic films limited the audience producers and distributors could hope to entice, early sex shops limited the market for toys and novelties. Jane Everywoman was not about to venture into a filthy back-alley hovel teeming with perverts in trench coats. The popular construct was based in fact, and it did not present a pretty mental picture to female consumers.

While the modern adult toy and novelty market produces more than $2 billion in sales annually, acceptance of this division of the adult entertainment industry has not always been easy. Mainstream America, especially women, has become more open about the use of sex toys in recent years. Transparency about sex, women's liberation and the gradual erasure of taboos have empowered women and lessened their sexual embarrassment. Many women no longer consider sexual relations a marital duty, but instead find sex a delightful diversion to be enjoyed with or without the bonds of matrimony.

The hit TV show *Sex and the City* did more for American commerce than sell Manolo Blahnik shoes by the boatload and familiarize shoppers with brands like Prada, Christian Louboutin, and Jimmy Choo. The series also sold the now-famous Rabbit Vibrator in bulk. A product definitely has gone mainstream when it's a regular resident of Carrie Bradshaw's Fendi handbag.

Susan Colvin, CEO of California Exotic Novelties, thanks the TV show that was a pop culture phenomenon in more ways than one. "After *Sex and the City* came out and promoted a sex toy, the Jack Rabbit on the show itself, every woman wanted one. It was so easily accepted. It is the number one all time selling product. It's incredible what that show did for us. It was also a first. Here were the characters talking about this product on a show people watched and loved. It was a breakthrough and it was the beginning of a culture shift. Now adult toys and masturbation are talked about on regular basic cable sitcoms."

As with any product related to the adult entertainment industry, sex toys have a long and rich history dating back to historic times. The Ancient Greeks discovered olive oil made a great lubricant, and early stone-like dildos have been discovered at archaeological sites the world over. But to focus on how modern toys' have stimulated our economy in recent years, it is necessary to consider what has taken place, primarily with women, since the onset of the Sexual Revolution.

The modern pornography market has boomed since men and women started becoming comfortable with the notion that sex should be enjoyable. The sex toy market has grown exponentially since women realized men aren't required for sexual fulfillment…as long as one has batteries. In fact, that women are empowered enough to take charge of their own pleasure and their own orgasms with or without men frightens social and religious conservatives the world over. The choice is up to the woman, and her ability is enough to keep traditional misogynists shaking in their boots.

Essentially, while sex toys are made for both men and women, it is women who have embraced the market since the early 1990s. Today, the majority of sex toy companies and marketers—both retailers and manufacturers—appeal directly to the female consumer. Many adult novelty companies are owned by women who are raking in the bucks by appealing to female buyers *en masse.*

Originally, the sex toy market was controlled by large companies like Doc Johnson and Good Vibrations. That isn't the case anymore. Many women-controlled businesses are making enormous names for themselves in today's market by following the same business model Tupperware pioneered in the 1960s, appealing not only to the female consumer, but also to the woman who is looking for an earning opportunity. Passion Parties, one of the industry leaders, works not only to educate women about sexual issues, but also to make them comfortable with the normality of owning and using vibrators (amongst other merchandise), while also trying to sell them on the idea that they can control their own destiny by becoming a distributor. The company, headed by Pat Davis and based in Las Vegas, Nevada, is one of the primary entities in the space, appealing to women who classify themselves as stay-at-home moms in committed relationships, twenty-something singles, or fifty-year-old divorcées. Additionally, the parties, which usually host anywhere from one dozen to two dozen women, typically bring in from $500 to more than $5,000 per one-hour event, have become known as great revenue generators.

The concept is a complete departure from the way sex toys were marketed prior to the 1990s. Previously, the message was focused on men, employing images of graphic sex, naked women, or other features that relayed a hardcore, male-centric message to the consumer. Today, however, women and small business owners have repackaged their products, making them more accessible and comfortable for female consumers while also playing up the notion that the toys can be used with a partner. The perverted, pornographic image of the sex toy has been dismissed, making a vibrator as normal as a hair dryer and just as necessary.

The numbers don't lie. According to a 2004 study combining information from Chicago's The Berman Center sexual health and wellness project and sales statistics from online retailer Drugstore.com, 44 percent of women between the ages of 18 and 60 have used a sex toy. Of the women polled, 78 percent were in active relationships.[5]

Widespread acceptance of the sex toy industry has been enhanced by the Adult Novelty Expo trade show, which presents the novelty industry as though it were any other business, eschewing the hardcore pornography associated with its sister show, the Adult Entertainment Expo. Both shows, coordinated by the AVN Media Network, take place in Las Vegas each year. The industry has become so mainstream that pleasure products now may be found at retailers ranging from Walgreens to Fred Segal. Additionally, merchandisers have focused on potential crossover appeal by creating products like flavored body lotions, cosmetics, body glitter, and other types of female-centric offerings that make sex toys go hand-in-hand with beauty, pampering, and luxury—a part of life that is to be enjoyed and becomes as second nature as putting on lip gloss.

Changes in Technology:
The Future of the Sex Toy

There's no denying modern human beings are technology junkies. There really isn't a facet of our individual lives that we haven't considered automating, and truth be told, our sex lives are included in that mix.

Sex toy technology has improved by leaps and bounds since the days of the first rubber dildo or simple battery-operated vibrator. As big a splash as the Rabbit made after its debut on *Sex and the City*, the device is sadly primitive by today's standards.

Who could have imagined that one day we would be connecting our sex toys to our computers and allowing other people to control the devices over the Internet? Does that sound a little too sci-fi for you? Well get rid of that thought, because the toy is a reality.

Called the Sinulator, the handy little device allows users to name their toy and set up an interactive online personality. Anyone who knows the name of your little friend can make it work whenever they see you online.

Interesting, yes? The Sinulator redefines the meaning of "interactive." Women aren't having all the fun, though: New sex toy technology is for men as well.

Enter the Interactive Fleshlight, which is based on the traditional concept of a vibrating sleeve. A transmitter embedded in the toy measures the intensity of thrusting movements and communicates directly with the accompanying software. The male component of the Interactive Fleshlight directs the female component, intensifying what the woman on the other end of the computer connection feels in accordance with the man's action. The use of these two pieces of equipment together redefines cybersex and creates a completely new, and virtual, experience between two users.[6]

The Adult Entertainment Expo is one trade show that stays ahead of the curve when rolling out new sex toy technology and keeping consumers abreast of the very latest in the pleasure products industry. There is little the trade show doesn't address. Recent unveilings have included the World's First Sex Robot, which cost its developers an estimated $500,000 to $1 million to create. Those who are interested in purchasing an electronic companion can work hand-in-hand with the producer, TrueCompanion.com, and have a robot customized to fit their desires and needs. This isn't some bulky *Jetson's* robot from the 1960s. Instead, the faux human can be modeled to fit the consumer's idea of what their perfect mate would look like…down to eye color.

How's that for innovation?

The sex toy division of the adult entertainment industry is as vibrant and ever-changing as mainstream technology companies like Apple and Microsoft. Just as traditional pornography has worked to find the latest trends and techniques when connecting with consumers, adult toy manufacturers aim to keep pace with consumers' needs and wants when it comes to enhancing and complementing their sex lives. As the world continues to get smaller and online platforms continue to connect people around the block and on opposite sides of the globe, the adult entertainment industry and sex toy producers serve its technology-driven customers. After all, cybersex, through the use of the Internet and sex toys that work virtually, might just be the safest form of sex yet.

The Dawning of the Internet:
On-Demand Entertainment...24/7

The Internet changed the world. There is no denying its impact on business, commerce, and communication. The Internet is also responsible for recreating the entire adult entertainment industry. While there are positives and negatives associated with what the Internet did to porn and how industry professionals repackaged themselves and their business models to utilize and harness this new technology, the Internet shook the adult entertainment industry to its core. All the changes the adult entertainment industry experienced before the Internet Age composed barely a blip on the radar compared to the way the World Wide Web revolutionized the market. Suddenly, profit margins disappeared...because content appeared on the Internet for free.

With the advent of new online technology came a parade of amateur pornographers, producers, distributors, and marketers. All were determined to cash in on the new way of delivering sex to consumers. Almost overnight, large production houses found themselves with a tidal wave of competition. What's more, this competition had little or no overhead and could duplicate or pirate material and sell it for next to nothing or publish it for free, all to the obvious chagrin of the Old Guard producers.

The emergence of the Internet caught some industry professionals by surprise, as for years their focus had been on selling films and appealing to their consumer base through a controlled supply and demand chain. That model disintegrated in a blink, and many industry bigwigs were left scratching their heads over how to combat or otherwise control the flow of content while turning a profit with the new technology.

Even with the confusion within the industry, the Internet and pornography were an immediate fit. If not for the insatiable sexual appetites of consumers, the Internet might not be as vast as it is today. Say what you will about morality, but the meteoric rise of the Internet can be attributed in many ways to the adult entertainment industry.

While I have dedicated an entire chapter to the Internet and its role in the adult entertainment industry in this book, it is important to note a couple of items for background purposes. The Internet, as a whole, completely changed the adult entertainment industry from top to bottom. Many professionals were caught off-guard by entrepreneurial techies who quickly were able to exploit their knowledge of the Internet in the early days in order to fill their pockets with wads of cash. Online pornography pioneers were able to capitalize on the Internet right away, but many longstanding industry professionals eventually caught up and began utilizing the tool to continue building their fortunes.

Some of the statistics associated with Internet pornography are shocking. In 2006, $3,075.64 was spent on Internet porn during every second of every day. During that same second, an average of 28,258 people viewed pornography online, and 372 Internet surfers typed in adult-related search terms on Google, Yahoo! or another leading search engine. Approximately every 39 minutes, a porn site was published in the U.S.[7]

The same 2006 report showed revenues generated by pornography topped the combined revenues of Microsoft, Google, Amazon, eBay, Yahoo!, Apple, Netflix, and Earthlink.[8] How's that for positive earning capability?

Today there are approximately 4.2 million websites that offer pornography or some other form of adult entertainment. These websites serve 72 million viewers around the globe; 40 million of those viewers happen to be American. Another interesting statistic: one-fourth of all Internet searches on a daily basis have something to do with pornography or adult entertainment.[9]

Statistics aside, what makes the Internet and its relationship to pornography so compelling is that there are nearly unlimited ways to use the technology. Today's World Wide Web offers a wide array of porn websites, from the amateur with a webcam in his bedroom, to porn stars who showcase their own stable of talent, to the production houses that concurrently release both DVDs and online movies. Of course, the business model behind all of this is a perpetual moneymaker. Although a host of free sites that offer amateur or pirated content have disrupted the cash flow in recent years, the online adult entertainment community has devised a series of strategies for convincing consumers to pay for high-quality content instead of settling for free, low-quality material. Some producers' strategies have been successful, and others fight the figurative 12-headed Hydra: They contain or control one pirated/free site, but 12 more spring up in its place.

Of course, Internet pornography also has paved the way for a variety of attempts to regulate or censor legal content, from controlling who can access the material to defining what may be displayed. The first attempt at curtailing online pornography occurred in 1996 when Congress passed the Communications Decency Act. CDA attempted to criminalize indecent or "obscene" online expression. Free speech advocates took up the fight, working tirelessly to overturn the law because, suddenly, the use of dirty words, the display of sexually explicit materials that were perfectly legal in print, and even sexual health and medical information could have been defined as criminal in some situations. Although age-restriction provisions of the law stand, the Supreme Court struck down the most controversial aspects of CDA in 1997.[10]

A variety of other attempts at controlling the virtual realm have entered the legal arena since then, proving there is a fine line between out-and-out censorship and protecting the free-speech rights of people older than 18. No legitimate adult industry business wants to exploit children, yet "Protect the children!" remains the rallying cry of social conservatives. The important point here, as the government has discovered, is that it is extremely difficult to define "offensive" and "harmful," at least where the Internet is concerned. What is obscene to one person could be a turn-on to another consenting adult.

The Internet, as a whole, presents a unique opportunity for members of the adult entertainment industry. Never before has pornography been more accessible to consumers. On the other hand, the consumer now runs the show, challenging content producers to keep their work fresh and entertaining. At the same time, where there is incredible opportunity, there also is room for epic failure. In order for the adult entertainment industry to survive, members must figure out ways to work together while staying abreast of changes in technology and keeping viewers interested...and paying.

PART THREE

The Screen Siren
The Emergence of the Porn Star

It's hard to think of adult entertainment without envisioning the "bombshell" who has the ability to make your every fantasy an onscreen reality. Women like Jessica Drake, Sunny Leone, Joanna Angel, Stormy Daniels, Jesse Jane, and of course, the über-famous Jenna Jameson have had a hand in making the industry what it is today. In the process, they have reaped the rewards of sexual superstardom.

The modern porn star is a unique woman. Many female performers work within the industry, but few are able to protect their longevity and achieve celebrity status. Stars are those who have established their image as a brand and garnered a loyal fan base, consequently driving the kind of revenue over which studios salivate.

"The [porn star] idea is exclusive only to a small group of women in this industry," stated Larry Flynt, publisher of *Hustler*. "Out in L.A. you have so many girls who are looking to break into show business and they try adult. However, the majority are burned out in six months. That is not the making of the star."

Most of the successful adult industry performers are hardworking professionals who are as devoted to their craft as professionals in any other field. Regardless, an incredible amount of mythology surrounds the women, and the men, who work in porn, their reasons for entering the business, and their roles in the bigger picture.

Steve Hirsch, founder of Vivid Entertainment and the mastermind behind the concept of the "contract girl" came up with the first marketing model around the screen sirens themselves. "We realized that we had to promote one main person. And that is where we came up with the concept of the Vivid Girl. We decided to sign a girl to an exclusive contract and market her that way."

The evolution of the porn star has been gradual, and might be attributed largely to the mainstreaming of the industry as well as the shifting of female attitudes towards sex and pornography. Female performers have their detractors and supporters. One side is critical, claiming porn stars are nothing more than prostitutes. The other side sees porn stars as empowered females, embracing their sexuality and ultimately controlling when, where, and how they have sex, as well as any profit to be made.

The Porn Star as a Cultural Icon

Porn stars evolved from the classic notion of the pin-up girl. Typically models or actresses, pin-up girls entered American consciousness during WWII when GIs pasted pictures in lockers and painted scantily clad women on airplanes before entering battle. Betty Grable, Lauren Bacall, Ava Gardner, and Diana Barrymore were among the most celebrated pin-up girls of their day. Marilyn Monroe, a former pin-up girl who became one of the biggest stars of all time, graced the pages of the first *Playboy*.

The idea of a performer who was known specifically for her role in adult films did not become prevalent until the movie *Deep Throat* was in theaters. Linda Lovelace is considered by many to be the first porn star; in fact, she was named among the 50 Top Porn Stars of All Time. From a commercial standpoint, Lovelace doesn't carry some of the punch other contenders do. She made only four movies over the course of her career and eventually revealed a thorough dislike of the industry, claiming she had been forced into performing in the first place. Her allegations about coercion and abuse were called into question after she voluntarily appeared in the January 2001 issue of *Leg Show*, an explicit adult magazine.

Ginger Lynn, one of the most popular porn stars ever, made her debut in the 1980s.

"Ginger [Lynn] was the first, we marketed her exclusively," stated Steve Hirsch. "Our first movie at Vivid was 'Ginger.' She gave us something that we could really focus on and know that if we were going to spend the dollars promoting her and developing a fan base that when the consumers wanted to see her next movie, they would be purchasing it through us."

Lynn was the first Vivid Girl, a system Vivid Entertainment, many industry insiders say, was based on the studio contracts popular during Hollywood's Golden Age. Lynn appeared in a total of 173 movies. At the height of her popularity, she was known for hardcore and risqué acts which had not yet become prevalent on the scene, such as anal sex and double penetration.

"Ultimately, the business is about sex and Ginger [Lynn] was extremely sexual. She might have looked like the girl next door, but she really worked hard to develop her look and sexually, she delivered," stated Hirsch. "And she wasn't afraid to promote her movies."

While Lynn did take a break from the industry to pursue some mainstream acting opportunities in B-films under her real name, Ginger Lynn Allen, she eventually returned to porn, where she received an enthusiastic welcome home in 1999.

"People might have said it was this type of Old Hollywood-style contract that we wanted to offer, but really, it wasn't that, I just wanted someone that I could put the Vivid stamp on, someone who was exclusively ours," stated Hirsch. "I wanted someone who could be the face of the company, someone that we could take out and who would be a spokesperson. We were fortunate that Ginger thought the same way. She could have probably made more money by shooting for a lot of companies, but she thought that that it was important to create a brand. So the stars aligned that way."

Now, no discussion of porn stars would be complete without considering the most well-known porn star of all time, Jenna Jameson. Called "the world's most famous adult-entertainment performer,"[11] as well as "Porn Queen," Jameson first gained notoriety and mainstream acceptance when she appeared in Howard Stern's movie, *Private Parts*, as herself. Originally under contract with Wicked Pictures and then Vivid before starting her own company, Jameson paved the way for porn stars who long to be household names.

"Jenna was our second contract girl," said Wicked President Steve Orenstein. "It was a huge turning point for us as a company, because we were two years in business. The question was out there, 'Did Wicked make Jenna or did Jenna make Wicked?'"

Jameson's star was not without rust. Tabloids loved her often messy personal life, which sometimes was made messier by the unfortunate perception that women who have sex on film don't deserve privacy. Professionally, though, Jameson was a dynamo. Through Club Jenna, her holding company, she cultivated a stable of actresses who performed under her brand. She authored a *New York Times* bestselling book and developed a line of merchandise ranging from clothes and lingerie to sex toys and cosmetics. And she created and operated a robust web-based business that continues to bring in millions of dollars in revenue every year.

"It all started with Jenna. Here was the first time that you had a star who had other women look at her and say, 'That is who I want to be.' Jenna took the embarrassment factor out of the business. That was the beginning of girls taking themselves seriously in the business," stated Hirsch. "But today, it's very hard to build a star. Of course, there are girls people know who can sell movies. But ultimately, you have to invest a lot of money into a girl in order for her to work exclusively for you. And you have to determine if she will be able to generate more revenue than another girl."

Talent Earnings

Like any profession within the entertainment industry, adult or mainstream, a popular misconception holds that just because a person is a performer, they must be reaping fat paychecks. Vast riches do not automatically go hand-in-hand with being an onscreen performer.

Admittedly, individual stars have made fortunes and managed their finances well, but others have made very little money and blown every penny. On-screen talent typically is paid per scene or per day. Payment per scene is defined by the type of action the scene entails (i.e. position, oral sex, girl-on-girl, three-way). Typical per-scene rates range from $250 to $3,000, and a scene can take anywhere from two to twelve hours to film depending upon the number of people involved, whether there is a script, etc. According to the adult talent agency L.A. Direct Models, female performers may earn $200 to $400 for oral sex scenes, $400 to $1,200 for straight sex scenes, $900 to $1,500 for anal sex scenes, $1,200 to $1,600 for double penetration, and upwards of $2,000 for double-anal scenes. Of course, this depends on the female, her popularity, and whether she is under contract with a studio. Female performers who work in niche markets can earn 15 percent more than the base rates previously mentioned. Not considering recent economic challenges that have affected talent earnings, an adult actress who works regularly can expect take home between $50,000 and $100,000 per year, depending on the demand for her name and her reputation for reliability and work ethic.

According to fetish performer and director Bobbi Starr, the performer who is easy to work with is more likely to stay employed. "Directors and studios like to hire people who have a good attitude," she said.

Performers don't make their livings from scenes alone. Most also make in-person appearances, attend in-store DVD signings, appear as featured dancers at strip clubs, and interact in live online chat rooms. All of those are paid gigs.

Kevin Beechum, president and owner of KBeech.com and a 30-year veteran of the manufacturing and distribution end of the industry, said, "These [female performers] don't make that much money anymore doing movies. They make their money going out on the dance circuit or doing appearances. However, the only way that they can make money [on the dance circuit] is by being featured on the box covers of their movies."

Even with Beechum's apparent double-edged sword, adult entertainment is one industry where women have the ability to out-earn their male counterparts. According to male adult actor, Barrett Blade, guys are just "a living prop. You only ever see our hips, amongst other things. The woman is the star of the show."

Men typically earn $300 to $400 per scene, with beginners finding themselves in the $100 to $200 range. The average male porn actor earns a median salary of about $40,000 per year. However, men who are in demand because they are reliable sexual performers, have made a name for themselves with fans, or are particularly easy to work with may earn as much as $100,000 annually.

To be successful in the industry, performers must understand there is much more to their job than simply showing up and having sex on screen. The usual workday requires a performer to have face time with producers and directors, engage in contract negotiations, be part of a photo shoot for an upcoming project, communicate with fans via social media, and attend to personal marketing and branding chores. Some days also include attending industry events and making other personal appearances. Frankly speaking, adult entertainment is not a party every day, and only performers who recognize the business side of the business will succeed.

This is where many on-screen talent members, especially women, enter rocky territory. Women who are inexperienced in the nuances of traditional business, including negotiating contracts, creating terms, and acceptable working conditions can find themselves taken advantage of.

The Road to Adult Entertainment:
The Life of a Porn Star

Few women, when they are little girls, dream of one day of becoming a porn star. But sometimes that is exactly what happens.

Most of the women who think they want a career in adult entertainment decide within days, weeks, or months that there are easier, more socially acceptable ways to make a living. The cream of the crop, though, combine opportunity, ingenuity, marketing savvy—and yes, sex—to mold a unique, and uniquely rewarding, career.

Among the latter group is Bobbi Starr, an artist by nature and training. A graduate of San Jose State University, Starr holds a music degree and plays both piano and oboe. She was auditioning for a spot in graduate school when she "stumbled into" a career in adult entertainment. A man she was dating introduced her to swinging—sometimes called polyamory or "open relationships"—and that introduced her to bisexuality. She began to experiment with a side of herself that craved release from the constant pressure of the academic audition circuit.

"All the music I was doing at the time, I was very emotional and it consumed my entire life," Starr said. "At the time, the only outlet I had was sex. And so when I would go to parties with him, I felt as if this was something really fascinating. I had no idea that world even existed.

"I wanted to experience more for myself. Before I had been with [the man I was dating], I had never even seen pornography before.

"He told me, 'You have to watch porn. You have to see what you are missing.' So he showed me a Belladonna film, an old Elegant Angel movie that was on VHS, a Joe Gallant DVD. It was a lot of really hardcore, girl-girl, anal," Starr continued. "And as I was watching this, I was really struck by the fact that these people were powerful. I decided I wanted to experience this, but I didn't know how to do that."

Starr's boyfriend had a connection with someone at Kink.com, a network of BDSM websites, and agreed to introduce her.

He also encouraged her to be sure she understood the ramifications of her actions. Even sex tapes made by couples for their own use end up in the public eye, and her appearance in even one professionally produced porn scene likely would follow her for the rest of her life. She wouldn't be able to keep the secret. Ultimately, Starr decided to go ahead.

"I identified the reasons why I wanted to do [pornography]," she said. "I am very in charge of my own sexuality, and I was curious and fascinated by the people and the industry. I wanted to learn about kinks and fetishes, and I knew that if I didn't do it, I would have regretted it."

Starr moved from Northern California to Los Angeles to pursue a new path at the age of 23, after deciding that if adult entertainment didn't work out, she could reapply to graduate school and incorporate a new understanding of sexuality into her academic life. Today she is an award-winning performer and director who heads her own division of Kink.com and at Evil Angel.

And she never thought porn would be more than a brief diversion.

"In 2006 [when I entered the industry], I never thought of making a career out of [pornography]," she acknowledged. "Instead, I felt it was more of a 'study' for me. I didn't foresee a career, but ultimately, I'm still here today."

Her "study" didn't come without a specific set of goals. Starr said her list of goals looked something like this:

1.) Work with Belladonna.
2.) Sign for John Stagliano's company, Evil Angel, at the Adult Entertainment Convention.
3.) Begin a website if economics permit.
4.) Make my own films, either through my own website or by directing for another company.

Thus far, Starr has accomplished everything she intended to do, and then some. In 2010 she won an award for Most Outrageous Sex Scene in *Belladonna: No Warning 4*. She also has worked with Evil Angel both on-camera and as a director, and she began her own website in 2011, which ultimately resulted in a 2012 AVN Award for Best Porn Star Website.

"I have decided I just want to experience this industry as I go along," she said "In school everything was very stressful, pressured and planned out and I got a little burned out, which is one of the reasons I ended up [in adult]."

Another academic, Joanna Angel, also ended up in adult entertainment by chance. Like Starr, Angel had no prior knowledge about the industry, its scope, or its size. A graduate of Rutgers University with a degree in English literature, she started her website, BurningAngel.com, in 2002 while still attending school.

"I was at this stage where I wasn't sure what I wanted to do with my life, and really it was my roommate's idea," she said. "[The website] was brought up as a joke, and then the joke became reality, and before I knew it I was walking around asking my friends if they would pose nude for me so I could put it on the Internet. The great thing about the web is that you can start businesses really quickly.

"When the company first started, the website only had stills; we didn't have any video or anything. And because I was still in college, the website was only getting updated once every six weeks," she continued. "What's crazy is that people were still joining even when there was only one photo going live on the site every six weeks. That's compared to the fact that people update their websites five times a day now, and even then it's hard to get people to join."

It was a friend of a friend who originally suggested that Angel go to the AVN Adult Entertainment Expo, the annual industry convention in Las Vegas, in order to really understand what she could be doing with her website, and ultimately, her career. In 2004, Angel booked a plane ticket and headed west with the hope she would increase her understanding of the adult entertainment industry and where exactly her niche, and her website, could fit into the mix.

The experience opened her eyes to the world of adult entertainment. While she knew pornography was a moneymaker, she had no idea who the players in the industry were, the expansiveness of the product lines, and the potential that her website was not yet harnessing. She finally started to understand the business behind the industry.

"At first, I don't think that a lot of people knew what to make of Burning Angel," she recalled. "I was meeting all of these industry people who lived and worked in L.A. and here I was, this girl who is operating this porn site out of her bedroom in New Jersey with her roommate and not really making any money at it. It was a very strange concept to most of the people I talked to."

On the flight back from Vegas, she made a decision. While she didn't have a formal business plan, she knew it was time to alter the direction of the website. Angel decided she had to get into video as well as define what she and her friends were doing: they were making hardcore porn.

Burning Angel started to grow in 2005 as Angel and her team launched video on the website. It was at this point that the video production company, VCA Pictures, approached Angel about doing some films for the studio. The offer came with an opportunity to direct, allowing her a chance to expand the Joanna Angel brand with the backing of a major studio. Angel took the contract, viewing the relationship as a way to promote her brand while playing with the studio's money instead of her own.

"I never saw myself working for someone else," she said. "At the time, had [Burning Angel] been a multi-million dollar company, I probably wouldn't have done it, but we were small and we needed help getting our name out there. Having my face and my name on other people's movies was a good push."

The first movie Angel made with VCA was *Joanna's Angels 1,* which came with a decent-sized budget. Angel felt it was an ample opportunity to learn more about the business, and VCA's cross-promotional flexibility with Burning Angel provided her the chance to do a form of porn "multi-tasking," increasing awareness about her name and her niche. As such, she attracted significant attention in the form of nominations for awards and subscriptions to her website.

In 2006 Angel was nominated for "Best New Starlet" and "Best Actress," and although she won neither, she called the experience she gained "priceless." Two years after Angel signed with the company, after directing several movies and gaining camera experience, she and VCA parted ways. VCA wanted a contract actress whose main priority was the VCA brand, and Angel's main priority always had been Burning Angel.

"[VCA] gave me a nice push, and I was able to get a lot of publicity," she said. "It was nice to have the opportunity to work with professionals, because before all of that, [the staff at Burning Angel] didn't really know what we were doing. Making a movie and being able to hand it to VCA and having them tell us what was right and wrong allowed us to get better and keep learning."

Angel's single-minded focus on her business is not the norm among performers. A divide exists between the adult film stars who show up on the set, do their jobs, and go on with their day and entrepreneurs like Angel who create companies around their brand of sex. Angel understands that her longevity thus far into her career has less to do with having fun in front of the camera, and more to do with a commitment to the business she has built and the employees who depend on her. Ultimately, Angel is as much a small business owner as any other entrepreneur in any other industry, anywhere in the world. Her job just comes with a benefit she considers "as good as a day off": Every now and then, she gets to put on a cool outfit and have sex in front of a camera for half an hour.

Vivid Girl Sunny Leone also chanced into her career when she caught the eye of the late Bob Guccione, the founder of *Penthouse*. Leone is quick to state that she never envisioned a career in adult entertainment, but now has a hard time thinking about a life outside of it.

"I didn't have a plan at all," she said. "I didn't think it was a short-term thing; I didn't think it was a long-term thing. But good things happened. When Bob Guccione was alive, he used to review all of the pictures, all of the layouts, and he personally picked his *Penthouse* Pets. He saw something in my photo that he liked. Thanks to him, I am where I am today. He would be sitting in his house, clicking through his slide projector, and I just happened to capture his attention. Within the first few months of my career [in the adult entertainment industry] I was named a *Penthouse* Pet. When all of that started, everything seemed to snowball from there." Penthouse, as a company, is very brand-conscious, just like competitor *Playboy* and powerhouse studios Vivid and Wicked. *Penthouse* Pets are marketed as part of that brand, traveling extensively to appear in person. With Leone's new role came an endless amount of traveling, across the country and all over the world. She started on a circuit of radio shows, TV interviews, photo shoots and other personal appearances. While she didn't intend to become a jet-setter, that aspect of the *Penthouse* Pet life immediately attracted her and kept her attention.

"It still shocks me when someone wants my autograph," she commented. "It's absolutely insane to me. It was great to travel the country and meet all of these people. I was only 18 or 19, so it was a big shock."

Until Leone signed with Vivid in 2006, she represented herself. She did her own bookings, worked with photographers, scheduled meet-and-greets, the whole gamut. Only after she became a contract performer and her schedule exploded did she enlist the help of a public relations professional.

"I was the girl who collected everyone's card, and I called them," she reflected. "I told these people they had to hire me. I was very diligent and very persistent, and I am sure there are some photographers out there who would say, 'She never left me alone until I shot her!'"

She attributes her success to follow-through and commitment to being the best at what she does.

"It doesn't matter what you want, what industry you are in, what you are doing," she said. "It doesn't matter if you are in adult entertainment or own something as simple as a printing company. If you are not persistent and determined about what you want, you are never going to get it."

Unlike the performers mentioned previously Jessica Drake was a reluctant entrant into adult. Currently under contract with Wicked Pictures she got her start in the industry in 1999 while she was working as an exotic dancer and attending college in El Paso, Texas.

"It's certainly somewhat of a cliché beginning," Drake said. "I was a stripper. I wasn't going to college for anything specific; I was going because I knew I needed to go to school. I didn't want to be stuck stripping."

While working as a feature dancer, she was introduced to a couple who had ties to the adult entertainment industry. They wooed her, so to speak, and encouraged her to take a look at the industry itself. Young, blonde, and gorgeous, Drake's initial impression was that porn probably wasn't for her. While she didn't shun the idea or judge her new friends, she kept the notion of performing at arm's length but stayed in touch with the couple.

One day, she accompanied the couple to a photo shoot in New Mexico. After sandstorms cancelled the shoot, Drake ended up receiving an education in all things adult via extensive conversations with everyone on set, from the talent to the director to the personal assistants.

It was only when she encountered some problems trying to balance work, school, and other commitments that she decided to turn to the relationships she made that day, for support if nothing else.

Drake's first on-set experience was as a personal assistant…or to use an industry phrase, she served as the "Condom and Lube Girl," holding all the supplies needed for the scene. The film was a Jill Kelly production, and Drake stood off to the side, watching the actors have sex as the scene unfolded. Everything seemed so normal, she said. This was a real business with real objectives and goals. The crew had a schedule; everyone acted as a team. She wanted to be part of the experience.

"I was so surprised by the amount of professionalism by the people on the set. People make assumptions about this sort of thing when they don't know about the industry. But everyone was so great, so comfortable. Sure they were naked and having sex, but I was in love with the atmosphere. It wasn't long after that until I was approached with a movie ready to be made, and people I was comfortable being around and I said, 'You know, I would *love* to do it'," reflected Drake.

In her very first movie, Drake performed two scenes: one with a man and one with a woman. She admitted that in retrospect it seemed a bit odd just how comfortable she was with the cameras and having sex on set. Ten years later, though, she attributes much of her success to that comfort—plus what she calls a tendency to be a "ham on camera."

All four women are savvy, progressive thinkers. While they may have different goals, they are excellent examples of how to be successful in the adult entertainment industry.

The Porn Star as Entrepreneur

Just as with any industry, the woman who opts to make a career out of porn isn't always a blinding success; an entrepreneurial spirit and mindset are required. Success depends on how involved a woman decides to be not only in her own career, but also in the industry as a whole. Attaining achievement in adult entertainment requires focus on how a woman chooses to market herself after she has generated a following and started to become popular.

Some performers, like Angel, create brands around their names. In Angel's case, the brand includes a viable company with several divisions, product manufacturing, a distribution partnership with Hustler, and an active employee base. The problem, she's since discovered, is that she and the company are so intricately linked, she's literally married to her work. Angel eats, breathes, sleeps, and dreams her business. She owns every piece—and the responsibility that comes with it.

"I can't just leave; it's not just me," she noted. "When you are a performer you have an agent and you are a work-for-hire person, and I am certainly not putting down the girls who do that. I think there are a lot of [work-for-hire] girls who have great careers, but your only responsibility is to yourself. If you are working and you find that porn is not right for you, the only person that decision is going to affect is you."

In contrast, Angel's employees pay their bills because of her brand. Angel employs five full-time people in addition to herself and her business partner: a publicist, a photographer, a videographer/editor, a web designer, and a general administrator.

"People make their living off this company," she said. "One of my employees has a child, and you know people depend on me and I depend on them. This is a real company; it doesn't come with the light hearted thought of 'Oh, I want to be in a porn movie, or I don't feel like doing this today.' There is a lot of time, money and hard work that gets put into this. I own a business. Everything I do is part of this company.

"Just like any business owner knows, sometimes it's difficult," Angel continued. "I know I can't be on camera forever, but I own this company and I want it to last. I spend so much of my day making budgets or writing scripts or watching Google Analytics or understanding what is selling and what isn't selling. And truthfully, I love all that stuff. It's empowering and it's fascinating to run a company."

Lucky Smith, former agent and webmaster for the adult industry, commented on Angel's position and how many other performers look to Angel as a model for success. "[Joanna's] really been a vanguard. There are a lot of people both inside the industry and out that have mimicked what she does, her model."

Bobbi Starr, on the other hand, has limited her role as an entrepreneur to independent contractor. The decision was intentional, she said: She wants to be able to choose what she does without working for someone else or being tasked with the responsibility of employees. She didn't consciously try to "build a brand" around herself. Instead, she took the opportunities that came her way, and her popularity increased, seemingly on its own. She works with an agent and also has a distribution deal with Evil Angel. Her website was launched in July 2011 with the help of her business partner, Richard Avery, and she is determined to grow conservatively and keep operation as small and as in-house as possible until revenue generation spurs something bigger.

"I have created various and different partnerships with people and companies," Starr said. "That's because I want complete control over my brand and don't want anyone telling me what I can and cannot do."

Jessica Drake, who largely operates under the Wicked Pictures umbrella, agrees that a performer doesn't have to have a large production house to be successful. She said she believes the industry has benefitted because of small business owners like Angel's. "I don't think there is a divide between contract performers and freelancers, so to speak," Drake said. "There are contract performers who work for some companies that have the business mindset, and there are a lot of gonzo performers who have [that mindset] as well and really have boosted the business of the industry as a whole."

As a contract entrepreneur who represents both Wicked Pictures and her brand, Drake concurs with Angel, at least in part. "There are times you wish you could clone yourself. I realize I have so many different opportunities, and I start thinking, 'Okay, if I get on a plane at this time and take the red-eye to this place, I can make this show and fulfill this booking.' And then you throw something else into your schedule, and well, it can be tricky," she said.

Much of the key to success within the industry is diversification. For instance, Angel works to generate different revenue streams within the Burning Angel brand. Web subscriptions compose 80 percent of her company's revenue, and the website's e-store adds revenues from movies, t-shirts, and other merchandise. The DVD distribution partnership with Wicked Pictures, signed in 2008, also encompasses television broadcast deals with the Spice Channel, New Frontier, and the Erotic Network. Pay-per-view revenues from those sources also contribute to Burning Angel's bottom line.

KBeech's Kevin Beechum said the way Angel runs her company speaks volumes about her business savvy. "She's a smart [woman]. The mere fact that she went out to partner with [Wicked] on distribution means she understands that she might be giving up some of the profit, but her time is more valuable and more well spent focusing on [Burning Angel] as a company, rather than some of the nuances of running both manufacture and getting her products to customers."

Leone follows Angel's model as well, even though she is under an exclusive contract with Vivid as a performer. She said performers who also aspire to be business owners need to keep an open mind and subscribe to the idea that you must always be learning. With that in mind, she restructured the terms of her contract as she developed her business in order to ensure her name is independent of the Vivid label. "If you don't pay attention to the little details or if you are not empowered enough to ask questions, then things are going to happen to you that you do not like," Leone said. "I don't think there are victims in this industry more than there are in any other business."

She also said it is important to be able to call the shots as a business owner. After she signed with Vivid, she knew she wanted to market her own name as well. "I walked into Steven [Hirsch's] office and said, 'I want to make my own movies, I want to own them, and I want you to do the distribution.' So I signed an exclusive contract to shoot all of my boy/girl movies, and Vivid would do my U.S. distribution. I am contracted with Vivid as a 'Vivid Girl,' but not with the regular contractual obligations that a typical contract star would have."

Leone is a big believer in strategy as it relates to company direction. "Before I was with Vivid, I owned and ran my own website, which was a very successful endeavor. [Now] I have hired outside contractors to do tech work on the site. Additionally, our company has grown so much in the past year that we are now required to really think about who we are going to hire. We know we can't handle every single thing that is happening to us. If we tried to, and didn't hire someone, it would hurt our company instead of helping us grow.

"At some point you have to evaluate whether you try to fit more things into an already crowded schedule or hire someone who can handle [some things] and actually make the product better and help the company grow. And we have done that, and it's such an amazing feeling to hire someone who is excited about what they do and who is inspired when they see numbers double or triple."

Any performer, who takes the reins in his or her career, and whether they own their own company or work as a contractor, realizes they are embarking upon a big commitment.

"It's a 24/7 job," Angel said. "I don't stop, just like any other small business owner. I love what I do. We just have to keep working, keep getting better."

Drake tends to agree with Angel on this point, as well. "Some of [these women] are so business minded," Drake said. "They might work for the big two or three companies or they might not, but they are so focused, so busy, and so structured. Much like everything else, this business is what you make of it. I have seen success come from girls who are very determined, very hard working, and very smart. They run small businesses in every sense of the word."

Keeping Customers Happy: Communicating with Fans

The longevity of a female performer goes part in parcel with generating a loyal fan base. In today's 24/7 technology world, there has never been a better time to be a porn star when it comes to communicating with fans. The success of a website is integral to achievement within the adult entertainment industry.

Joy King, vice president of special projects for Wicked Pictures, said, "[Wicked] recently partnered with a new web developer. We have areas on the website where consumers can leave feedback. They can comment on movies, talent, what they like, and what they don't like. Once a week, I go into the site and read through all the comments, and I don't hesitate to take into account positive and negative feedback. [Wicked] will implement consumer suggestions on what they want to see and what they do not, unless it goes against our brand and who we are."

The contact option on Starr's website delivers an email directly to her, and she monitors posts and comments to make sure the content people want to see is being produced. "I also do monthly one-on-one question-and-answer video chats. Fans will send me questions, and I will pick five and answer them in a video," she said. "It's difficult for me, sometimes, to keep the ongoing communication open, because it's a lot of work, a lot of emails, a lot of questions. I do my best to make myself available, but also try to remind the fans that I do run a business and wear a lot of hats."

Starr looks up to other established performers in the industry, for instance Belladonna. While it was a goal of Starr's to perform with Belladonna when she first entered the industry, she also notes that she emulates much of what the older actress does. "I think [Belladonna] has built her brand very well while maintaining a personal approach to her fans," Starr reflected. "People will go up to her and she will take the time to speak with them and interact with them. She's a regular person, and I think that's very admirable and a great way to build an adult entertainment product."

Jessica Drake thinks social media like Facebook and Twitter are great ways to stay connected. "That is the great thing about Twitter and Facebook," she said. "You can keep your hand on the pulse of what is happening in the industry and also stay in touch with fans. I tweet in line at the grocery store or when I am in traffic. It takes me seconds to make sure my fans know I am thinking about them."

Angel is another tech-focused member of the industry. She may not leave her apartment over the course of a weekend, but that doesn't stop her from promoting her work. "I'm on Facebook and Twitter all the time, and my reach is really extensive with that," she said. "I don't close myself up indoors all the time, but I know I can spend time on either of those sites, talk with fans, get feedback, and keep my brand in front of them, while also making them happy about the fact that they are talking with me."

Indeed, fan interaction is key to being successful as an adult performer, and frankly this is one area where the industry has mainstream Hollywood beat. As any visitor to the Adult Entertainment Expo knows, it is the adult film star who welcomes you, interacts with you, flirts with you. Adult stars know their careers depend on fans coming back for more.

The Making of a Star

While adult entertainment is synonymous with the women who perform in front of the camera, it would be disingenuous not to mention some of the women who make the industry tick. One of those women is Joy King, hailed as an executive power player at Wicked Pictures.

Another case of happening upon a career in the industry "by accident," in 1984 King began working at Caballero Home Video, a general video production and distribution company. Caballero, at the time, worked with a variety of film genres and King, who started in the children's division, found herself looking at a move into the company's adult sector.

"I wasn't afraid of the adult side, so they moved me over," she said. "I was fortunate to have grown up with very supporting parents who never limited my beliefs and what I believed I could accomplish." That background carried over to how she handled herself in her career. "I believed I could do anything. I had no fear, and I also was coming into a business without any preconceived ideas. Many of the people at Caballero were convinced that [if you worked in adult] you were limited and that belief was really prevalent. I didn't have that. I walked in kind of bright-eyed and bushy-tailed."

King set out to shake up the status quo at Caballero, and much of her attitude was based on a belief that adult films didn't have to be handled delicately and could have a place in a public forum.

"The one thing that stands out is when we first shot a movie called *Night Trips*, and I wanted to do a public screening because it was just a beautiful movie," she said. "The owner of the company said, 'Oh, you can't do that.' But I proceeded to go to the Director's Guild on Sunset and got the screening set up. I told them I had a movie that I wanted a screening for, asked them how much and basically got all the details. Then two days before, I called them to say [the film] was a triple-X movie. I said that I was sure they wouldn't want to censor my production because of First Amendment rights and the fact that they had already cashed my check for the deposit. It got very quiet, but they agreed to move forward with the screening."

The screening turned out to be a huge success. Indeed, no one had attempted to get an adult film screened in a public venue, and since King's coup d'état, no one has been able to do it again. Director's Guild policy now forbids adult film screenings.

"This was a real confidence builder for me," stated King. "What's more is that the owners of the company didn't even show up because they were convinced it would be shut down, but it wasn't and it was great."

The achievement made King realize she could be very good at her job, regardless of the fact she was a woman during a tumultuous time in a controversial industry.

"I certainly ran into people in the industry who didn't have a high opinion of women, and I know I did get my feathers ruffled, but I ignored all of that," she said. "I glossed over it."

King met Steve Orenstein in the late 1980s. Orenstein is the founder of Wicked Pictures, but before that he worked as a video buyer whom King saw regularly at industry events. King and Orenstein struck up a friendship that eventually presented a business opportunity for King when Orenstein launched Wicked in 1993. However, challenges stood in the way of King becoming a part of the team: Orenstein couldn't afford her.

"It took a couple of years after [Orenstein] started the company before he figured out what he could have me do," commented King.

And that opportunity came in the form of a young, talented, eager actress who walked into Orenstein's office stating she wanted to become the most famous porn star in the world. Her name was Jenna Jameson.

"There was a combined opportunity with Jenna, because I had been selling to Adam and Eve and had a unique perspective in how I dealt with them," King said. "At that point it was the best of both worlds: I could both market Jenna and create revenue for [Wicked]."

King has been credited with developing and growing the marketing strategy around Jameson, who was a decidedly different actress than her counterparts in the industry at the time. Motivation and determination, coupled with beauty, brains, and the charm of the girl next door, led Orenstein and King to conclude they were working with someone special.

"Jenna [Jameson] was a huge turning point for the company, and that's why I hired Joy," Orenstein said. "The funny thing about Jenna was that she had already done fifteen movies in the business, and when we signed her and put out a big ad introducing her at the [AVN Awards], we had companies who called us asking us, 'Who is that girl?' So if you want to talk about marketing perception, there you have it."

Jameson's outlook on her career fascinated Orenstein and King, and they began work to make her vision a reality.

"As much as we assisted her, it was her driving force that made it happen," King said. "She could carry herself well in the media. She was an outstanding model and we initially had some pictures done of her and created an entire marketing plan around her and her brand."

When King began promoting Jameson, King realized that she wanted to push the line once again, setting out to create opportunity for her client in the mainstream media. Jameson was featured in the E! Channel's *Wild On* series with Brooke Burke, on *Entertainment Tonight*, and was a regular component on the Howard Stern radio show, even playing a role in his autobiographical movie, *Private Parts*.

"The first thing we did with her," Orenstein said, "was go to the Cannes Film Festival, because back then, they still highlighted adult films. So we took out an ad that said, 'Come meet the new star in adult,' knowing that her first movie [for Wicked] wasn't even out yet. But it was this which got the E! channel to call our booth and schedule an interview. The woman who ended up interviewing [Jenna] had an ear-to-ear grin the entire time she talked to Jenna because [Jenna] was just that good."

However, Jameson's skyrocketing career didn't come without challenges—especially because King and Orenstein simultaneously were working to propel Jameson's career and develop the Wicked Pictures brand as a production company.

"We weren't completely prepared for the level of success that came, both for her and for Wicked as a company," King said. "So as we got busier, it became more difficult to handle everything. When we started on this journey, it never occurred to us just how successful it would all be. So, there were things that happened that we looked back on that made us say, 'Oh, we should have done that differently.' Obviously, it all worked out, so it doesn't matter now, but we were so busy building Jenna as the brand that somewhere along the way, we forgot to do the same for Wicked."

King acknowledges it is possible to create an incredibly successful talent career in the adult entertainment industry, but she also believes that in order to accomplish the feat, an actor or an actress must treat the endeavor like a business and take it seriously. In her book *Get Into Porn*, King notes that while many actresses [and actors] want to create a "brand" around themselves, they can't do that just by performing in films.

"You must have a professional approach to everything that you are doing: honoring your word, being genuine, doing what you say you are going to do," she said. "There is nothing more frustrating in business than working with someone who doesn't deliver. And if you can be consistent and you have good people around you, then anyone can be successful given that they have other elements present: they are attractive, they are smart. It's more than just one thing over another. It's a combination of having a professional attitude and treating this like a real business."

The industry itself has become much more female-friendly and focused since the early 1980s, and King believes the savvy many women have developed is required in order to become a mainstay in adult entertainment. As a woman who created a career for herself in what had traditionally been a male-centric industry, King said the opportunity for women has greatly expanded, and the stigma associated with being a member of the adult entertainment community, whether in front of the camera or behind the camera, has significantly reduced.

"I think the Internet certainly opened up a lot of opportunity, both from the standpoint of working in the industry and actually accessing the materials," she said. "It sort of started becoming this cool, pop-culture thing. For instance, when Jenna and I would go places, she had just as many female fans as she had men. It was kind of surprising. But I think at that point you had these college-age students that were a little more open minded in terms of their own sexuality. Women in general were becoming more okay with the entire thought of pornography, where before it was this horrific thing at the Pussycat Theater that came with the reaction of 'Oh my God, whose man goes to that?'"

King believes the mainstreaming of the industry began when greater access was given to females, whether they were able to walk into a store and buy adult materials without feeling dirty, or they were able to buy toys and other goods online anonymously. This accessibility encouraged female consumers to open their minds and develop a new perspective about adult entertainment. That caused production houses, including Wicked and Digital Playground, to begin promoting themselves as companies looking to engage distaff consumers.

While King doesn't wish to portray the industry as immediately accepted by all people, she did note much of the progress seemed to follow generational patterns: Younger women embraced their sexuality and enjoyment of sexual content without societal guilt, and as they aged, the next generation continued to embrace what was offered.

"The more it became acceptable, the more women began seeking employment not just in front of the camera, but behind it as well, which helped create more opportunity, for more women," King observed.

King gives considerable credit to several female entrepreneurs not only for creating careers for themselves, but also for developing independent brands, marketing others, creating jobs, and taking on the role of ambassador for the industry.

"I think Joanna Angel is incredibly savvy, intelligent; she handles her business," King said. "Also, Lisa Ann has done a fantastic job of creating her brand. Stormy Daniels is another example. I have had the opportunity to work with her [at Wicked], but she is another person who, if she says she is going to have a script to me by a certain time, she is going to have the script to me by that time. If she says she will have a budget done by the end of the day, I will have that budget."

King believes respect and professionalism is what determines whether a woman in the talent community will be able to create a career that lasts.

"Of course, that goes for any business," she said. "But in this industry you have a lot of people who end up here by accident who don't take it seriously. So when you find someone who is and does, it's refreshing."

Because of the role King fills as an executive at Wicked and an advocate in the public forum, she has served as mentor (or as she states, more like a "mother-figure") to many of the women with whom she works. She said she takes pride in helping them make the best choices, teaching them they can say "no," and ultimately assisting them to avoid negative situations. She also said she has talked more women out of the industry than she has talked into it.

"[Performers] have to realize that you have a choice about everything you do, and there are such things as boundaries and limitations, even in this industry," she said. "I also always stress the consequences and what [working in the industry] means. This career choice is one that lasts forever. Families and friends will look at you differently. I just think that it is so important that anyone who decides to enter this industry come into it with their eyes wide open and have an understanding of how it is going to affect them."

Much of society is more open, but anti-pornography people and groups remain, and they can be vicious. King has developed a way to respond to those who criticize her work or accuse the industry as a whole of exploiting women.

"Surprisingly, this doesn't happen as much as most people believe it happens," she said. "I have a fairly disarming personality; I'm certainly not what most people picture when they envision a porn producer. I'm normal. I don't get as much feedback as you might think. However, I have been asked, 'What would you do if your daughter wanted to do this?' and those types of questions. But it all comes back to the fact that this industry is about people making choices for themselves.

"Women are exploited in this industry just as much as they are in beer commercials and *Sports Illustrated* swimsuit editions. But in this industry, exploitation ends when a woman has the ability to make the call on what she wants to do. It stops being considered exploitation and should be looked at as women who are taking charge of their own careers.

"I get offended when someone tries to tell me what is going on in my own business," King said. "I have been here for a very long time, I have seen women come into this industry and create amazing, lifelong careers. The opportunities for women in this industry do not exist anywhere else."

Considering the changes the industry has undergone the success King has experienced during her career, it's fine for her to be opinionated about the role the adult entertainment plays in society. At the same time, she is a great example of the type of advocate the industry, and companies like Wicked, need in order to thrive.

Agents to the Infamous

Lucky Smith, former manager for actress Juli Ashton and others, found himself in the middle of a changing industry in the early 1990s as a recent law school graduate. Smith, who is now known for managing a maximum of six girls at a time in order to attend to each one as an individual, in the early days did everything from set visits to contract negotiations to babysitting for both his clients and the studios that employed them.

"I got started by chance, really," he said. "I represented a woman, Alexis DeVell, in a traffic case. Some months later she called me and said she decided to get into the adult movie business and she wanted me to go to Los Angeles to negotiate the contract. Legend was the first company I worked with."

The front office of the production house originally thought Smith was DeVell's boyfriend. Managers were not common; boyfriends were. When Smith asked to see the contract and began taking a red pen to the document to rephrase or rewrite certain clauses and statements, the studio realized they were dealing with a performer who had representation.

Smith went to his first shoot as a by-stander after DeVell signed. He was fascinated by the moviemaking process and ended up staying through four days of his client's stint on screen. After flying back to Boulder, DeVell returned to his office lamenting the way the shoot had turned negative.

"She said, 'After you left, it was just awful. They wanted me to do scenes that I didn't want to do. I hated it. I want you to come out every time I shoot,'" he recalled.

It was then that Smith decided to investigate how he could create a career as a talent manager. He called a fellow lawyer who had experience at the job and was told he could expect to receive 15 to 20 percent of his client's earnings. During the early 1990s when porn was booming, an agent could earn a decent living.

When Smith took on his next client, Shayla LeVeaux, he also helped book additional income-earning opportunities at strip clubs and other shows where the girls could increase their exposure and pad their bank accounts.

"I used to say that I was selling very pretty shoes," he said. "All women, frankly speaking, have the same biological parts. The products at the end of the day are homogenous. I had to convince studios and production companies that my girls were better, more beautiful, more talented. That was the trick to it and another reason why I kept my client list very small."

Smith also was able to get adult star Juli Ashton cast on the show *Night Calls*, which ran on Playboy TV from 1995 until 2007. Playboy, as a company, has been notoriously opposed to casting adult stars for their programs. When Smith was approached by a vice president of Playboy about Ashton, he turned down the offer for that reason. Playboy persisted, and in November 1998 Ashton signed on to co-host *Night Calls*.

Smith began earning his agent commission right away when Playboy set about promoting the show in a way that didn't serve Ashton's best interests. Before one personal appearance, co-host Tiffany Granath, who was a *Playboy* Playmate, and therefore only ever posed nude for the magazine, emerged from wardrobe wearing an elegant, modest evening gown selected for her by show executives. Ashton's attire, on the other hand, consisted of Victoria's Secret lingerie. Smith objected immediately. "You either put them both in evening gowns, or they both wear lingerie," he said. "You aren't going to put the porn girl in her underwear."

Smith understood how easily studios could bully or coerce contract performers into doing things they didn't sign up for. He saw his role as enforcer, protecting his client's interests, or at the very least saying, "Okay, we are willing to consider that, but you are going to pay more if you want her to do that scene."

Smith helped his clients find work and negotiate pay in three primary areas: feature dancing, films, and an "other" category that included magazine spreads, trade shows, and novelty item sponsorships. Once he and his clients determined the core areas in which the client would participate, Smith approached building an actresses' career and managing the rest of her life step-by-step: "This is how we are going to pay your car payment, and this is how we are going to pay your rent."

Furthermore, Smith was not overly concerned about the first contract written for a client. He wasn't aiming to make someone a millionaire on the first shot. Rather, he wanted to establish the client and make sure she got return work, and he did that by helping her demonstrate she was professional and could be relied upon. When her contract came up for renewal, he could up the ante.

Contract negotiations in adult are more difficult than in Hollywood, primarily because the adult entertainment industry views actresses the same way a car dealership considers new cars: The moment a car leaves the lot, its value depreciates. In adult, once a woman shoots her first sex scene, she is not as valuable. Studios also see a great deal of risk in new talent: The performer might decide she hates the business; she might be horrible on screen. A million different things could happen to leave the studio in the lurch. Smith considered this with each of his clients and aimed to make the deal attractive to both the actress and the studio—he negotiated "out clauses" in each deal he oversaw. After the first film, both parties had the option to say "thanks, but no thanks."

Smith also said he talked more women out of entering the business than he ever did into it. Because becoming an adult performer is such a serious decision, he believes women of 22 or 23 shouldn't rush in. "Porn is around forever," he said. "It's always going to be there, so you have to realize the choice you are making."

Keeping it Up:
The Life and Times of Male Talent

Male porn star. All day, you get to have sex with beautiful, desirable women in front of the camera for the world to see. Sounds like a dream job, right?

While the role of male porn star does have its perks, male performers, for all intents and purposes, are mostly accessories— biological pieces of the pie that are necessary to create a final product.

In contrast to the popular misconception that male porn stars must have a lot of fun, the majority of male talent discovers that the job is harder than it looks. Just like women in the industry, men who work in front of the camera must create a career that ensures longevity and provides security against the inevitable march of time. With the exception of a few notable icons like Ron Jeremy and Peter North, even men must acknowledge there will come a time when they no longer will be camera-ready.

Headliners and well-known women in the industry have the ability to pick and choose their jobs, they have established a reputation for themselves as having a good attitude, are easy to work with on set and don't go around acting like a diva. Men also are tasked with developing a good reputation, especially if they want to succeed. However, few men have the ability to pick and choose their own jobs like many of their female counterparts.

Men traditionally operate in the industry as independent contractors and rarely find themselves under contract with a production house. There have been a few male contract performers, but on the whole the industry does not actively recruit male actors. Consequently, it is much harder for a man to break into the industry than it is for a woman.

The easiest way for a man to get a break in the industry is to find a female actress who shows potential and is willing to insist she will work only with him. Even then male talent face a difficult road. Few production companies will hire a male actor without experience and references, and few talent agencies are willing to represent men.

One of the best known U.S. talent agencies that handles male actors is World Modeling, based in Van Nuys, California.

In light of all of the difficulties men face in the industry, it is important to note that men typically are much more viable than women once they have established themselves in porn. Even with all of the female beauties out there, Ron Jeremy tops the 50 Top Porn Stars of All Time list.

Jeremy, who broke into the industry in 1978, has performed in more than 1,600 productions and directed more than 100 films. He has a signature line of sex toys and has worked as a consultant for mainstream movie productions such as *Boogie Nights* and *9 ½ weeks*. Jeremy originally broke into the industry with his girlfriend's encouragement: She submitted a picture she had taken of him to *Playgirl* magazine in the hopes of seeing Jeremy in a "Boys Next Door" photo spread. The entry was accepted, and Jeremy then decided to consider pornography as a way to support himself after striking out in New York theater.

Today, more than 30 years since he entered the industry, Jeremy is considered one of the best known actors and personalities in adult. Furthermore, he has experienced considerable crossover success in mainstream television, movies, music, books, and video games. Jeremy has also served as a spokesperson for the Free Speech Coalition and People for the Ethical Treatment of Animals (PETA).

Indeed, Jeremy is a male icon in the industry. His success, while uncommon, is a testament to men's ability to create a career in porn.

Barrett Blade also has experienced a good deal of success as an adult actor. Blade has discovered there is a place for him when he decides to stop acting: He can direct.

Another accidental porn star, Blade entered the adult industry in 1999 and spent several years acting before expanding his horizons to the production side. "I was signed to Warner Brothers as a member of a music group called Dial 7 back in the '90s, but we were dropped by our label," he said. "At one of our last shows in Hollywood, I met a porn girl named Devon who was signed to Wicked Pictures at the time, and I ended up hanging out with her because I didn't have much going on. When you come from the music industry into the porn industry, it's pretty funny how easy it is to jump in there, and without sounding cocky, see where the flaws were and know what needed to be fixed."

Blade began to work with Devon (who goes by her first name only), helping her manage her career from behind the scenes, until one day she invited him to do a scene with her. Initially, he turned her down. She persisted and eventually, upon reflecting that his music career was at a standstill, decided "why not?"

The relationship with Devon was short-lived, however, and even though he had performed in several scenes, Blade found himself without future prospects in an industry that was not overly hospitable to new male actors.

"I began calling directors that I knew, asking for work," he explained. "I offered my services as a personal assistant. I said I would pick up condoms, I didn't care, I needed a job. It was then that one person came back to me and said that I should do scenes since I had been there before. I asked about the pay and was surprised to learn that it was more than I had been making, so I decided, yeah, I guess so. I started performing."

When Blade first began working, the way men expanded their careers was to be placed on a girl's list of actors she would work with on camera. The more girls who felt comfortable with a male performer, the better it was for the man's career. Producers frequently asked actresses "Who is on your list?" in order to find men that might fit the roles they needed to cast. In today's adult entertainment world, agents play a larger role in casting, so the woman's say in who she will be filming with has decreased. While she may provide a "no" list, or a list of men she refuses to work with, women no longer have the ability to say, "I'm only working with so and so on this project." Consequently, some men work heavily with agents to increase their bookings. Blade is not one of those men. He said he has been effective at forming relationships and does not feel he needs to pay an agent to book him. Hence, he books all of his work himself.

"In traditional Hollywood, the agent works for the actor," Blade said. "In porn, the actor works for the agent. It's reverse, and therefore not always favorable to the interests of the actor."

Blade attests to the fact that women make more money, but their longevity is much shorter. Men, on the other hand, might make less, but they can work more and over a longer period of time.

An example of a man's longevity in the industry is Nick Manning, who had a budding mainstream career as a semi-pro baseball player, Wall Street broker, model and actor prior to beginning in adult entertainment.

"I was working on Wall Street, playing ball in my spare time and going to graduate school and I hated it," stated Manning. "So I quit and I went down to the local modeling agency near where I was working. The first few places I went told me that I was too old since I was 28 at the time. However, I landed a role in Kevin Costner's *'For the Love of the Game,'* and then *'Any Given Sunday.'* After this, I went onto do a *Playgirl* spread. I found my groove with this. I started working with *Penthouse* and some other adult media. I knew I wasn't going to be Tom Cruise, but at the same time I had no idea that after 600 magazines and 2,000 adult movies, I would still be around."

Manning goes on to agree with Blade that from an emotional standpoint, the business is much harder on women than it is on men, and that also plays a significant role in the length of women's careers.

"I have the ability to work every day if I want to," stated Manning. "There have been times where I have worked 250 days a year. Not many women in the business do that, it burns them out and for good reason. But this is one of the ways how a guy in the industry gets attention paid to them. Women are the stars, but men can be noticed if they put themselves out there."

However, the women who have been successful, Blade noted, are the ones who treat their work like a business and can separate themselves from the emotional trappings that usually come with sex.

"The ones that are doing it for the wrong reasons are the ones that tend to come and go more quickly," he said. "And unfortunately, many of them are doing it for the wrong reasons and tend to exploit that. It's a fine line. As a guy who loves women, I hate to see that. What bothers me the most is when a girl does it to support her boyfriend or a drug habit. I have always been a firm believer that this business should be 21 and up, because I think the girls at 18 or 19, while there are some who can handle it, the majority are not prepared to be making thousands [of dollars] a week and knowing how to take care of their money, and put it away, and pay their taxes, and do what they are supposed to."

From the male perspective, the business itself is much easier; however, most young men cannot handle the physical requirements when they are 18 or 19 years old, at least in Blade's opinion.

Currently, the industry boasts few male performers who are under 22 or 23 years old, except in gay productions.

"When women come to me looking for advice, I tell them to treat it like a business and not a party," Blade said. "This isn't your hookup time, your dating service. If you took a job anywhere else and showed up drunk or high, you aren't going to have a job. If you go in as a professional, on time, with a good attitude, you are going to keep working."

Keeping a focused business mentality is one thing Blade learned early in his career, and he said that has influenced the way he treats women. The advice came from his mother, who told him, "Treat the women right." He decided those words were some of the best advice he could have received, because he realized that without women, he wouldn't have a job.

Some men, regardless whether they are homosexual or straight, turn to gay porn. That is a course Blade has said he never considered, even though gay roles tend to pay better. Not only is acting in gay porn an obvious challenge to a straight man (even though some men in the industry do it), but many women refuse to work with straight men who have performed in gay films. According to Blade, some producers of gay movies do not test for HIV the way producers of straight adult films do, as the policy is at a number of gay studios is "condom only."

"I have a problem with that," Blade said. "And unfortunately, if I say 'no' to doing a scene because of an issue with an actress who has done a scene with a man who also does gay porn, they are not going to replace the girl. They are going to replace me."

Blade believes that there are other challenges to remaining active in the business. First, the transition from "young hot guy" to "seductive mature male" can be difficult without falling into the no-man's-land of "creepy old man." In addition, a male performer's greatest physical asset tends to become less reliable as he ages. Both of those things worry Blade.

"It is possible to cross over into that 'old guy role' gracefully, but obviously, even though your penis may work, the jobs are not as regular," commented Blade. "Randy Spears is a great example of [a guy who worked in spite of age]. He worked well into his fifties."

But Blade knows that staying in front of the cameras forever is not a guaranteed option, even though he feels he still has years before he needs to consider surrendering to age completely. He actively works to market himself and create other streams of revenue based upon his personal brand. In the past he operated a website that sold individual scenes he filmed and performed in, and he allowed a mold of his penis to be made in order to produce a line of dildos.

Outside his role as a performer, Blade actively embarked upon improving his education about what happens behind the camera, planning ahead for an alternate career once his acting days are over.

"I went through a slump, had some personal problems where I realized that I needed a backup plan," he said. "I needed something to cover my ass, so I went to editing school. There was a big-name director back in the day, Nick Andrews, who taught me a lot, and I started shooting behind the scenes. I started learning about the cameras and still photography, really all of it. For a while I was shooting, lighting, doing the stills, all of it, myself. It was my goal to learn everything I could so I could do whatever job anyone came to me with."

Blade began marketing himself to companies and production houses asking to direct, film, or take on any other behind-the-scenes position that was available. While he admitted crossing over from in front of the camera to behind it is difficult because the powers that be are reluctant to take performers seriously, he believes his hard work and persistence have paid off. Over time and by proving himself through delivering good work, he has created a viable career path for when he decides to stop performing.

Overall, Blade keeps his job, and his career, in perspective.

"I know why I am being recognized," he said. "It's because I am selling sex. It's nice to have recognition for the work that I have done, but I know I am not the next Tom Cruise. When you start patting yourself on the back for everything, you start to have a problem of ego. Thank the fans. Without them, none of us would have a job. Keep it a business."

What a Contract Girl
Really Looks Like

Contract girls are a unique breed, and frankly, there used to be more of them in the industry. The production houses, with their stables of stars during the heyday of pornography, mimicked the old-school glamour of Hollywood during the 1930s, when certain stars were known for their affiliation with certain studios.

"When Ginger [Lynn] decided that she didn't want to do adult movies anymore, [Vivid] started examining our business in the idea of 'are we the Ginger company? Or are we Vivid?' That is when we brought on our second contract girl, Jamie Summers, and we started shooting a series of movies called 'The Brat Series' and they did every bit as well as the Ginger movies and I thought that we were on to something. We decided to expand and bring on a group of girls that we could build a company around and start calling them 'Vivid Girls.' We decided to send them out as groups and take over," said Steve Hirsch of Vivid Entertainment.

Jessica Drake is one contract girl who takes her role very seriously; consequently, she's a boon to her studio, Wicked Pictures. Part of her strategy when she signed with the studio in 2004 was removing herself from visibility in the industry prior to signing. Ultimately, taking herself off the market for two years before the deal made her more valuable in the eyes of Wicked management, because the studio could re-introduce an established name with a track record.

"There are a lot of benefits to being a contract girl, and when Wicked came along, I was actually in the process of negotiating with another company," Drake said. "Right before I was going to sign [with the other company], I received some phone calls inquiring as to my status. That's when Wicked wanted to meet with me. I sat down and spoke with [owner] Steve [Orenstein], and we were on the same page with everything."

With Wicked, everything came together. Drake was able to set her terms and talk about what she expected from Wicked. She wanted to work with a company that was not just going to book her for sex scenes and promote her for a limited time, essentially saddling her with a shelf life. Wicked offered something different: Orenstein's company offered Drake support and the opportunity for professional growth, whether that growth occurred on-screen or behind the scenes. She wanted the ability to express herself creatively, however she saw fit. Additionally, never once did Wicked propose taking ownership of her trademarked name "jessica drake." She's always owned the brand, and she always will.

Drake left Orenstein's office knowing she was going to sign with the company, and she did, the following week.

"Think what you will about Jenna [Jameson]," Orenstein said. "Yes, she was successful. But I would rather have five more Jessica Drakes any day. Girls like Jessica do not come around every day. When you sign a contract with a performer, it's like a marriage; you have to know who you are signing because it is a minimum one-year deal with that person. I sign girls that want to be here. I will not sign a girl who made her decision on being here because of the money. Jessica is that person."

Since starting with Wicked, Drake has realized she and the company share a vision. The production house, she said, does not simply sign a girl because the girl is hot or because she looks good on camera, but based on the type of relationship the studio and the actress can foster together.

"I have signed about twenty girls over the past twenty years, and there is no one like Jessica, nobody." Orenstein said. "I have gotten it right sometimes, and other times, I have gotten it wrong. I ask performers to evaluate what they have done for the company come contract renewal time, and Jessica is one person who always is able to verbally state the value that she brings. She gives all of the credit to the company."

Drake is not only a cheerleader for Wicked Pictures, but also for her contemporaries at the company.

"Consider Stormy Daniels: She has gone on to be an incredibly successful writer and director [for Wicked]," Drake said. "It's all about the other things that we can do, not just about the idea that here is another pretty girl. During the interview process and when we [Wicked] decide to sign another contract girl, it's really analyzed. Not to make this sound bad, but we aren't going after the 'bad girl' or the salacious story. We aren't going to sign someone just because they made some news on *TMZ*. That strategy may work initially, but anyone who signs with a company on those terms is a flash in the pan, and in this business, it's about longevity."

Drake is consistent in her work with Wicked. Since the time she signed with the company, she has done seven movies per year. She performs a handful of scenes here and there, based on whether she is interested in the concept for the movie or wants to work with specific actors or actresses. Generally she keeps herself in starring roles that come with her face on the box cover. Ancillary work related to writing or directing is a completely separate area. Drake is not a contracted writer for Wicked, but she is adamant that she would never write for anyone else.

"I don't write really well on assignment, so when the mood strikes me and I have an idea, I write," she said. "I direct features for Wicked, not incredibly often, but like I said, when the mood strikes me. A movie I did last year called *Three Days in June* was one that I wrote, directed, and starred in. For all practical purposes, it was probably the first big feature that I did, and it got a lot of nominations at the AVN Awards. It didn't win anything, but as they say, 'It's an honor to be nominated.' What I am focusing on now is actually a line of instructional sex DVDs for Wicked called *Jessica Drake's Guide to Wicked Sex.*"

Drake embraces a passion helping people in areas where sex and reproductive health may still be taboo. As an adult film star, she's in a unique position to make a difference: Take away the glitz and glamour associated with her role at Wicked, and there is an opportunity for outreach where resources, and education, are limited. She feels her new line of educational videos allows her to "give back" in appreciation for all she has received and to be a part of something bigger.

"Jessica is really amazing, because she is very appreciative of the opportunities that she is provided," Orenstein said. "No matter if it is something in the industry or outside of it, she's genuine in her approach."

Throughout her career, Drake has traveled to sets and personal appearances in exotic locales. Somewhere in the middle of all the airports and convention centers in which she has spent time, she began to realize she was missing the heart and soul, the "realness," of areas many people only know as spots on a map.

"I was in South Africa, and I hired a private tour company to take me out and show me Johannesburg," she said. "One of the things I was interested in seeing was Soledo. It's a big township in Johannesburg. The tour guide said he couldn't take me through, but he knew some kids who would be able to guide me. I took some time to go through an orphanage and a nursery school, and I was struck by the conditions, the children and the poverty. I had an ah-ha moment. That was really it for me. I decided that I wanted to do more charity work."

She became affiliated with an overseas organization that focuses on building homes and providing clean water to people in poverty-stricken and remote areas. She believes the farther away a location, the more she tends to get out of the experience and the more benefit she feels she brings to the people she is working to help.

"I was in Cambodia last year and spent three weeks in a little village outside of Siem-Reap. That was an amazing experience," she said. "And then I was in Kenya, about four hours outside of Nairobi, in the Rift Valley, and after that I was in Tanzania for a week."

Despite all of the effort that she puts into her humanitarian globetrotting, Drake is quick to point out she keeps her "day job" secret from the charities with which she works. While she doesn't speculate on their potential opinion of her involvement in the adult entertainment industry, she doesn't want to chance her work getting in the way of good deeds.

Drake recently formed a 501(c)(3) non-profit to assist in domestic efforts. This, too, is separate from her role with Wicked and the "jessica drake" brand, as it is important to her that no one thinks she volunteers her time as part of a public relations campaign. Her charity work is done anonymously.

Anonymous or not, Drake also thinks she can help humanitarian efforts in some of the most stricken places on Earth by doing what fans say she does best: sex. Or at least talking about it.

Drake is working to become a licensed sex educator and sexual coach. While she's doubtless already an expert at "sex ed," she believes certifications will assist her charity efforts, especially in the areas of HIV/AIDS and teaching safe-sex techniques in Africa and Southeast Asia. These areas are known for their lack of reproductive education and have some of the highest HIV/AIDS rates in the world. Drake, as a performer who always has been condom-only, believes that much can be done through progressive outreach and education.

"I do sex workshops all over the world," she said. "I really love the humanitarian work. When I go to a country like Kenya, you have to realize the area that I was in has a sixty-four percent HIV infection rate. One of the reasons that I chose to do the course to become a licensed sex educator, was to give me more credibility when I go to these areas and when I reach out to non-profits and other [Non-Government Organizations]. In every country I visit, I try to seek out their version of Planned Parenthood or a family planning clinic, and it really blows my mind when I think about some of the stuff I have seen.

"One of the things I am interested in accomplishing with my non-profit is to find some condom sponsors who are willing to go into these areas and teach the women about how to discuss safe sex with their partners. There is a huge stigma attached to that in some areas, and it's not that the people aren't smart enough—it's just that they do not have the resources at all."

Drake recounted her experience at a family planning clinic in Cambodia. The sole facility in a huge geographic area was responsible for providing reproductive education and services to a grossly underserved female population—and everything was accomplished in a ramshackle structure with a thatched roof.

Considering she has seen firsthand what happens when women are denied necessary sexual education and resources, Drake is especially concerned about the climate towards reproductive rights and sexual health at home in the United States.

"I think the government choosing not to fund Planned Parenthood is incredibly destructive," she said. "We have already found that without [resources], the teenage pregnancy rate goes up, the rate of HIV/AIDS infection increases, [sexually transmitted infections] skyrocket. Whether it is because of opposition by different groups or lack of other funding, it handicaps us in the long run. I don't get it, as a woman. For me it's such a personal topic, and it's crippling."

In light of all of her passion opinions, and the good deeds she does every day, Drake still gets some negative feedback about the charity work she does.

"I have been asked 'How can you do that? You're a porn star,'" she revealed. "I realize my job entails me having sex on camera, but I counter with the fact that I do have some celebrity status that I combine with resources I am ready to put forward on my own dime.

It's important for me to stand up for what I believe in. I believe that you can still be a role model and be a porn star. The two roles are not mutually exclusive. I have spent my whole career battling these stereotypes, and it got to the point where I decided that I am going to do the things that I am interested in; I am going to do the things that make me happy, critics be damned. My positive efforts go further and benefit more people than their criticism of me."

Orenstein, frankly, couldn't be happier with Drake and more pleased with all of her efforts. "She's truly amazing," he said. "She follows through on commitments, she's always professional, she's dedicated, she driven, she's compassionate. She could be doing anything in the world, but she's doing this because she loves it. Wicked is lucky to have her."

Another performer, Sunny Leone of Vivid Entertainment, attributes her success as a contract girl to the fact that during the time that she was looking to grow her career, the industry was in a very public recession due to overall economic challenges affecting not only porn, but the business climate as a whole. She remembers being privy to a lot of complaining about DVD sales and not making money and piracy, as well as a host of other issues. Frankly, she said, she turned a deaf ear and didn't allow the naysayers to get her down.

When Leone decided to get into the industry, she did it through a careful analysis of the players who mattered. Finally, she chose Vivid.

"I figured if I was going to make adult movies, why shouldn't I go to the best company in the industry? Vivid had the best reputation for the way they deal with girls, their work ethic," she said. "And it worked. I have one of the best relationships with Steven [Hirsch] and every person in that office. It's such a blessing to have such an amazing circle around my brand and my company. [Vivid] wants to see me succeed. I have always been told the company is behind me 100 percent."

Leone is one of the busiest women in adult. After expanding her own company during 2011, she was invited to host the 2012 AVN Awards.

"I've been having some of the best years of my life, this year included," she said. "2011 has been the most successful business year I have had thus far in my career, and I attribute that to being creative. It has been ten years now that I have been involved in adult entertainment, and I still have my drive, which I think is rare. I still want to keep moving past yesterday's goal."

Even though she's under contract with Vivid, Leone has been very involved in creating her own brand. She has owned her website since Day One, and she has never depended on any other company to host or maintain it for her. While she has gone outside for technology advice, Leone is adamant about making sure she has control over the site and its content.

"Vivid is absolutely amazing, and Steven [Hirsch] provides such resources to my individual brand," she said.

When she signed with Vivid initially, Leone was embarking on a different road in the adult industry, one that pushed her business model along and spurred additional development. The contract with Vivid propelled her career, her brand, and her image simultaneously.

Steve Hirsch of Vivid said, "Sunny [Leone] is special. She was one of the last girls who made it really just working with girls on camera. And she is so stunning and such a hard worker that she really stands out and has done a phenomenal job. In an industry with so few 'stars' Sunny is one person who is right up there with Jesse Jane and maybe one or two others."

"Until the time I signed with Vivid, I had not done any hardcore boy/girl or girl/girl films," she revealed. "The way my business has developed is based on the idea that the less I do, the more people want. It's about supply and demand, and I personally believe that if you are going to take your clothes off for money, you should be the one that makes the majority of the profit. It's your body, it's your image, and it's your brand. Every girl in the industry has her own business plan for how she is going to be successful. I know some girls out there shoot for everyone, and they are very successful and win tons and tons of awards for shooting for all of these different people. I see myself as a bit of an anomaly, because I have done very little and have achieved every level of success that I could possibly dream of."

She believes that in order to be successful, performers must be comfortable on set as well as when negotiating work contracts. Comfort, for Leone, includes choosing scene partners. She is very selective about whom she has sex with and says 90 percent of the performers with whom she has worked are people she wanted to be on screen with: She had an established relationship with them, knew them, and saw something there that made sense from a business perspective.

"I would get offers from people, and they would encourage me [to] 'shoot with this girl. She is really popular,'" she said. "And I would say absolutely not, it's not happening. I either didn't find the girl attractive or I knew too much about her or there was something else that turned me off on the prospect of working with her. People want to see you having a good time, and it's such an intimate thing, it should stay that way."

She is also quick to argue with those who say she is being exploited. Leone thinks exploitation is present everywhere, regardless of industry. The women in the adult entertainment industry have the power, she insists, but she also is firm on the position that anyone who allows someone else to make her choices for her is not smart enough to stay on top of industry trends and changes. In a nutshell: Anytime the performer is not involved in decision making, there is opportunity possibility she will "get screwed."

"I don't think there are many victims in this industry," Leone said. "You have the right to say yes or no. Now if you say yes against your better judgment or morals or whatever you are feeling just so you can make a quick extra thousand dollars, then that is your choice. At the end of the day, if you are unhappy with something, you are the one that signed the contract that agreed to the terms. Additionally, you said on camera before you shot that you agreed you were going to be shooting this scene, that you are of sound mind, that you are not on any drugs, and that no one is coercing you to do this. That is standard procedure. If you don't have the balls to stick up for yourself and what you want out of life, you deserve what comes to you."

Leone also believes many women who enter the industry would benefit by learning a thing or two about business, and specifically contracts, or by keeping someone they trust as a confidant. Contracts are designed to benefit the production house or serve the purposes of the individual shoot; hence, reading each and every detail is of paramount importance. Leone said anyone can't or won't do this needs to enlist the help of a trusted someone who can or will. Ultimately, assuming something or being overly trusting never benefits the on-screen talent.

"You have to read every single line and have a lawyer review it," Leone confirmed. "At this point in my life, if I wasn't working in the industry, I might go back and enroll in law school. That's how familiar I have become with contract-speak."

Leone has been a part of many mainstream endeavors, but she remains dedicated to her craft and the opportunities the adult entertainment industry has provided to her.

"I like to produce, I like to be on-screen," she said. "I do so well in producing and making movies, and through my company, my partner and I put a lot of effort into my brand. We are starting to see how much it is growing, how it is affecting our fan base, and that creates opportunity not only for us, but also for the employees we have to hire. [The brand] is doing so well that I would not want that to go away [to pursue mainstream]. I love my life."

Based on her own experience, Leone feels positive about where the industry is headed and what her role within it is going to be. She understands she is not getting any younger, and in this business, age matters. Her strategy right now will provide opportunity over the next decade, though, she believes. Tying in all of the expertise she has gained— production, launching and marketing websites, and other roles—will suit her future interests well.

"At some point I know I am going to have to hang up those heels," she said. "I don't mind if I am not in the spotlight, as long as I am working in this industry. I am a forward-thinking business owner.

I see so many girls enter this industry, and I think some appreciate what I have done and what my company represents," she added. "They ask me for advice. But then there are others who lack the follow-through and do not have the business sense. I know I can't help everyone. Adult entertainment is like any other business, there are leaders and there are followers. My father instilled me with a great work ethic. He taught me that hard work pays off, that it's important to plan ahead, to save money, to live within your means. He told me 'You have to create your own plan. You cannot depend on others to do it for you, and this is what will make you successful.' Yes, I'm an adult entertainer, but the theory holds true regardless of business."

PART FOUR

All in the Comfort of Your Own Home
From Movie Screen to Home Theater

No matter the product, if you can't get it to the consumers who purchase it, you won't make any sales. The adult entertainment industry is no exception to this rule. However, because of the wide array of products produced, coupled with major competition within the business, manufacturers, distributors, sellers and other marketers have their work cut out for them when it comes connecting to the consumer base.

The commerce of the industry doesn't stop when the cameras are shut off. In reality, that is just the beginning. Many of the roadblocks experienced by the business in modern history have less to do with the overall production and more with working with the end user. Challenges related to format and technology as well, as local obscenity laws and shipping requirements, are just some of the issues.

Distribution is broad and works within the following channels:

- Electronic methods such as cable, television, direct broadcast satellite, the Internet, and mobile applications
- Print media such as magazines and trade publications
- Video or film offered as VHS tapes, DVDs, and Blu-ray™ Discs
- Novelty items and adult toys

Within the adult space, distribution methods have evolved as mediums have changed and technology has improved. While there are a variety of distribution methods today, before adult entertainment became multi-channel, few studios or production houses put much thought into their distribution process. Consumer access to porn was limited, usually to a movie theater or adult store. However, as the industry opened up, the production giants had to reconsider how to reach customers. Smaller, independent companies entered the space, unveiling new distribution methods that required less overhead. New audiences appeared, demanding content be delivered on their terms, not by whatever method was most convenient for producers. With the emergence of the Internet, adult entertainment companies were confronted with a new reality: The consumer called the shots. Connecting with customers was key, regardless whether the business was a large production house or a small mom-and-pop adult store.

Distribution: Budgets, Dynamics, Models, Challenges, and Market Size

There are two primary distribution channels within the adult entertainment industry: business-to-business and business-to-consumer. For a long time, business-to-consumer marketing implied unsavory adult video stores located off a highway exit ramp or in a seedy back alley. That's not so much the case anymore, as rarely, if ever, do consumers need to leave their homes in order to get access to their favorite adult stars.

Ease of use meant more than a simple expansion of the market for adult content. The opportunity created major challenges. As content delivery continues to change, distribution channels have to stay on top of their game in order to remain in business, let alone profitable.

During the early days of distribution, producers of adult content made the majority of their profit from sales of VHS tapes. The majority of the sales, and then rentals, came from video stores. Profitability at this time was great, both for manufacturers and sellers. Manufacturers made their money because their product was in high demand, and they controlled output. The seller, or the video store, was able to generate a healthy profit on each tape whether they sold or rented the product. Renting allowed a tape to be paid for after the first two or three rentals, and subsequent rentals paved the way for return on investment to be multiplied several times over. From the perspective of a video store owner, adult films had a low overhead cost.

The VHS opportunity paved the way for another group of people to make money in adult: distributors. Scott Field began working for his father's adult studio, Fat Dog Productions, in 1982. At the same time, because he didn't want to get directly involved in the manufacturing side of the business, he started his own distribution company. Field liked the idea of distributing because he wouldn't be limited to pushing only one product, and therefore could broaden his profit opportunities. Still, he admits distribution is a cutthroat business. Manufacturers and distributors can be polite adversaries. After all, the advent of distribution companies added another expense to manufacturing even as they simplified manufacturers' lives.

"Manufacturers care about [distributors] to a point, but they would rather cut the distributor out of the deal and do it themselves, keeping more of the profit," Field said. "It's nothing new; this has been going on forever."

The manufacturing and store relationships Field nurtures today were formed over the span of two decades. Distribution is not a glamorous piece of the business, especially when considering the everyday backstabbing that often occurs between rival companies. Field doesn't subscribe to that way of doing business, and sees no benefit in marketing only one company's movie, or focusing on one brand. He looks to market anything that sells. The bottom line: If there is an audience for a product, he will work to get it stocked in his customers' stores.

Distributors have seen drastic changes in their business since the Internet came to be. Technology has provided the opportunity for manufacturers to connect directly with consumers, edging distributors out of the movie-marketing process almost completely. Manufacturers often are able to charge less for their products online than what a distributor charges wholesale clients.

Beta vs. VHS and the Rental Market

Remember Betamax? Most of us probably haven't thought about that technology dinosaur in ages. However, that awkward little device opened up the adult industry and provided an outlet for explosive market expansion.

Betamax, developed by Sony, and subsequently, VHS, developed by JVC, were introduced to the technology market in the late 1970s, and suddenly consumers had an alternative to viewing adult movies in seedy movie theaters. With the virtual elimination of the embarrassment attached to viewing pornography in public, the adult entertainment audience increased exponentially. Mainstream Americans now could watch all the porn they wanted in the privacy of their own homes, and nobody had to know.

But nobody said the transition would be easy. With the emergence of competing home-video formats came the obligatory format war.

Although Beta actually offered better quality, severe limitations on the amount of content that could be housed on a tape hampered adoption of the format. The recording length for a Beta tape was sixty minutes—fine for recording your daughter's ballet recital or your son's soccer game, but it posed a significant problem for movies, mainstream or adult. Sony probably could have worked through this and been the victor in the format war, but the company made one serious misstep: It released proprietary information about how the playback machine functioned and how it was built. This faux pas allowed JVC not only to get its VHS product to market quicker, but also allowed them to improve upon the challenges that Sony had experienced in recording length. VHS tapes had the capability to record three hours of video—perfect for movies. Plus, the playback machine was less expensive to manufacture.

"When I first started in this industry, we were selling Beta and VHS [tapes]," Field said. "Beta was very expensive. At that time in 1982, we were selling Beta for $65 to $70 a movie. VHS was selling for $50 to $55 per movie. Back then, there were no rentals; stores were simply selling the videos. So, for instance, I would get an order for 100 copies of *Deep Throat*. Today, a store calls up and buys one copy, because they are renting that video out."

Although recording-length issues composed the official explanation for Beta's eventual failure in the market, pop-culture gossip presents another reason. In much the same way Apple Computers discourages adult material on its products, Sony reportedly was averse to their tapes carrying pornographic content. JVC allegedly did not have such a hang-up.   There is little substantiated evidence to support the alternate reason for Beta's downfall, because adult videos were, in fact, available on the format.

"Beta and VHS were the same actual format; the same principles went into both," Field said.   "But VHS tapes were more affordable, and they took off in a way Beta didn't.   To this day, I still have stores in the Midwest who will call and order VHS tapes.   They haven't gotten into the DVDs yet.   These are little stores or truck stops that call up and order twenty-five tapes.   You still have truckers who have VHS players in their trucks."

KBeech owner Kevin Beechum also got his start in the industry during the format war.   He recalls selling a variety of movies on Beta tapes early in his career.   Even after the adult industry migrated to VHS, some consumers still wanted their porn on Beta.   Because distributors often took on the responsibility for putting the finished movie on the appropriate medium, the format dichotomy opened new revenue opportunities: Distributors essentially could sell the same title twice—once in Beta and once in VHS.

"I started as a sales manager selling videos, Beta specifically," Beechum said.   "Then we moved into VHS.   I spent maybe four years tops working for someone else, and then I opened KBeech Video.   That allowed me not only to handle the sales and distribution, but also to get into the manufacturing side of things.   Things expanded from there.   We kept our hands in all areas."

VHS rentals offered virtually unlimited revenue opportunity for retailers; you could make hundreds of dollars on one cassette if the movie was popular and in demand.   Furthermore, renting offered retailers a way to ease consumers into comfort with pornography.   A video rental was not only discreet, but also temporary; the guilt associated with having a porno in your possession was minimized.

"Back in the day, you could find three video stores on one corner, and all of them sold adult [movies]," Beechum said.   "My company alone was the largest distributor for Family Video, and they are still around today.   The VHS market and video rental [business] was just huge."

Business Boom:
Big Demand Leads to Bigger Growth

When VHS finally got its foothold in the market and adult content manufacturers and distributors realized the opportunity available to them, it didn't take long for business to boom and for industry professionals to realize their supply needed to keep up with demand.   The market had opened up considerably when the videocassette recorder became affordable enough for every American to own one.

"When VHS was introduced, business was just booming. And it didn't matter what [the movie] was. If it was on VHS, stores wanted it," said Beechum.

First Amendment attorney and industry defender Lou Sirkin agrees. "VHS really became popular in video stores, and mom-and-pop [stores] really started to come into their own because they realized there was a market for adult. It really started then that people felt comfortable going into a video store, going to the adult section, and taking movies home."

Statistics show that beginning in 1988, approximately 1,300 hardcore titles were released for public consumption; by 2005, that number was up to 13,588 titles, long after entertainment mediums evolved from VHS. [12] Additionally, adult video sales and rentals in the United States effectively doubled between 1992 and 2005, moving from 405 million units sold to the crushing number of 895 million units sold.[13]

"VHS was such a popular format, and there are still people today who are loyal to the format because of the size of their collections," noted Mark Franks, founder of Castle Megastores.

Beechum fondly remembers those good old days, too. "When I was working in sales, the person on the other end of the phone line [ordering movies] became your best friend," he said. "I had women who ran these video stores, and I would call them 'Mom.' I would call them up and say 'Hey Ma, I have these five new releases. You need them,' and they would order five of each. It was like taking candy from a baby," reflected Beechum. "Now, it's different. If you look at the business today, there are a quarter of the stores. Blockbuster is crashing, Movie Gallery went under. Family Video is kind of stuck where they are.   And the existing stores are all experiencing a decline in their adult market in general."

The Advent of the DVD and
the Death of Blu-Ray

The demise of the VHS videotape began in 1996 with the introduction of the Digital Versatile Disc (DVD). According to *AVN*, sales and rentals of adult videos hit an all-time high during the same year, increasing 100 percent from $2.1 billion in 1992 to $4.2 billion in 1996. [14]   At that point in time, adult videos made up approximately 19 percent of the inventory in all video retail stores.

Despite being more portable and holding more content than videocassettes, DVDs were slow to catch on with consumers.

"The transition to DVD was gradual because the first DVD players were pricey," Castle Megastores' Franks said. "Then manufacturers realized that in order to gain market share, they needed to get the cost down on the equipment."

Beechum remembers another stumbling block for the medium, at least where adult content was concerned: Because DVD players were expensive; consumers bought only one and installed it in the living room or family area, not the bedroom.   So American households would buy family-oriented DVDs to watch in the living room, but they continued to buy adult content on VHS tapes.

"We're still selling DVDs, even today. Sure we run the website and we sell movies and [adult] toys there, but [business-to-consumer] only accounts for a quarter of our business, the other three quarters comes from DVD and movie [business-to-business]sales," stated Beechum.   "There is still a big business out there, but it's so saturated, and so many of the big players just aren't in business anymore."

And then came the advent of Blu-ray. Marketed as The Next Big Thing in Home Entertainment, Blu-ray Discs, developed by Sony, increased the capacity of optical storage even beyond that of DVDs. The extra capacity allowed content producers to fill the discs with another Next Big Thing: high-definition movies—films so vivid viewers could almost touch, taste and smell them. The leap in quality was seductive, but it proved to be a double-edged sword.

"The top producers always talked about quality," Franks said. "And that's why there was a focus on Blu-ray. One of the problems with Blu-ray was that it gave *too much* quality. In close-ups, you could see where the girls had shaved and it was detail you didn't want."

The few movies that were marketed on Blu-ray Discs went nowhere. Not only were the discs expensive to produce, but the quality of the platform actually diminished the experience of the end user.

"Blu-ray was really expensive for the studios," Beechum said. "And only wealthy people actually had the machine to run it when it first came out. Sure, the price dropped on the equipment, but by then the production companies had already lost money, so no one was producing Blu-ray anymore."

A few studios still release titles on Blu-ray, but the technology is not a primary focus. Large studios practically give their inventories away just to get the product out of their warehouses.

"People won't by them," Franks commented. "There is no value or market in Blu-ray. You can charge more for DVDs, even with the Internet around. The technology with regard to HDTV and LED TVs has really improved in what you can see on your screen, so this is in direct competition with what Blu-ray has to offer. I can tell you I was hopeful that it would take off, but in regard to adult movies, it absolutely has no value. People who put a lot of money into Blu-ray just got slaughtered."

Changes in Production and
Decline in Profitability

Numbers don't lie: Porn is still being produced, but production has changed considerably in recent years. Beechum, who in addition to distributing runs several production companies, said his operation's production is down to two movies a week, resulting in approximately $2 million in annual revenue. Ten years ago the company raked in approximately $10 million annually and produced six movies per week. The market has shrunk tremendously, he added: Ten years ago, he had 150 buyers for each movie; now he has 20.

"If you can't make your money back, there's no reason to keep producing," Beechum commented. "But I still have to laugh when people sit back groaning about how business is so bad. People are still making money, but instead of two million a year, they are only making a million. It's not like they are standing in line at a soup kitchen, you know?"

Adult Internet pioneer Greg Dumas, the man responsible for taking Hustler online, agrees with Beechum. "A lot of company owners have told me, 'I'm living hand to mouth right now,' and if anyone knew that, if it was public, there would be a shit storm," he said. "The industry is all smoke and mirrors." According to Beechum, the adult industry is a victim of its own success and misguided self-promotion. The easier pornography became to acquire, the more people realized there was money in the business. Very public discussion about the amount of money in porn encouraged a lot of new producers to join the industry. Even though VHS and then DVD and then the Internet each expanded the consumer market, the market did not expand enough to support an unlimited number of studios. A few companies still rustle up the budgets to make blockbuster films, and there is a loyal audience for flashy, scripted, big-budget features. Everyone else, though, is mass-producing gonzo films—low-budget offerings that offer wall-to-wall sex but no storyline, costuming or set dressing. Gonzo titles sometimes sell and sometimes don't.

"When Digital Playground made [*Pirates*], [producer-director Ali] Joone's brother worked at the mainstream film studio that was producing *Pirates of the Caribbean*," Beechum recalled. "[Digital Playground] was smart enough to jump on the bandwagon and put a bunch of money into [*Pirates*] and release it just before the mainstream film came out, so they couldn't get sued. [*Pirates*] had all the stars in it and was just a larger-than-life kind of film, and it was a big hit. They made a fortune.

Beechum compared the showmanship surrounding *Pirates'* release to the impact *Deep Throat* made during its original release. *Deep Throat* represented a seminal moment in adult entertainment, because no one had made that sort of movie before. In the same way *Deep Throat's* success encouraged other studios to release scripted, almost Hollywood-like films that happened to include explicit sex, Digital Playground's contemporaries attempted to duplicate the success of *Pirates*. Wicked, for example, has succeeded to a degree with films like *Fallen*, starring Jessica Drake, but the company also has invested a lot of money in films that went nowhere or experienced an initial sales spike only to plummet into obscurity within weeks. Part of the problem, according to distributors, is that there's a disconnect between prices studios have to charge in order to recoup their investment in a big-budget movie and what consumers are willing to pay.

"[Wicked] tried selling *Speed* for $70 per DVD, and that's ridiculous," Beechum said. "It's way overpriced. Who is buying a porno for $70 these days?" That's the thing on these big-budget movies: A lot of people are still trying to do it, but it's not working the way it used to."

Beechum fondly recalls a time in the not-too-distant past when consumers walked into adult stores looking for specific videos. If the store didn't have the title he wanted, the consumer would drive around town looking for it. Now, Beechum said, if a store doesn't have a specific video, the consumer will buy something else or simply go home and browse the Internet. Adult movies are easy to come by, and most of them are interchangeable. That's a large part of the reason for the overall decline in the industry, and the "substitution quotient" has caused Beechum to reconsider his entire business model. He has scaled his marketing budget to zero and no longer attends trade shows or other industry events because most business-to-business marketing is a waste of money.

"It doesn't pay to advertise [within the industry] anymore, because trade magazines are only available to people in the [San Fernando] Valley [where most of the studios are located]," Beechum said.

Of course, the manufacturing market is also about trends and what's hot in the marketplace. Fifteen years ago, Beechum focused his business primarily on making parodies of mainstream movies. The tactic was successful until the market became saturated with porn parodies. The trend recently returned, but trends are cyclical. The parody craze will be gone again soon.

"You can come out with something good, but in five years it will be dead because everyone decides to do it," Beechum lamented. "This industry kills anything good that comes around."

The New Life and Times of the
Video Distributor

While statistics indicate that people still buy DVDs and VHS tapes, there's no denying those media are on a steady decline. Even distributors like Scott Field, who have been in the business longer than most, know their business model is threatened by the non-stop advancement of technology. Field cites online distributors as part of the problem and believes payment models like micro-billing, a financial transaction usually completed online that involves a small amount of money usually under $10 are part of the reason why his profits, and business, have declined.

"The fact is, the manufacturers gave permission for companies [like AEBN, a major online video-on-demand provider] to stream their product [via the Internet], and they gave it to them for such a low price per minute, like two and three cents," Field said. "Why on Earth would anyone want to go to a video store and rent a video or buy a video for $39.95 when they could buy the entire movie online for $1.60 or so to see the entire sixty minutes? The industry shot themselves in the foot when they allowed these people to put it online for nothing. They should have insisted that the price be $5 a minute, or something like that."

The distribution community believes there must be a way to make people revert back to hard-copy formats of adult products. What if, for example, the government was to begin taxing the Internet? There probably are no short-term solutions to the distribution dilemma, as any transition in the adult industry takes several years to manifest a positive, or negative, result.

"The day of the distributor will be gone; the day of the video stores is practically gone," Field lamented. "In mainstream, you can stream Netflix on your TV. All of these other companies out there can do the same, including in the adult space on your computer. Once the manufacturers in adult decide to sell a movie directly to DirecTV or another cable provider, or once convergence of computers and TVs occurs, video is over.

"Distributors are being made irrelevant," he continued. "And a lot of it, in my eyes, is generational. I think certain age groups still like the touch and feel of buying a product, holding it in your hand. While I do shop online, and I shouldn't say that, I do try to buy in stores. But the fact is, you can save a lot of money by buying on the Internet, and that's what the current economy dictates must be done, regardless of industry."

Still, Field insists his particular setup is unique. Because his business is small, operated by him and his wife, he doesn't incur tons of overhead expenses that usually are associated with the distribution role. He has flexibility to order and offer what people are buying. If consumers aren't trending towards Evil Angel one week, he focuses on Wicked, or Jules Jordan, or whatever the porn *du jour* happens to be. He says he does roughly $2 million in sales per year, and that figure hasn't changed more than a couple percent in recent history. Compared to some of the manufacturers who are losing upwards of thirty, forty, or fifty percent of their sales per year, Field said his business thus far "is amazing."

Field is not a fan of the Johnny-come-lately element the Internet introduced to the adult industry. In business since the 1980s, Field believes many of the new companies and technology mavens have not revolutionized the business, but instead destroyed it. He especially resents their willingness to present themselves as experts and announce "all is alive and well in adult."

"These people have no idea who is who or anything about [the business]," Field said. "They don't know about the manufacturing part of things, they don't know the process, what it's been through, where it's going, and maybe that's not important—but it is my opinion. Ninety-five percent of industry people out there don't care; they are just interested in pushing product out. Why should any store be interested in buying videos that are pushed out every single week when they know that next week there is going to be a video just like this week's released?"

Field believes all of the big companies are guilty of flooding the marketplace—Digital Playground, Vivid, Wicked, you name it. And it is this product dissolution that contributes to bargain-basement pricing. But he also said there is no alternative, as the studio heads "have to keep pushing content to keep up with the payments on their expensive houses and in-your-face lifestyle." He does give particular credit to Andrew Blake of Studio A, who comes out with a new movie every six or seven months. Blake's release schedule leads to a significant number of pre-orders and recurring orders for Studio A movies, and the company doesn't saturate the market.

"Unless there is a movie that is put out that is absolutely amazing, these [one-a-week] films don't sell out or get reordered," Field said. "Digital Playground put out some amazing work in *Pirates*, and so has Wicked, but they also put out a lot of everything else."

As a distributor in today's online-search-engine-targeted world, Field also recognizes the value in understanding his customer base, knowing what niches trend, what consumers want, and what or who they want to see in an adult film. He says that he watches different areas of the country where he has clients; he consults with his store owners and does a lot of research to understand what is going to sell. He says a "blanket approach" to stocking shelves is not the way to go, especially since that stock could potentially sit there unsold if people in the area aren't interested, he opined.

"I watch trends," he said. "For instance, certain areas of Florida might like a certain actress, or what the high end stores want, or what the mom-and-pop liquor store wants. There are some stores who don't care what they get, and the cheaper the better. But the really good stores have an assortment of great movies. And in reality, eighty percent of the industry puts out a really great, high-quality product. However, it's that remaining twenty percent that brings the quality level down and cheapens it for everyone else."

Evil Angel: A Case Study in
Business Done Right

Considering how it seems the majority of adult manufacturers in today's economy are simply working to make ends meet, there are some studios that are doing it right and who have combined a variety of veteran experience to make sure they not only stay viable, but also profitable. Evil Angel Studios is one of those brands, and the people in control are neither new to the business, nor do they feel that their heyday is over.

John Stagliano founded Evil Angel in 1982 when he began promoting a glossy magazine under that name. In 1983, the company turned to producing movies, which Stagliano then sold to other companies. Evil Angel became a manufacturer in its own right in 1989. Throughout the history of the company, Stagliano has placed much importance on the viewpoint of the director. Consequently, fans know Evil Angel for its directors, not its performers. The model is unique to the industry, launching careers for industry icons including Jules Jordan.

"From the beginning, we have always had a focus on the directors," Stagliano said. "Certainly it's true that talent is very important to the scene, but for me, as a consumer of porno, I noticed that some directors exposed the girl in a particular or better way compared to other directors. This is what I based our business model on."

Bobbi Starr, now a director for Kink.com, worked with Evil Angel early in her career. "They are a great example of a group of people who really make pornography for themselves," she said. "They really explore their own fetishes, their own kinks and sexuality. And they direct their own content, which I feel is very honest.

"I respect that John Stagliano has always invested in his directors," she continued. He has looked for directors who are really kinky, who are really into their fetish, who are dedicated to their own sexuality. They make porn that they want to watch themselves. This is what I feel is very important—not to lose yourself in what the industry says will sell. If you do that, I feel that you run the risk of losing your integrity."

Christian Mann, the general manager of Evil Angel and Stagliano's right hand, has an extensive history in adult entertainment. Beginning in the industry in 1979, Mann has worked in almost every aspect of the business, from magazines to mail order, production, distribution, sales, and marketing. Prior to joining Evil Angel, Mann owned Video Team, a video and DVD distribution company that also moved into content production under a private label and eventually sold to Metro Interactive in 2006.

"When John [Stagliano] called me into service, he was probably the only guy that I would have gone to work for in an employee capacity," Mann said. "Having owned my own company for so many years, and being around the industry for so long, it's somewhat humbling and challenging going back to work for someone else. His company was the one studio, even in light of what was happening economically in the industry, which was thriving."

Mann is quick to say that he takes no credit for the brand recognition Evil Angel currently experiences, saying he joined the company because he felt his particular skill set could assist Stagliano as the company moved forward. Mann notes that Stagliano runs the production house with a focus on making sure employees' skill sets and competencies are not duplicated.

"The things I bring to the table are items that were not present at Evil Angel," Mann said. "Either John felt that he couldn't handle a certain project or he didn't want to."

Mann is known primarily for his ability to market a brand and considers himself self-taught. Plus, he also comes with 30 years of established industry relationships, something that he attributes to his ability to not burn bridges. He is quick to point out that the only way to last as long as he has in the industry is to stay on people's good sides. Of course, that is true in any business.

"Another thing that is hard to find in an employee, even in a general manager, is the sense of ownership," he said. "I don't own [Evil Angel], but I feel invested in it. The decisions I make and the recommendations that I bring to John always come from the point of view of what would I do if I owned this company."

Mann attributes much of his role to the fact that he has been around to see a bevy of monumental changes in the industry. He lived through the learning curve as the business move from adult movie theaters to videotape, then to DVD, and now into the online arena. He points out that his education and knowledge have morphed as changes occurred because he was determined to remain relevant.

"The thing I know after 30 years is that while the public has a desire for sexually explicit material, no matter what happens to the delivery method, people still want it," Mann commented.

From a marketing point of view, Mann believes the biggest change in the industry is related to a sort of Attention Deficit Disorder (ADD) that permeates society as a whole. He recalls when movie making was just that: making a full-length movie. Maybe there was a plot, a storyline, etc., but now, the majority of the focus in adult has moved to gonzo, a style that focuses on a variety of clips or a compilation of scenes. Gonzo filmmaking is at the core of Evil Angel's business model.

Marketing gonzo product is completely different from marketing features. Gonzo film clips typically are sold online in small snippets that cost a few dollars apiece, whereas traditional DVD buyers still an entire feature for a much higher price.

Evil Angel, therefore, seeks a different market than the market sought by production houses that primarily create feature-length films. Mann says that while the feature movie market remains a healthy business, delivery still is largely accomplished through DVD sales. Few people are willing to sit at their computer for two hours and watch an entire film from start to finish.

"The movies that [Evil Angel] produces are more sexually driven," Mann said. "Our customer is less likely to want to watch a feature where there is twenty minutes of dialogue before a twenty minute sex scene."

Evil Angel's short-scene-based approach to filmmaking and marketing also benefits from—and buttresses—the studio's director-centric attitude.

"[Stagliano] built [Evil Angel] around the directors, not the stars, and he made those [directors] famous," Beechum said. "And people love what he produces because of [his approach]. He will do a distribution deal with each director and establish a fan base behind each of them. He's made a lot of people a lot of money based on this model. For instance, Jules Jordan was created by Stagliano, and now Jules [Jordan] has his own company and went off on his own."

Although Evil Angel continues to produce DVDs, Stagliano is well aware that as DVD revenues decline, revenues in other areas must increase in order for his company to stay afloat. Stagliano and his staff are quick to recognize and adjust to consumer purchasing trends.

"Our revenue has significantly changed since the advent of the DVD," he said. "Instead of making 90 percent of our revenue from DVD sales, we now make 50 percent." The 50 percent of revenue that does not come from DVD sales derives from online sales, licensing, and broadcast pay-per-view. The company produces new material all the time, and it sells.

"Despite the huge amount of material that is available, I really think that there is still a market for new material," Mann said. "People are still asking for new content to be produced. Even though, with the amount of material that is available, no one could possibly ever see it all, the demand for new production will never stop."

Regardless, Evil Angel does not jump on any trend or bandwagon that happens along. The company, while it is dedicated to quality, is also dedicated to a certain type of content. "There was a time when I started at Evil Angel that I went to John with the name of a director who was just hot, hot, hot at that moment," Mann recalled. "I said, 'We should sign this guy because he is really in demand right now and he approached us about distributing his goods and I know it will sell.' John turned to me and point blank said, 'I don't care. I don't want you to ever tell me that we should distribute because it will sell well. I don't need the money; I don't care. Only tell me if something is good. Make the compelling argument for why it is good, which is the reason why we would bring it on.' He told me that he would rather distribute something that is a sales failure, but which he knew in his heart of hearts was a good product instead of distributing something that comes with financial success, but is not a product that he personally believed in.

"I remember thinking that was kind of a backwards way of looking at the issue, but then again, why is John the president of a company that is kind of like the last man standing in this industry? I realized that it was that attitude on content and quality over marketing and sales which is actually the best marketing plan out there. People trust Evil Angel content because if we are distributing it, the material has passed the John Stagliano test."

Stagliano is adamant about his philosophy: Create a good product and then have faith the market will purchase it. The content, not some cheesy marketing message, is what sells. Cheesy marketing may produce short-term success, but long-term achievement accrues only with passionate belief in one's brand. "I will not produce or endorse something that I don't personally feel passionate about," he said. "I don't have to manufacture something just because someone else thinks it's hot. My dedication to this is validated in the form of lots of dollars."

Consequently, Evil Angel's pricing has never been affected by fear-based thinking. Stagliano has never slashed prices in order to remain competitive, the average price point, he said, is considerably higher than other products on the market. According to Stagliano, Evil Angel wraps the value of a consumer's experience into every price tag.

"You can buy our product for $40, or you can buy the other guy's product for $20," Stagliano said. "However, with Evil Angel there is also a guarantee that you know what you are paying for, and you get the type of experience consumers have come to expect from the brand. Who benefits from paying more? Maybe you bought the $20 DVD and found you can't even jack off to it, as opposed to buying the $40 Evil Angel DVD where you had a high-quality masturbatory experience because of the five scenes of stroke-worthy content on that disc."

The lesson is that by itself, price does not determine value. The lesson holds true for every product in adult, according to Mann, who sees potential for Evil Angel in other market segments.

"Right now, I am most excited about the crossover opportunity John and I are working on in the sex-toy business," Mann said. "It doesn't seem to have a lot of the issues that the movie business has related to piracy and content hijacking. As Paul Cambria, an attorney who represents the adult industry told me many years ago, 'You can't download a dildo.' [The novelty sector] is just a great and growing business. Because of a worldwide sexual empowerment movement among women, ladies own their sexuality in a very free and comfortable way, and that is reflected in their interest in sexual pleasure products. This is really interesting to me because there is such an opportunity for growth, and it is a product that people want. You don't have the government threatening you in this area; you don't have the Internet threatening you with extinction. And the product themselves, there is such a diversity.

"As someone who is interested in the psychology of sexual marketing, it's just a great place to be in," he continued. "Opposed to the movie business and this doomsday feeling that 'Okay, we are here today, but we are on our way out,' in the sexual products market there is a feeling that the best days of the business are ahead. Personally, I feel that's the case for Evil Angel in movies or whatever we are doing, because our market continues to grow based on politics and cultural changes as well as changes amongst attitudes in the younger generation."

Evil Angel, as a company, operates under a business mindset that is planted in Darwinism: It's evolutionary, not revolutionary. For Stagliano and his staff, size and strength have less to do with species survival than willingness to embrace change and roll with it.

PART FIVE

The New Novelty Business
No Longer an Off-Ramp Truck Stop

Adult novelties often get lumped together with adult movies. The novelty business, though, should be considered separately, even while novelties periodically cross over into adult movies and vice versa.

Novelty manufacturers usually work directly with stores or websites that sell the products, and distributors have little pull in this area. According to Field, some DVD distributors also offer novelties in order to increase market share, but he chooses to avoid this part of the industry completely. Although including novelties in a distributor's mix may open a few otherwise closed doors, there is little to no margin for the middleman.

Adult toy manufacturers typically give a volume-based discount off their published wholesale prices, and stores selling the products usually provide a price break to customers because there are other businesses selling the same toys. Large adult stores sometimes use novelties as attention grabbers or loss leaders: Their role is to get consumers into the store, where hopefully they will purchase other items with bigger profit margins. Boutiques and independent stores, on the other hand, focus on customer experience and customer service to raise their revenues. Their customers will pay full suggested retail for the products they want, which is fortunate, since boutiques and indies order smaller quantities and therefore pay higher wholesale prices than chains and megastores pay.

An example of a successful adult store chain founded on the brand of a large company is the Hustler Hollywood stores. Teresa Flynt, daughter of *Hustler* publisher Larry Flynt, is in charge of the operation and direction of the Hustler Hollywood chain.

"The [first Hollywood Hustler] store on Sunset Boulevard opened on December 3, 1998," stated Teresa Flynt. "And there is a political background to our opening. The first Hustler store was technically in Downtown Cincinnati, and Hamilton County, where the city was located wouldn't allow *Hustler* to be sold there. So Larry Flynt decided to buy a newsstand and take the issue to court so he could sell his magazine. Well, he won and ultimately that location was bringing in high revenue. Then, out here in Hollywood, this idea of retail was being played with and again, [Larry Flynt] wondered if it was something that could succeed as well [in California]."

Coming from humble, political roots, the Hustler Hollywood store chain was born. Teresa Flynt, who was filling a separate role at Larry Flynt Publications, the parent company of *Hustler*, offered up her assistance in the expansion. The primary reason for it? At the time, she had been married and had experience of walking into a few adult stores herself. She states that personally, she always hated the experience because of the fact that everything seemed to take on a shady pallor in a badly run adult store.

"I knew that anything my father would engage in, he would do it right. Look at everything he has, his home, his car, even his wheelchair, everything is top notch, I knew that if he was going to go the route of the adult store, it would be first class and I knew I could influence the direction," stated Flynt.

Flynt said that her father stated that his goal in the Hustler Hollywood stores, was to make it so a schoolteacher "would feel comfortable entering into one."

"The product selection, years after the original opening has changed, but that also takes into account that technology has changed," stated Flynt. "Originally, we had VHS tapes, both adult and mainstream. We had toys, Hustler clothing, books and some lingerie."

At that time there were not many stores that subscribed to a "boutique style" approach. Teresa Flynt began going to adult stores across the United States as well as attending the annual Adult Entertainment Expo to find out what other stores were doing in the space. It was from there that the Hustler Hollywood chain began to morph and evolve.

"The experience we offer to the consumer is one that welcomes them. You don't want into the store to immediately be faced with some supersize butt plug. You are greeted with lingerie and candles and as you progress into the store the merchandise gets hotter and more risqué," stated Flynt. "This way anyone who walks in the door has the option to progress farther in or they can stay within their comfort zone in the front of the store. I would say that we target couples who want to shop together to enhance their sex life. Our target is not the consumer who is looking for the peep show booth."

With this business model in mind, the Hustler Hollywood brand has seen their business grow. Because they appeal to new consumers entering the novelty market, it has been important for the chain to stay on top of trends in the marketplace and what consumers are interested in.

"We sell so many different things. For instance, right now the book *Fifty Shades of Grey* has impacted our business. We have seen consumers come in looking for the toys used in the book and the supporting items. That book has received so much publicity that it has also impacted the sex lives of individuals. People read about the balls, the handcuffs and the floggers, and they don't know where to go get it. And they end up at our store," stated Flynt.

However, while Hustler Hollywood is part of Larry Flynt Publications, some novelty companies, like JimmyJane, are careful to distance themselves from pornography while looking for the occasional crossover opportunity; other manufacturers prefer to maintain a close association with the more risqué elements of the adult industry. Doc Johnson, for example, produces signature lines for Jenna Jameson and Belladonna and markets all of its products with a hardcore pornographic message.

"The traditional toy market is just like the DVD market—it's saturated," said Beechum, whose business distributes both DVDs and novelties. "You have to figure for every company out there making it in novelty, there's five getting killed.   [Novelty manufacturing] is going to end up the same way as the video production market: You either need to do something different, or you are going to be weeded out. You have to look at the wider span of the industry: You have one group of people who are willing to spend $150 [for a vibrator], but then you have a huge group of people who can only spend $20 on a dildo. That market is huge."

Emerging brands are entering the space to answer a need or address a lapse in the marketplace, especially as consumer groups shift away from the traditional male customer and focus more on couples and women. A new breed of manufacturers is reshaping the adult novelty market and moving the business into the mainstream, which only helps all companies in the space gain acceptance amongst a wider consumer base.

"When I first started talking about what I thought was possible [in the novelty market], I was laughed at," said Ethan Imboden, president and founder of JimmyJane, a company that designs and manufactures sophisticated, expensive adult toys. "JimmyJane is now viewed in a completely different light." stated.

The market for novelty items is as diverse as the mainstream women's shoe industry, and the marketing plan for both is a lesson in sharing. Companies either offer practicality and low-cost pleasure, or sexual experience and lifestyle choice enhancement. The choice is up to the consumer, who chooses whether to shop at Wal-Mart or Neiman Marcus.

Redefining Mechanical Pleasure:
The Evolution of Sex Toys

The adult novelty industry is considerably smaller than that of the DVD or video market. However, because of entrepreneurs in the space like Imboden, the days of the "big rubber dildo" defining the adult sex toy market are, more or less, over. The profitability of manufacturers continues to grow while adult content producers watch their bank accounts shrink. The reason? Internet users can't pirate or "steal" a sex toy the way they can a movie, and there are few substitutions for unique novelty products.

When Imboden pursued an engineering degree at the prestigious Johns Hopkins University in Baltimore, Maryland, he never dreamed he someday would end up creating a business based strictly on sexual pleasure. Now president and CEO of JimmyJane, one of the leading (and most award-winning) producers of sexual enhancement items in the world, Imboden has dedicated himself to redefining stale stereotypes as well as inaccurate notions about what sex toys really are. He is profoundly sure of himself when he says sexual wellbeing is essentially for overall good health.

"After I returned to Berkley from Johns Hopkins with a degree in electrical engineering, I worked as an engineer on the Human Genome Project," Imboden said. "We were supporting the National Institutes of Health (NIH) in its bid to be the first organization to sequence human DNA. It was a pretty intense environment, and it was incredible to be in such a cutting-edge field. However, in the midst of all of this that I was doing, something was missing."

Imboden took a sabbatical, traveling throughout Europe for six months while he considered what he wanted from his career. Along the way, he met an industrial product designer who also was a professor at the Domus Academy in Milan, Italy. The institution serves as a cornerstone for the industrial design industry, and Imboden immediately became fascinated by the business.

He realized that while he liked the field he was in, he had no control over the projects he was assigned. Imboden wanted more variety; to be able to design products with more imagination. He didn't want to be part of a marketing cycle; he wanted to be able to help the end users of the products he created. By the time he was finished thinking things through, he knew he could do a better job if he were able to work closely with clients, eliminating the middlemen. Imboden left the Human Genome Project and created his own design firm.

"Within the first few months of having this independent design firm, I was approached by three different people about creating products related to sex," Imboden recalled. "At this point I had worked on lines of eyewear for Nike, cell phones for Motorola, furniture for Henry Miller, and all of these different things that normally crossed the desk of an industrial designer, but nobody had ever asked me about X-rated products. I thought it was interesting, and I felt as if it was a pretty obvious indicator that something was up."

To learn more about an unfamiliar industry, he attended the adult manufacturers' expo in 2002. For a person with limited experience with pleasure products, the show was an eye opening experience—a sort of crash course in Sex Toys 101.

"At first I was overwhelmed by all of the products and all of the imagery that was under one roof, and it wasn't even that big of a trade show," Imboden recalled. "Visually, it was overwhelming, and I didn't think that it was altogether that comfortable on all ends. I skirted my way around the outside of the show, feeling a little timid. There were all of these huge black, green, really in-your-face-type dildos and other products. But once I got over that and started looking at what was being done, I realized it was just business."

Imboden began to edge his way into the mix, spending time looking at the products, working to understand them and the way they were marketed. He immediately defaulted to his industrial design background in his analysis of the products before him, considering the design, the concept, and the delivery. Soon, it dawned on him that sex-related products needed to be looked at like any other consumer product. Thus, he happened upon the idea that there was significant opportunity not only to expand product offerings within the space, but also to enhance the consumer experience.

Even after he went back to his normal life and everyday work, he continued to think about the possibilities, not least because the subject of sex toys and sexual enhancement products continued to come up in conversation. When friends learned about his new design interests, they were eager to discuss products. Evidently, he'd stumbled onto a hot topic.

"It was coming up at dinners and cocktail parties," he said. "At first I tried to avoid the subject, but finally I opened up about my 'special' clients and then started talking about vibrators. Everything else would come to a halt, and suddenly we would all be talking about sex products and sexuality."

Imboden found that although people seemed eager to talk about the subject, they would not initiate the conversation without an excuse. Imboden's enthusiasm about his novelty design projects provided a reason for friends and acquaintances to interject their own opinions about the subject. And those opinions ran the gamut.

"Everyone seemed to have an opinion, and maybe it was an opinion on a product that I might not be looking for," he said. "But the point was, it was the right product for someone. What I kept hearing was that what people wanted was not what was being produced. The products produced were garish in design, either looking really goofy or like severed anatomy, and they were presented in a way that was affiliated with porn stars or with pornographic images. That was the prevailing presentation, and the products were branded in a way that I was familiar with and had worked on."

Imboden saw a disconnect between the producers of existing sexual products and consumers. What's more, he believed there was a large consumer demographic whose needs weren't being addressed at all. The non-addressed were very particular about the cars they drove, the clothes they wore, and they believed everything they purchased was a reflection of who they were.

"The vibrator these people wanted was not available," Imboden said. "There was a huge gap. These people were buying products that did not necessarily meet their needs or wants, but they continued to buy because that was what was available to them. But there was no excitement about their purchases. It was a mismatch of consumer wants and needs. This group of people was settling on a product, resigned to it."

The discovery fascinated Imboden, because he believes there is no greater form of self-expression and, ultimately, personal satisfaction than that which is received through sexual gratification.

"You never feel better than you do when you feel sexy," he said. "It is closely tied to self-understanding and confidence. Why isn't there a brand that reflects that? Why aren't these products aligned with these aspirations? What I believe had happened was on the product side, or manufacturing side, it was working—people were buying the products, so they kept making the products. But a lot of that design and engineering work was really incremental. It was pushing the ball forward a little, but there was still no one stopping to understand consumers and their changing needs and opinions."

Imboden recognized a vacuum into which a significant market segment had fallen by default. He lays the blame for the problem at the door of societal taboos: People were not talking about what they liked and didn't like, because they were afraid of what others would think. Designers couldn't listen to what wasn't being said, and few took the time to ask appropriate questions.

"You can trace all sorts of different shifts in sexuality and trends in sexuality to certain points in time," he said. "It does seem to be progressive. The United States is much different culturally than other countries in the world. I wasn't the first person to think something different needed to be offered. A lot of retailers at the time were trying to solve the problem, but it had to start with the manufacturing process."

JimmyJane, Imboden's brainchild, was born in 2004. The company's mission statement is simple: In order to create the best sexual experience with the best enhancement tools, JimmyJane strives to "support a healthy, playful, and intelligent enjoyment of sexuality by recognizing that sexuality is as much an intellectual and psychological interaction as it is a physical one."

The company identifies its customer base as "sophisticated, thoughtful, and respected" and supports the "right to present our view of sexuality, and the reciprocal responsibility to be respectful of the views of others."

"I don't think you can dictate 'this is what sexy must look like,'" Imboden said. "It's about opening up possibilities. In a broader sense, what we are looking to do is through the presentation of this product in an extremely forthright manner, we want to empower the consumer to have the conversations that traditionally have been hard to have."

According to Imboden, the industry as a whole cannot evolve without frank conversations about what works and what doesn't work. He believes there can be significant change only if consumers are incredibly vocal about what they want to see—a theory that has been put forth by many leaders in the adult entertainment industry, from manufacturers and production houses to retailers.

Imboden's marketing plan is as unique as his products. He does not target only women, the way some new, upscale entries in the space do. Instead, JimmyJane's sales are split 50/50 between men and women consumers, and marketing embraces a range of platforms. The company maintains a clean, chic, and sophisticated website at JimmyJane.com and has partnered with many specialty retailers like Fred Segal in Los Angeles, Selfridges in London, and the department store chain Nordstrom. JimmyJane had developed an international retail presence as well: its products are stocked by stores in Berlin, Milan, Hong Kong, Paris, and Tokyo. Furthermore, the brand has arranged promotion in hospitality and hotel environments, including The Delano in Miami and W Hotels, a worldwide chain.

Though the company has found mainstream acceptance, that milestone did not come without challenges.

"It was easy to come in from the outside world and underestimate just how much resistance there is, or was, in the mainstream accepting these products," Imboden said. "So we set out to redesign how the public viewed this. We launched our site to include jewelry, massage oil, and candles along with our sexual products under one wellbeing heading, which was [a new approach] in the [adult novelties] category. A lot of what we did was outside of traditional sex-toy marketing and distribution, but it was necessary in order to work with Nordstrom, Bed Bath and Beyond, Whole Foods. Getting them to understand the concept was a huge challenge."

While some of the retailers Imboden targeted understood what he was trying to do, implementation presented another roadblock. After all, finding a sex product in a place where it is not expected, such in the beauty department at Nordstrom, can create not only shock, but also aversion.

"We tried to reach out to [high-end] consumers, so if they walked into a place like Fred Segal, they would accept the fact that a JimmyJane product was being sold there," Imboden said. "We wanted to educate them about what this product offered and why it was relevant. We didn't want to change solely the retail dynamic, but also the context in which the product was viewed in retail, in media. Early fans of the brand, like Kate Moss, were seen buying the product, that news made it to Page Six, and suddenly people were talking about us. A consumer's first impression of the product was no longer negative."

Imboden is convinced there is newfound interest in private luxury products, partially because he and his company helped create that interest. He believes it is possible to create a luxury sex toy without cheapening the experience or the product delivery.

"There was a point in time where JimmyJane was very small, and because we were so focused on changing the conversation around this topic, we really spent a lot of time outside of the industry," Imboden revealed. "And I think there was a period of time where the company was not very well liked by those in the industry. I don't think we were being taken seriously or that we wanted to participate with the industry. I feel really good about the fact that now we are able to work with other brands in the category, our retailers, and other members of the adult community. Now we are asked to speak on panels at industry trade shows. Ultimately, a transformation of this industry is not something any one brand can accomplish, but I am pleased with what we have been able to do. Today, I see a lot of like-mindedness amongst [brands]."

Susan Colvin, of California Exotic Novelties, is another example of an entrepreneur like Imboden who was interested in revamping the "business as normal" aspect of the novelty industry. When she began in the largely male-dominated sector of the industry, she was shocked to realize that there was very little in the business that would actually appeal to women, even though the products were made with their anatomy in mind. Starting her business in 1994, she is now one of the largest novelty manufacturers in the country.

"When I started all of the adult companies in the industry were run by men, except for a distribution company by the name of Capital News," stated Colvin. "Therefore the toys were nothing interesting, the packaging was not attractive. The products themselves were ivory or black, there was nothing attractive about it and I wondered immediately why nothing had been made for couples or for women."

It was at that moment that California Exotic Novelties was born.

"My major competitors at that time were Doc Johnson, TopCo, Pipedreams, Benwa and NasToys. There were also some lubricant companies. These were companies that had all been around for a long time. Everyone else had been in business between ten and twenty years.   My business model was based on marketing the products differently. We came out with products that were pink and purple and really, everyone else thought I was just crazy because it had never been done before," stated Colvin. "We put more money into the packaging, taking beautiful photos for the packages themselves. We also invested immediately in new technology. As a female I noticed that the vibrators in existence at the time were noisy, they weren't very powerful and they weren't reliable."

Colvin's company looked at improving the products on the market and is credited with the development of the first rechargeable vibrator, the first "Rabbit" vibrator and the first remote control egg in the industry.   At the same time, Colvin became focused on promoting her products as part of a healthy sexual life.

"There has definitely been a transition in the novelty industry and part of that comes down to promoting healthy sexuality and the wellness associated with using our products. When CEN was born, there were no medical benefits to the products that we produced. Today, we have life coaches on our website that talk about the role a healthy sex life plays in overall health and well-being. We wanted to form a partnership with relationship therapists who were able to answer the questions individuals and couples had about healthy sexuality and the role of pleasure in relationships."

CEN through Colvin has teamed up with Dr. Laura Berman, a true pioneer in the area of women's sexuality. Through this exclusive deal, CEN has collaborated on specific toys promoted by Dr. Berman, a huge departure from the traditional adult-related toys promoted and branded under the name of a popular porn star.

"I feel that this is important, especially as the Internet has opened things up for consumers. There is a discussion that takes place and it's not just about promoting an adult toy. Couples and individuals are curious about pleasure principles that affect their lives and their relationships," stated Colvin, "and we wanted to make sure that we had qualified experts as part of our company who were able to answer their questions."

Colvin feels that the most valuable customer to CEN is the consumer who is able to make a well-informed decision about what they want in their sex life and what they don't. Moreover, she feels that this mindset has affected the way products are promoted. Like many of her competitors and colleagues have expressed, no longer are adult novelty products sold at some shady store on the wrong side of town.   Mainstream acceptance has put these products in malls, drug stores and specialty stores and has effectively opened minds and changed attitudes.

"Our timing was great getting into this business because we have been able to ride the crest of the awakening of women and couples.   We currently have 3,200 products and sometimes we are asked why we have so many products.   The reason for this is that we target certain products to specific audiences.   Some products are made for adult bookstores and their packaging shows this.   And then we have many products that are made to go into any store or are used at home parties, and they are softer looking," commented Colvin. "The adult bookstore model is still viable, but at the same time, there are other consumers who have needs that must be addressed."

Of course, while the face of consumers has changed, so has the competition, Colvin notes.   Where there were only five or six companies in the space when Colvin began CEN in 1994, today because of the Internet, there are literally hundreds.

"It's an unbelievable number of companies that CEN actually competes with.   While there is more opportunity because the consumer base has opened up, it still means that we have to work hard in order to succeed.   Every single day of the year we have to think about what the market wants to see next.   How can we produce better products?   What do people want to see available to them?   It keeps us on our toes," stated Colvin.

Another brand that has changed the marketplace considerably is We-Vibe. The company's owner, Bruce Murison, happened into the novelty business somewhat by chance after finding himself out of a job during the dotcom bust.

In 2003, Murison and his wife Melody, both of whom worked at Nortel, realized they soon would be out of jobs because of the high-tech crash. Even worse, the employment picture for engineers looked grim in their native Ottawa, Canada. With choices limited to striking out on their own or working in a coffee shop, the Murisons opted for creativity.

"I had started several businesses over the past twenty-five years and had multiple inventions, but at that time I didn't have the cash needed to move forward on some of my ideas," Bruce Murison said. "I have been an inventor since I was 15, and I remember back in the 1990s sitting in front of the TV saying, 'I invented that' but ultimately never pursued it. This gave us the faith and the gumption to go forward and mortgage our house and commit our life savings to a new venture—and that [venture] was a sex toy."

Murison patented the We-Vibe in 2004. The concept behind the product is simple: Murison's toy easily fits between a couple during sex.

"I used to stand around downtown Ottawa by the government buildings and ask people, especially women, about what they wanted in a sex toy," he said. "People told me they hated wires, they hated batteries. They just wanted something that would turn on when they wanted it to, no wires, no straps. Plus, people want to have sex as normal as possible even if they wanted a little extra stimulation."

Murison encountered lots of people who wouldn't talk about their sex toys, but when he found someone who was willing to talk, they were *really* willing to talk. He found the younger generation always open to speaking about their preferences while men tended to shy away from such conversations. Women, though, were eager to comment on what they liked and didn't like.

While Bruce handled product design, Melody went to work on a marketing plan. Because women were so passionate about going in a new direction with sexual enhancement devices, the Murisons felt that the key to success with the We-Vibe lay, at least in part, in beautiful and comfortable-looking packaging.

"It had to be aesthetically pleasing and essentially the polar opposite of how many sex toys were displayed and marketed at that time," Bruce Murison said. "Melody has a great eye for all things beautiful. We moved away from naked women on the packaging... distanced ourselves from the porn star aspect of the novelty market. So with the idea of elegance, reliability, and quality, we started to market the We-Vibe."

Initial marketing efforts consisted of sending product samples to iconic individuals within the mainstream entertainment industry. We-Vibe was featured on TV and in magazines including *GQ, Penthouse, Allure, Elle*, and even *O, Oprah's magazine*.

"We started to win awards, and I think a large part of this is the idea that once you develop a better mousetrap, word spreads, especially among women," Murison said. "People started walking into stores and asking for We-Vibe."

Murison insists his company always has taken a mainstream approach to business, so We-Vibe has never had to worry about an "adult entertainment" label or "crossing over" into the mainstream.

Sure, the product has been featured in *Playboy*, but it's also found easy acceptance outside traditional adult channels.

That can be both blessing and curse. The Murisons were completely unfamiliar with the workings of the adult novelty market, which meant they had a lot to learn.

"We had to learn how to work with our distributors without annoying them," Murison said, laughing. "We received absolute open arms from the [adult] industry, and it was a very friendly and helpful group of people who helped us learn the ropes."

One of the gaps in the marketplace We-Vibe hit head-on was a demand for waterproof, comfortable, powerful, rechargeable toys. Murison said once they saw the need, the solution was simple: create a product to fill it. The company focuses on quality, not quantity, offering only five products so far. The entire We-Vibe experience exudes a boutique feel—making it a comfortable fit for women consumers, whom research has indicated are responsible for 80 percent of a household's purchases. They also tend to be curious about new and better ways to accomplish things, Murison said.

"Men tend to be selfish enough to be satisfied," he noted. "They do what's good for them. Empowering women to be satisfied within a relationship really is the driving factor in our business. I genuinely think that having Melody in that [marketing] position has helped us attract women customers, because there have been times when I have come up with an idea and she has looked at me and said, 'No way.' Males are just wired different; they don't always get it."

We-Vibe primary demographic lies in the 30-60 age range— individuals who understand the value in spending $150-$200 on a toy and have the requisite disposable income.

"This age group understands the concept of getting what you pay for," Murison said. "They don't want something that is going to break in a few weeks, and they have the capacity to pay what we charge. There is an element of exclusivity, but when you think about it, a nice dinner costs $100, and the We-Vibe will last you five years. Melody's marketing is able to get a consumer to feel happy about their purchase; to paint an image in their minds where this purchase is held in esteem."

Rome wasn't built in a day, and brands are not built overnight. Achieving recognition and confidence among consumers is not as simple as advertising.   Murison said We-Vibe's best and most longstanding customers have been attracted via commercials, website advertisements, radio information, and—perhaps most importantly—by word of mouth, including product reviews and feedback from happy customers. The company's sales have doubled every year since 2004; by late 2011, cumulative sales topped one million units. Murison said the company has been virtually untouched by the global economic recession.

What's more, "there are four billion women in the world; we have barely scratched the surface," he commented. "We-Vibe is not such a prevalent thing, and we have a lot of room for growth to educate people on who are."

Like Imboden, Murison believe the biggest potential for growth lies in forming alliances with high-end mainstream retailers. We-Vibe's ideal market does not visit adult stores, and the Murisons understand those consumers because they're among the group.

"Melody is the classic conservative, three-kids-in-the-suburbs type of woman," Murison said. "And this is why I think that mainstream is the way to go. Before we got into this business Melody had never been in a sex shop, and this way we can appeal to people who don't frequent those stores."

Among the marketing tactics currently under consideration at We-Vibe is attracting a mainstream female celebrity to endorse the product line. Oprah would be great, but Murison also is interested in looking to a health and sexuality professional and how a partnership could be formed over the idea of how sex toys actually promote greater satisfaction and well-being in a couple's relationship.

"We haven't done any advertising in that area really because we have been so focused on building the company," stated Murison.

We-Vibe's non-threatening approach to sex and the marketing that surrounds it is a testament to the business that they do, and will continue to grow upon.

"[This is] a normal, legitimate business and most people in business see it as a business," he said. "I think we are leading-edge and we are a high tech company, but we just happen to be designing these toys that give people pleasure.

"When we first started, we were worried about what our neighbors might think of us," he added. "But there is no negativity. Our kids' friends will say, 'Wow, you have really cool parents,' and our neighbor's send us flowers to congratulate us on the success we have had."

The New Adult Store Business Model

Mark Franks doesn't have to imagine the future of the adult novelty business—he's already helping to create it, at least where retail is concerned. Franks, president and CEO of West Coast adult store chain Castle Megastore, stepped into a fading enterprise in 2003 and turned the then fifteen-year-old business into a thriving operation that revolutionized public perception of an entire industry.

Franks admits stereotypes exist for a reason. At one time, adult stores did indeed come complete with creepy clerks and dim back-room arcades that were more notable for their best-left-unremembered seediness than for the movies they showed. Traditionally, merchandise displays were thrown together up front to make the store look legitimate, but the stores made their real money off the back rooms, which were cash-only. Operational costs were minimal, usually consisting of building upkeep and a small selection of merchandise in addition to whatever finances were required to purchase and maintain the movie equipment in the arcades. In many stores, a separate company operated the arcades, incurring all the expense and sharing the revenue with the store's owner.

With the advent of VHS, adult stores segued into the video-rental business, buying videotapes and renting them until they wore out. At that point, they'd either sell the tapes to consumers as "previously owned" or attempt to return them to the manufacturer as defective. Franks equates the video-rental business to "selling air," because after three or four rentals the store recovered the tape's cost. Couple that with either looking for refund from the manufacturer or selling the tape used, and adult stores were almost pure profit.

"The Internet killed that though," Franks said. "There is still some tape business going on, but it's been gutted; it's nowhere near where it used to be." Today's adult stores are an entirely different animal, thanks in no small part to Franks, a veteran of adult retailing whose accomplishments include owning and selling video production companies, prosecuting Internet pirates in Australia, and running a distribution operation in Amsterdam. The modern incarnation of Castle Megastore is a bright, clean, airy establishment with friendly, knowledgeable staff and no arcades. Except for the merchandise, Castle stores could be any other retail outlet.

"The biggest trend has been the movement away from the traditional bookstore model," he said. "If you look at all of the big money made 10 or 15 years ago, it was from the entertainment side of things, the peep shows, not the toys.   There used to be a philosophy that said, 'The front of the store is where I pay the rent and the staff. The back of the store is where I make all my money.'"

While a few operations cling to traditional adult retail models, in general the game has changed, according to Franks. Current models trend towards boutique-style stores that take a more female- and couple-centric approach. In-your-face, hardcore porn is on the decline in the retail environment—and there's a good reason for that. According to Franks, 70 percent of the revenue generated by the Castle Megastore chain comes from a combination of couples who shop together and women customers who shop alone.

"A woman does not want to come into a store and see a guy coming out of a peep area, because she knows what he has been doing," Franks said. "Those two styles of stores do not mix, and I think store owners are realizing that you have to decide who you want to attract, who you are basing your business model on, and who you are going to be as a company."

The key to current success in the adult store industry is creating an experience for the customer. That requires hiring a high-caliber staff, carrying high-quality products, delivering a pleasant atmosphere, and staying informed about what customers are interested in buying.

Castle Megastore is among the largest store chains in the country, and each store is among the largest in its class. The locations range in size from 5,500 square feet to 20,000 square feet. The empire itself expands 17 locations in Alaska, Washington, Oregon, New Mexico, and Arizona.

All of them share a common demographic, Franks said: Customers are 18 to 35 years old and are as likely to be women as men. The shift from the traditional male patron didn't occur overnight but Franks admits the result was worth the wait. Women, he said, are "fun group of people to cater to."

"I owned a chain of stores by the name of Adam and Eve in Australia in the early 1990s, and we owned that trademark, too, on the continent of Australia," he said. "We had very female-friendly stores. Once a month we would do a ladies night and bring out the 'love bus' full of Chippendale-esque dancers. We'd haul out a portable runway, get a one-day liquor license, and then drive these crazy ladies home, too, so no one got into trouble.

"We made a lot of money," he continued. "They would be plastered, and back in those days we would do $3,000 on a Friday night. We would have a girl modeling lingerie, and then one of our employees would come on the loudspeaker and say 'Okay, girls: For the next fifteen minutes, everything in the store is twenty percent off!' Customers would come up with armloads of products. Even then we recognized the need to appeal to the female consumer."

A change in customer attitudes about pornography and other adult entertainment products had something to do with the eight-year presidential administration of William Jefferson Clinton, according to Franks. Prior to the Clinton era, soft porn and other sexually-explicit material almost didn't exist on TV and rarely was seen or discussed in public. Franks insists any blame for the subsequent sexualization of society lies not with Clinton and his penchant for association with sex scandals, but instead with empowerment of the Baby Boomer Generation and the expansion of the Internet. The Clinton Administration does deserve credit for provoking positive economic growth and a resulting atmosphere of goodwill, though. Franks said that by the time Clinton left the White House, pornography was more mainstream than ever before.

"The Clinton Administration led to many women becoming breadwinners in their families, and they have made more decisions in regard to sex," Franks said. Ultimately, gaining control of their professional lives led to gaining more control in the bedroom. More than ever before, Franks noted, women feel free to tell men when and how they want to have sex.

"It's like this: Women control the sex, and if a woman says that her guy is not getting laid, then the decision is made," he said, laughing. "So if you are married or have a girlfriend and she says, 'Let's go over to the Castle and get some sex toys,' you are going to jump your ass in that car and buy her whatever she wants. You won't be able to get that money out of your pocket fast enough."

Success doesn't happen by accident. Franks is the first to admit data plays an enormous role. Castle Megastore is so dedicated to data-gathering and -management that Franks can quote any statistic about which one is curious. He said the best companies in the space make an investment in their infrastructure, using the best computer systems and point-of-sale systems to track sales to the minute and define emerging trends. The company's methods earned it a best-practices award from the National Retail Federation, of which Castle is a member.

"I can tell you what the productivity is of every employee in my company," Franks said. "We track everything. The people who have the top companies are all investing in POS systems and analytics, because if they don't, they won't be around."

And Castle Megastore is living proof of that. When Franks took over, the chain was $56 million in debt and embattled in U.S. bankruptcy court. The situation presented a huge challenge, Franks admits, but also a huge opportunity to completely rebuild and restructure.

"They didn't have a retail system in there that worked," he revealed. "It was a custom system, but it was a piece of junk. Even their books and their accounting procedures, there was a lack of recording, which ultimately led them to bankruptcy. There was money missing, all kinds of hidden debt when I came in, but of course, that was harder to discover because of the bad recordkeeping.

"I put in a system back in 2004 to remedy this issue, and now people in the space, both direct competitors of ours and other retailers, have established systems comparable to what we have."

Franks insists a retail chain, regardless of industry, cannot be successful unless analytics and software tracking systems allow management to understand the customer base and how products perform.

"I can take a look at my product base and tell you what my female customers are buying, what my male customers are buying, what is going on with the business, what the trends are," commented Franks.

In the case of Castle Megastore, analytics have told Franks that vibrators remain the top-selling sex toy. But even though consumers like the old classic standby, technological developments have wrought important changes. The Internet, for instance, could have heralded the death of brick-and-mortar stores—and the web did deliver mortal wounds to some—but thanks to Franks' treasured analytics, Castle Megastore shifted with the tide.

"I think that you really have to be a multi-platform company to be relevant," Franks said. "You have to have an e-commerce platform, you have to have the website. Our DVD business is down, but we still carry products; we have a massive DVD selection which is competitive with Internet pricing. I'm not saying that you can't find something cheaper, but we sell mostly new releases and we are competitive. We have a very comprehensive DVD department that is split into Bestsellers, New Releases, Buy One Get One for the bargain shopper. We still do a significant level of business. But we have maintained that customer by staying true to what the customer wants.

"We did gain some market share because a lot of our competition is not doing the same thing that we are doing," he added.

Like distributor Field, Franks also believes a bargain-basement mentality prevails among adult store owners. He ascribes most of that attitude to the Internet. Internet businesses may have less overhead if all they do is operate in a virtual realm, but comparing Internet-based businesses to adult stores in the brick and mortar realm leads to a slashing prices mentality that just doesn't work in the real world.

"When you sell everything cheap, you lose customers," Franks opined. "You don't have to be the cheapest out there, because if you do business right, the customer who wants to pay for a good experience will come back. I have guys who come back every week for the new releases, the best sellers. My stock is well organized; the store is laid out pleasantly. I think we are doing better not only because we believe in what we are doing, we believe in our DVD sales, but also because a lot of our competition doesn't."

Franks said comparative analysis reveals that Castle Megastore dominates the DVD and VHS business in every market where the chain exists. Some of that strength he attributes to his background on the production side of the industry.

"I know the lines, I understand the business, and I know the customer," he said. "And I think that is an important factor in knowing how to present your products."

Castle Megastore also places extreme emphasis on employee training and retention. Castle's people are not the creepy clerks of old, but a new breed of confident professionals who take pride in their work. Employees are the "face" of a company, so finding and keeping the best people makes a difference, Franks said. To that end, he hired a human resources professional to direct hiring practices and manage the staff across all stores.

Stringent hiring practices help the company ensure it selects only the best job applicants. Castle Megastore engages in extensive background checks and has a no-tolerance policy for drug use. Franks said he runs his business like any Fortune 500 company, and violation of company policies is ground for immediate dismissal.

"We have high standards, and this has allowed us to attract and recruit from big retailers like Macy's, Dillard's, Toys R Us," he noted. "That used to be a lot more challenging for us to do. When I first took over Castle, it was a mess. There are maybe seven people left from the original crew. We had to rebuild. Now, we didn't fire all of those people, but when we started ramping up our policies and procedures and became more focused on our message and how things were going to be run, the original crew jumped ship. They couldn't keep up with what they were required to do or didn't like the culture we were putting in place. After that, it was a case of getting decent people from mainstream industries to recognize we were legit. Now we have won every major award from within the industry that you can win. We won XBiz Retailer of the Year in 2009 when we were in Chapter 11, and they didn't even know about it.

"Today we have a very corporate atmosphere, with an employee base in excess of 200," Franks continued. "Every employee adheres to a written job description. We have a policy and procedure for virtually anything and everything we do, and we handle processes the same each and every time. This helps us run our business, because it holds our employees accountable to our company mission. It brings significant clarity to our business and how we get things done. "In 2005, Franks started Castle University, a training program that received national attention and may have been the first of its kind. Classes, which originate in a television-like studio at the corporate office, are delivered to the stores via closed-circuit TV. In addition to training sessions, the TV channel also communicates product changes and roll-outs to a staff that is spread out geographically. Franks said the program assists in maintaining a uniform environment chain-wide.

All of this has led to some uncommon honors for a man in the adult industry. Franks has been nominated for several mainstream business awards, including the Ernst & Young Entrepreneur of the Year in 2010. Although he enjoys being acknowledged for his business skills, the people who get the job done every day deserve to be commended, he said.

"I can remember when we were rebuilding the chain and one of the original employees who stuck around after the transition said, 'Wow, look at this store, it's incredible,'" Franks recalled. "And I told him, 'Look, man, anyone can buy a store and stock it with products. A monkey could do it. The factor that is going to make or break this company is the people.' The infrastructure that has been built is because of the people who believe in what we do."

Perhaps that's why he also believes many adult entrepreneurs have caused their own problems by not establishing a corporate mission, or any sort of vision outside making a buck. Franks believes these are the same people who complain about the impact so-called tube sites have on adult content producers. He brushes off that criticism as blame-shifting.

"Sure the Tube sites have hurt the business, but what I think has hurt things more is that there are so many in the adult business who don't put any value on what they do," he said. "They undercut themselves, lowering the value of their products. I have asked people, 'Why should I pay you $10 for a DVD if you are giving this stuff away online? If you have a good product, you don't need to control the price.'

"I'll give you an example," he continued. "Take a look at Stagliano, Jules Jordan, Digital Playground. We buy their products, we pay their price, and they are the best-selling products. Their stuff is not being whored off. Other companies, they have whored off their products because they are greedy and it's backfired on them."

Of course, Franks has come under criticism in his career for keeping his prices where they are, and refusing to offer deep discounts to vendors.

"When I was producing, we would put out nine features a week, 1200 movies per year. I had people call and complain that they wanted a better price. I would tell them that I don't have a better price, that they are already getting the best price that I can offer. I had people say, 'You know, I buy every one of your fucking releases.' I would tell them that I greatly appreciate their support, and then they would call me an arrogant son of a bitch and I said that's how I value my product. I told them they always had the option of not buying what I made, but they would say that they needed the product. Even though I would sell them a product for $25 dollars, they would sell it for $59 or $69 bucks. They were making a profit;

they just wanted me to lower my prices so they could make a bigger profit. That's the way business works."

Franks relies heavily on the National Retail Federation for advice about trends and changes in the retail market. One study completed by the trade organization outlined the necessity of being a multi-platform retailer by 2013. The report spoke to all markets, adult and mainstream, Franks said, yet he imagines few adult retailers have read it because few belong to the federation. He's a firm believer in looking outside the adult industry for education and information and predicts store owners who don't adopt a similar policy will go under.

As for the future, Franks said innovation is the only way forward. The company is developing a version of its website that will be compatible with mobile devices. The finished product will be a native website, not a mobile application consumers must download and install on their phones.

"We discussed an app, [but] we just don't know if this is something that is valuable for us because the app market is absolutely cram-packed and flooded," he said.

The company is very active on social networks and has developed a large following on both Twitter and Facebook. "None of our competition is even close to us on Facebook in terms of participants on the social network," Franks said. Social networking is just another way the company engages customers. Each piece of the puzzle may not result in an earth-shattering response on its own, but taken together, the benefits add up.

"Our business is up year after year, which probably puts us in a minority in the adult business, or retail as a whole," Franks said. "But I think it is our customer engagement that provides this. The selection that we have in our store is unparalleled, but you have to be relevant; there has to be a reason why people want to shop with you.

"The cream has been rising to the top," he continued, "and a lot of people who have been around for a while are going to go away. There are a lot of stores closing, and few opening. Castle is looking at expanding; we're going to keep going."

PART SIX

A Rocky Road Ahead
Legal and Social Issues

The adult entertainment industry is unique in so many ways, and it has been an incredible ride to be involved in such an interesting business. The industry is also unique in the legal and social challenges it has faced, faces now, and will continue to face. Few other businesses incite such ire or so many calls for outright eradication. It's easy to wonder how members of the adult entertainment industry can contemplate promotion, marketing, and longevity when their very existence is under fire.

History is rife with examples of efforts to regulate and ultimately criminalize sexually explicit entertainment. In the America of the1920s, cohabitation and sex outside of marriage were crimes. Although most sexual behavior carried on in private is legal these days, anti-pornography groups and movements remain alive and well in the United States. Many argue that the enforcement of a moral code on the inhabitants of a country is not the role of government, but there is an equally verbal side determined to protect people from themselves.

"I've always said the word porn is a stupid word used in representing the industry," said Lou Sirkin, a top obscenity lawyer who regularly represents the adult entertainment industry in court. "It has a connotation that is negative. There are people in the adult entertainment industry who are making these movies for people to watch in private, because nowadays there are really not any adult theaters around the country, so these products are for home entertainment. The people in [the movies] are actors and actresses, and there is thought put into the making of the movie, especially in some of the full-length [adult] features out there. It's part of the world, and that is what art is. Art develops and follows current fads."

Steven Orenstein of Wicked is not fond of the terminology, either. "The word 'porn' comes out of my mouth and I hate it and I try to correct myself, because really you should say 'adult material' or 'adult movies.' [Wicked] has traditionally gone out of its way to say we make adult movies. We are not sleazy pornographers."

As adult entertainment has developed, so have the challenges facing the industry. And just as Sirkin said, the movies have changed over time. No longer are topics like anal sex, gay sex, or lesbian sex taboo. Viewers would be hard-pressed not to find at least one of those subjects in most contemporary adult movies.

"There used to be a time where there was a mainstream faction in porn, and then there was everyone else," Orenstein said. "If [Wicked] was the mainstream, suddenly we were lumped together with the people who were doing more hardcore productions and suddenly everyone was classed as 'porn.'"

There isn't an easy answer to any of the problems faced by the adult entertainment industry, but it is important to understand how diverse the challenges are in both the short- and long-term. It's also safe to say the majority of these problems will never go away, no matter how vigilant industry watchdogs try to be.

Or, as Sirkin said, "Obscenity is in the eyes of the beholder. It all comes down to that one thing. Obscenity is a form of speech that some people may not like. But what you think is obscene and what I think is obscene are two different things. We don't ban the teaching of political philosophy, and people have wide ranging opinions on that topic. Adult entertainment falls into that same category."

The History of Obscenity:
Dirty Pictures in Pompeii

Adult entertainment, or the currently preferred term "erotica," has a long and healthy history going back to prehistoric times. It's safe to say our distant ancestors had a much healthier viewpoint regarding human sexuality than our society does today.

The word "pornography" descends from Greek antecedents and literally means "writing about prostitutes." The term acquired its contemporary linguistic baggage in mid-1800s Victorian England during archeological excavations at Pompeii. Destroyed by the volcanic eruption of Mount Vesuvius in AD 79, Pompeii's ruins revealed what Victorians considered an inordinate—and unhealthy— fascination with sex and sexuality. Victorians looked upon sex as an unfortunate and distasteful but necessary means to an end, at least where women were concerned: Sex was for procreation, not recreation. More than one Victorian mother, confronting her daughter about the physical obligations of the marriage bed on the eve of her wedding, delivered the sage advice "Just lie back and think of England."

Artwork uncovered at Pompeii, part of the ancient Roman Empire, immortalized graphic, and evidently gratuitous, sexual activity. The discovery upended the well-ordered sensibilities of the Victorian elite, who saw themselves as the philosophical heirs to the intellectual and artistic traditions of ancient Rome. The upper classes feared explicit depictions of sexual activity, sometimes involving multiple parties as well as vivid displays of genitalia, held power to corrupt the working class, who were considered more animalistic and impulsive than the educated wealthy and peers of the realm. Women and children, too, needed protection from such licentious evidence of man's baser nature. During an era when the mere sight of a woman's ankle was considered scandalous and arms and legs were referred to as "limbs" so as not to offend contemporary mores, the ruling class set about hiding Pompeii's relics by demonizing the material and its creators. The word pornography, unknown in the English lexicon before about 1840, came into its own.

Secrecy Breeds Scandal

So how did the Victorians deal with the stash of porn found in Pompeii? By creating a "Secret Museum" in Naples, Italy, where archeologists could deposit what they found. Access to the wide array of masturbatory material was forbidden to all except upper-class scholars, and then only for "research purposes." But Victorian determination to protect society as a whole from the potentially devastating effect of Pompeiian porn didn't stop there.

The Society for Suppression of Vice, founded in 1802, earned the ear of lawmakers with the claim pornographic or erotic material, radical Jacobian ideas, atheism, and free speech were interconnected and all had the ability to threaten the very foundation of humanity. The Society for Suppression of Vice also deemed access to contraception and education about human biology dangerous for the working class. Needless to say, with all these threats to its very existence imminent, at least according to the Society for the Suppression of Vice, the government set about outlawing all of the above.

Although sale and distribution of "obscene" literary works— like *Fanny Hill*, the controversial 1748 English novel with pornographic roots—already was prohibited, the laws of the time treated publication and distribution of obscene material as a common-law misdemeanor. The Society convinced lawmakers a tougher stance was needed if the creation and distribution of obscene material was were to be controlled.

In 1857, Parliament passed the Obscene Publications Act. The nation's highest-ranking jurist, Lord Chief Justice Campbell, famously compared pornography to poison, warning that pornography was much deadlier. The Act, which gave law enforcement statutory power to seize and destroy any material considered obscene, was the first law to criminalize pornographic material. Like similar modern statutes, though, the Act provided no definition of the word "obscene," allowing for subjective interpretation.

Modern Obscenity Interpretations

People have evolved over the past 250 years, or so we would hope, but puritanical ideas about sexuality continue to influence lawmakers and challenge the adult entertainment industry.

Sirkin—who has defended adult entertainment producers including Rob Black, Max Hardcore, and John Stagliano against criminal obscenity charges—harbors strong opinions about modern obscenity and why in this instance, the government has too much power and opportunity to be judgmental, especially when it comes to personal freedoms and the right to privacy.

"Why I have been so active in defending the industry is because, to me, [pornography] is protected free speech," Sirkin said. "I have always considered the adult industry to be the last defenders of free speech, because in many situations they have been the soldiers and have taken a lot of the shots to bring about action on liberty, freedom, and right of association. They have developed substantive material in order for me to exercise my freedom to express my own sexuality, and a lot of the tolerance now with regard to same-sex partnership is a direct result of the adult industry.

"People don't give [the industry] credit, because [critics of the industry] always want to make something salacious out of it," he continued. "But it is this industry that has made very deep, personal sacrifices and taken criticism while they were out there fighting."

The American adult entertainment industry operates primarily in California, so the notion that pornography is protected by the First Amendment of the U.S. Constitution seems logical. The notion is true, in a general sense. Adults may own pornography and look at it to their heart's content, and if they feel daring, they also can produce it and publish their work. However, the First Amendment doesn't provide a blanket protection for pornographic work and creates a loophole for child pornography (and rightly so) as well as a designation for obscene material. Obscenity is not protected by the First Amendment, but neither is it defined in any substantive way by U.S. law.

"Criminal law is not on the side of the industry," Christian Mann said. "It is not going to protect adult movies. The only area of criminal law that purports to protect the adult entertainment community is in the criminal component of copyright law. The vagueness of American obscenity law is a double-edged sword compared to other countries like Canada or Australia who might say, 'showing [a specific sexual] act is illegal and deemed obscene.' It's hard for the government to prosecute an obscenity case in America, but it is also hard for a content producer to know what could be considered illegal in the eyes of the federal government."

Federal and state prosecutors often consider material depicting anything beyond simple nudity fair game for the label "obscene." Largely, the attitude is based on a 1973 U.S. Supreme Court ruling in *Miller v. California* that held "nudity alone is not enough to make material legally obscene." Not coincidentally, the ruling also is one reason why the adult entertainment industry settled in California.

The *Miller* case is well-known in the adult entertainment industry, as it sets many of the standards for production and distribution today. In a nutshell, Marvin Miller, who operated a large, California-based mail-order business, marketed his appropriately labeled adult content using printed advertisements that featured graphic images of naked men and women. Convicted of knowingly distributing obscene material, Miller appealed to the U.S. Supreme Court, alleging all sexually explicit material was protected by the First Amendment as a form of Free Speech. The Court disagreed to a point, noting the potential danger that states would use the ruling as blanket authority for reining in all sorts of unpopular speech under the label "obscenity."

While the court did not attempt to define obscenity, it did devise a litmus test justices hoped would prevent overreaching by the overzealous.

The result became known as the Miller Test, which requires prosecutors and courts, when considering obscenity, to determine:

- Whether the average person, applying contemporary community standards, would find the work, taken as a whole, appealing to the prurient or sexual interest.
- Whether the work shows or describes, in a clearly offensive way, sexual conduct as defined by the laws of the state where the materials are located.
- Whether the work, taken as a whole, lacks serious literary, artistic, political, or scientific value.[15]

"When *Miller* came around, the adult industry was petrified," Sirkin observed. "They were really worried about needing serious literary, artistic, political, and scientific value. The question was whether they would be able to sustain the industry with that ruling. Then the sexual revolution came about in the 1970s, and there was this realization that sex was something that wasn't necessarily 'bad.' That's when you saw the emergence of *Deep Throat* and *Behind the Green Door*, movies that had a storyline and really advanced the notion that this genre is legitimate filmmaking."

Miller expanded upon precedent set by an earlier case, *Memoirs v. Massachusetts*, which in 1966 defined obscenity as "utterly without redeeming social value." *Miller* also set the stage for the "community standards" challenge, which in today's digital age provides significant room for interpretation...as in "whose community?"

"Community standards has been brought up to me before, but I always argue that [AEBN] doesn't have to be [locally] zoned or regulated because we don't make movies," said Scott Coffman, president of Charlotte, North Carolina-based Adult Entertainment Broadcast Network (AEBN). "All we are doing is coding material for use on the Internet. Community standards are the easiest way to target a manufacturer, and there is no law on the books that defines obscenity. Of course, I would never make a movie here in Charlotte; I would hate to be in front of that jury. Even [AEBN's] contracts are governed by California law. We don't even want our contracts written in North Carolina [because residents of the state tend to be socially conservative]."

The Rules Regarding Everything
from Dirty Magazines to
Homemade Sex Tapes

Government concern about what individuals do behind closed doors is not new. While the majority of Americans feel they have the unquestionable right to do engage in whatever sexual behavior they choose within the privacy of their own homes, pornography significant number of the same people do not believe everyone else should have the same unquestionable right.

"For a while there it was easier for me to try movies that were gay or lesbian, because you could make the argument, that if [jury members] had any thoughts or were leaning one way or the other, they could find out that people do engage in [same-gender sexual relations] and they don't drop dead from it," Sirkin said. "Or they could access this information if they were curious to find out what people of the same sex do with each other. That approach broke the argument down into simple terms.

"I have always argued that there is value in [pornography], because if a couple can sit down and watch a sexually explicit movie and discuss what they liked about it or what they didn't like about it and can honestly express what they might want to do or not want to do, then they can communicate about anything," he added.

The government doesn't always share Sirkin's view. In the case of Robert Eli Stanley, an investigation of illegal bookmaking led to obscenity charges when federal agents uncovered a private stash of pornographic films while serving a search warrant. By the time the Supreme Court was finished with *Stanley v. Georgia*, the justices' ruling invalidated all state laws that criminalized private possession of potentially obscene material. Chief Justice John Marshall called such laws a clear violation of the First and Fourth Amendments which guarantee citizens of the United States the freedom to express themselves as they as they wish, at least in private, without fear of unreasonable search and seizure of their property.

Ever since the *Stanley* ruling, "law enforcement is usually interested in commerce regarding adult entertainment, not possession," said Mark Kernes, senior editor and legal analyst for

AVN, the adult industry's original trade magazine. "You cannot be prosecuted for owning pornography. The Supreme Court said you can even own obscene material in the privacy of your own home. This does not include child pornography, but pretty much anything else. No matter how it got there, you can own it. To my mind, [*Stanley*] makes almost any of the interstate commerce or obscenity laws absurd. I mean, if you are allowed to have it in your own home, how did it get there? Someone had to sell it or trade for it or send it."

According to Sirkin, the *Stanley* ruling gives adults permission to fill up their computer hard drives with porn, stockpile adult magazines and movies, and view as much potentially obscene material as they please, provided none of that material involves people younger than 18.

"For the first five or six years that I was involved in defending adult producers, I was raising the right of privacy [as the primary defense]," Sirkin said. "Some of this was laid out in *Stanley v. Georgia*, that I have the right to express my sexuality with myself or the partner of my choice in any way I want in the privacy of my home. This was the beginning of the skyrocketing rise of sex toys and the feeling in this country that masturbation isn't sinful. [Back then,] we would walk into cases saying, 'Look if it is okay to look at this in the privacy of my own home, then how did it get there? Obviously you have to buy it, and I have a right of privacy there.'"

Sirkin would be the first to admit U.S. law is rife with baffling contradictions. Take this one, for example: While possession of potential obscenity is legal, production, even in private, may not be. Although every celebrity on the planet seems to have made a bedroom sex tape during the first decade of the 21st Century, unless they did so in California, New York, or New Hampshire, they could have faced prosecution the moment they committed sexual activity to film. Residents of conservative states like Alabama, Mississippi, Louisiana, and Florida are particularly susceptible to the whims of law enforcement and their neighbors.

"Those two factors are tied together because law enforcement would typically only know about adult filmmaking if a complaint is made," Kernes said.

That issue becomes more convoluted if when a homemade sex tape winds up on the Internet.

"If you put it on the Internet, you in essence [engaged in] interstate distribution with the tape," Kernes explained. "The Internet being what it is, people who see your tape would be seeing it in other places outside of where you live, probably, so you could be violating the interstate transportation concept [as it applies to obscenity]. And if you charged [Internet users to view the sex tape], that would violate prohibitions about commerce."

Making life even more precarious for amateur pornographers and hopeful sex-tape stars is a section of the United States Criminal Code devoted to ensuring anyone filmed *in flagrante delicto* is above the age of majority. Known colloquially as the Recordkeeping and Labeling Law, Title 18 U.S. Code §2257 provides prison time and steep fines for anyone who creates or distributes explicit film, video, or photographic materials without collecting and maintaining specific government-issued, photographic identification documents about the participants, including birth name and any aliases ever used, physical address, and other information. In addition, the finished product, even if it's not for public consumption, must be labeled in specific ways. The law applies not only to actual sex, but also to simulated sexual activity of the type sometimes seen in Hollywood movies, although law enforcement has yet to aim the statute at Hollywood.

"The government has essentially said that even though you may be making this tape for your own private benefit, you still have to keep these records," Kernes explained. "Not only that, but a 'custodian of records' must be named—someone who is in charge of managing any and all adult films. And that custodian must be on hand at least twenty hours a week in case the FBI wants to come in and inspect those records.

"I don't think of this [the Recordkeeping and Labeling Law] as much of a problem anymore other than the fact that it is an incredible expense," he continued.

While the idea of inciting the ire of the U.S. government by creating a sex tape in your own home is slightly melodramatic and for the most part unlikely, U.S. law enforcement bears a long and illustrious history of pursuing creators, distributors, and sellers of pornography. As recently as the late 1980s and early 1990s, the Justice Department cracked down on mail-order distributors of adult entertainment.

"What they did was target a particular company and have FBI agents and postal inspectors order products to be shipped into conservative jurisdictions," Kernes said. "Their favorites were Utah and Virginia. The point was to bring federal obscenity charges [in jurisdictions where prosecutors thought they could win cases]. Once they had four or five charges against one company, they would go to the company and say 'Look, we will drop all of these charges if you go out of business,' and that was successful in six or seven situations."

Mail-order giant Adam & Eve, based in Hillsborough, North Carolina, was one of the targets. Founder and chief executive officer Phil Harvey suddenly found himself faced with several dozen charges, all in different jurisdictions with different laws regarding obscenity.

"What was special about this case was that the Justice Department got overzealous in their pursuit, and Adam & Eve came back and said, 'You want to bring a case, bring [one] case and we will defend it, but we are not going to defend a dozen cases at the same time,'" Kernes recalled. "The company sued the Justice Department and won. There was a federal district court judge, Joyce Green, who said, 'Pick a jurisdiction and make a case there. Whether you win or lose, you can go on to the next one, but none of this multiple indictment crap.'"

Adam & Eve's victory over the U.S. government was a big win for the company, and by extension every other mail-order company that operated within the adult entertainment space.

"Phil had the wherewithal and finances and a big enough company with the reputation needed to fight those things," Sirkin said. "That helped him, and it was a great victory. But the situation that he ran into is not uncommon. I have a lot of people come to me with the idea, 'Let's try this, because if we win this case, [the federal government] will leave us alone.' And the very sad thing is that I have to tell them that it doesn't work that way. [One victory doesn't solve the problem], because there is no guarantee that in the next six months or seven months a new charge won't be brought up. And this has happened."

Google It: The Changing Face
of Community Standards

Attorneys who work in obscenity law argue that with the emergence of the Internet, the tenets of *Miller* are not as relevant as they once were. Sirkin, who defended Rob Black's now-defunct studio Extreme Associates in 2009, put the matter succinctly: "We just think [*Miller*] is an outdated concept with the Internet. In 1973, there was a difference between New York and Jackson, Mississippi. The country is not as isolated as it once was." [16]

Sirkin speaks from experience: *United States v. Extreme Associates*, aftershocks of which continue to rumble through subsequent obscenity prosecutions of adult industry mainstays like Ira Isaacs and John Stagliano, was among the first widely publicized cases to test *Miller* in the Internet Age. Black and his wife, a performer-director known as Lizzy Borden, were charged with a variety of crimes including interstate transportation of obscenity via the Internet. Admittedly, some of Black's and Borden's adult material was controversial even within the adult entertainment community because it incorporated realistic depictions of violent rape, sexual brutality, dismemberment and other offensive themes presented, according to Black and Borden, precisely for that reason: to offend. Black complicated matters by publicly daring federal officials to prosecute him. They did, with relish.

The case captured headlines for more than year, not least because Extreme Associates' content wasn't the only thing on trial. So was the *Miller* Test. At the heart of the matter stood a seemingly simple question that proved exceptionally difficult to answer: In an era when everyone is connected to virtually everyone else via the World Wide Web, what constitutes the "community" by which community standards are judged? Ultimately the question went unanswered when Black and Borden accepted plea deals, closed their company, and served time in prison.

"I think the *Miller* Test is fine, but what needs to be redefined is 'local community standards,'" Sirkin said. "This could ultimately be one region, or it could be the whole country. I would be afraid to go back to the court today to look at this, because the question of defining obscenity would also probably come up and no one is really sure of what the court's opinion would be on that."

Anecdotal evidence suggests Internet obscenity may be even more difficult to define than the corresponding concept in the real world, assuming the "community standard" derives from the cyberspace community as a whole. During a 2008 obscenity trial in Pensacola, Florida, defense attorney Lawrence Walters surveyed Google search records and discovered the average resident of Pensacola is more likely to search for the term "orgy" than "apple pie."[17] During the same year, a Harvard Business School study of online habits concluded people living in conservative, ultra-religious states tend to consume more online porn than those living in more liberal states.[18]

"When you talk about how the Internet has changed the idea of 'community standards,' you have to understand that we are talking about the *World Wide* Web," Kernes said. "Quite frankly, the majority of countries don't care if you can access pictures of sex. Then there are some countries where showing a picture of a naked breast is scandalous. There are countries in Europe who say 'Who cares' about all of it; they sell it at gas stations.' With the *Miller* case, the Supreme Court rejected a nationwide standard for obscenity, preferring to leave decisions up to the local community. The Internet though, negates that concept, or actually makes it much harder to define."

Indeed, critics of *Miller* argue in favor of a national standard, especially as the influence of the Internet expands and the community standard requirement becomes more diluted and obtuse.

"The case law is pretty clear," said Sirkin. The local community is "where [the product is] made, what it travels through, and where it ends. Even if the server is in Timbuktu, if you can see [the pornographic material] in Tampa, that's enough [to determine community jurisdiction]. If you can prove [the material traveled] over the Internet and ended up in Alabama, then you can [prosecute the case] there regardless if the point of sale was somewhere else.

"It's really crap on behalf of the government if this is what they are arguing," Sirkin continued, noting that such a rationale essentially negates the concept of jurisdiction altogether. "You can't call that community standards."

The Internet: Good and Bad
for Business

Adult entertainment and the products produced are a form of commerce and the Internet has opened up, new markets and created new customers for adult entertainment. But what at first appeared to be a godsend has muddied the legal waters where commerce, regulation, distribution, piracy, and access control are concerned.

"Now that you have the Internet, prosecutors can isolate what they want to go after, and because a trailer or a sample might only be a five-minute clip, this makes the work of the defense team that much harder," said Sirkin, adding that producers and their attorneys face a monumental challenge when attempting to demonstrate a brief, salacious film clip is of serious literary, artistic, political, or scientific value. No matter how well a website, considered as a whole, might hold up under the *Miller* Test, enterprising prosecutors can cherry pick bits and pieces that don't stand up to the test on their own. That's another question that has yet to find a definitive answer: In the case of websites, what composes "the work, taken as a whole?" "The Internet has caused a dramatic change in adult entertainment, and that plays a factor in the courtroom."

Title 18, Section 1465 of the U.S. Code prohibits the "production and transportation of obscene matters for sale or distribution" including by means of "an interactive computer service." One way in which adult companies are attempting to limit their exposure to criminal obscenity prosecution is by employing online billing forms that require consumers to confirm they understand what they're buying before they're allowed to view the material. The content offered for free in an adult website's public areas—content meant to convert browsers into buyers in the same way store window displays entice consumers in the real world—usually is what provokes prosecution.

"In order to get to the material on an adult website, you have to pay money to access it. So essentially, that provides a firewall," Kernes said. "The Feds usually do not want to pay whatever the entry fee is to access the material on the website; hence, the people who operate those websites are actually kind of safe, even though there have been exceptions to this."Rob Black is one of those exceptions. The obscenity charges filed against Black and his wife stemmed from a movie called *Forced Entry,* which was available online. The movie was highlighted in the 2002 documentary *American Porn,* which aired on PBS's *Frontline.* Black was interviewed in the documentary and sent out a challenge to then-U.S. Attorney General John Ashcroft. Black's "come and get me," delivered on national television, evidently convinced Ashcroft's Justice Department that making an example of a high-profile pornographer with a very apparent disregard for religion and other social conventions would be worth the cost of a subscription to Black's website.

"The mistake Rob made was operating under the naiveté that he is mainstream and thinking that *Frontline* would make the interview and his footage look positive," Sirkin reflected. "That doesn't sell. What sells is making [a report about the adult entertainment industry] salacious. What I *can't* believe is that Rob making some insulting remarks about Ashcroft is what ultimately got him indicted. To the industry, that became their excuse not to help him."

Black and his wife were charged with distribution of obscenity in 2003. Although the industry kept an eye on the case because of its potential to set precedent that could impact everyone, few rushed to the verbal, figurative, or financial defense of the accused. The ramifications worried the industry, and many insiders were quick to distance themselves from Black for fear the Justice Department would take aim at them next. Six years after the indictment, exhausted by the legal wrangling and extensive financial cost of the trial, the Blacks pleaded guilty and were sentenced to more than one year in prison apiece.

"That case lingered around for so many years, and this is where the adult industry started to become more selfish than ever before," said Sirkin, who was part of the Blacks' defense team. "Before [that case], the industry was a tight-knit group; there was some strong leadership and they fought for each other. When Rob [Black] got hit, it was because he was sort of a maverick. [The industry] said, 'Stay away from him, he's bad for us.' Here are these people, this new generation in the adult industry, who is judging someone else in the same industry. A true believer in the First Amendment realizes that you may have the right to not like something and not look at it or read it, but you have to show some level of tolerance to it. People became very judgmental of Rob, and they left him out there alone."

Evil Angel's John Stagliano also found himself and his studio indicted for obscenity based on videos purchased online. Commonly referred to by his infamous sobriquet Buttman, Stagliano is known for pushing the envelope when depicting fetishes including anal sex, bondage, enemas, and urination. When the feds went after him for obscenity, they targeted the fetish films *Milk Nymphos* and *Storm Squirters 2: Target Practice* as well as a trailer for a third video. All three items were accessible only through a purchase on Evil Angel's website.

The case once again tested the notions of jurisdictional boundaries and community. The content was produced in California, but the investigating FBI agent made his purchase through an Internet connection in Pennsylvania. Because the transaction was conducted across state lines via the Internet, the Justice Department claimed jurisdiction in Washington DC, so that's where Stagliano was indicted in April 2008. Had he been convicted, the sheer volume of charges leveled against him would have incarcerated him for the rest of his life.

Stagliano wasn't convicted. In July 2010, U.S. District Court Judge Richard J. Leon called the Justice Department's evidence "woefully insufficient," dismissed the charges *en masse*, and threw the case out of court. In the process, he reprimanded the government officials in charge of the case for mishandling and attempting to reinterpret decades-old federal obscenity laws, Internet commerce laws, constitutional free speech guarantees, and the legal business standing of criminal defendants.[19]"When Stagliano's case came up, we had a really great defendant," said Sirkin. "John is a fantastic guy. He's bright, he's entertaining, and he's very creative, challenging and intellectual about the subject matter. Here is a guy who is successful with his business, but he's not outrageous; he's soft spoken. We had a great defense team and the ability with John to explore a lot of ideas that we had been considering for years."

Stagliano is literally at the center of the adult entertainment industry, both philosophically and leadership-wise, and a negative verdict could have shaken the industry to its core. After all, the case against him was predicated upon an FBI agent's purchase of adult content through distribution channels that were thought to be legally sound and ethically safe. Stagliano took extreme care to ensure his business adhered to industry best practices and the letter of the law— and still found himself targeted for prosecution. He believes the case had less to do with legality than morality. "I believe the government should stick to governing and not moral policing," Stagliano said. "Every time there has been a situation where the government wants to enforce a moral code of conduct or religion, it ends badly for someone."

Despite beating the obscenity charges in such a resounding— and embarrassing for the government—way, Stagliano maintains significant concern for the future.

"If an extremist on the order of a Michelle Bachman were to become president, I think that would spell trouble for the industry as a whole, because you would have an individual who would make pornography a dividing line in society," he said. "But even without that, you always have the chance that a prosecutor in some part of the country will decide [a hard line against pornography] is a good way to make a name for himself. The idea of Evil Angel being a target is always on my mind."

Max Hardcore, too, knows something about being a target, especially after spending approximately eighteen months behind bars on an obscenity conviction related to the Internet. A former journalist turned gonzo pornography producer, Hardcore stars in his own videos along with women who pretend to be underage (although all are older than 18). In an environment where protecting children is a common rallying cry against perceived social ills, Hardcore's material is not just scandalous—it's inflammatory and polarizing.

In 2007, Hardcore was indicted for obscenity based on website videos that incorporated fisting, urination, and other fetish acts. The charges were brought in Tampa, Florida, which is where the investigating agent accessed the Internet in order to purchase the offending website content. In Hardcore's case the issue of community standards presented no conundrums, because the Internet served that stored and served the charged videos *also* was located in Tampa.

"What it came down to was where the servers were housed," *AVN* legal analyst Mark Kernes said. "If they had been in Europe, the prosecutor might have had a harder time convicting [Hardcore], but this was an incredibly conservative county. Community standards was a big issue in this case, again because of the location of the servers. The issue was considered local, as opposed to material found in cyberspace."

As happened with Rob Black, the adult entertainment industry couldn't distance itself from Hardcore fast enough. No legitimate adult entertainment enterprise knowingly traffics in material featuring underage performers, but Hardcore was enough of a rebel to believe that as long as he clung to the letter of the law, even if his material seemed to pander to a demographic others avoided, the law wouldn't attempt to run him out of business on other charges.

"Max Hardcore received much of the same treatment by the industry that Rob Black did," Sirkin noted. "He was outrageous to the rest of the industry. People were saying, 'Well my stuff is better than his,' but that's like saying J.D. Salinger is a better writer than William Faulkner, so I am only going to push for Faulkner to be removed from public schools, but not Salinger. Here are the people who don't want to be censored engaging in censorship. We went to trial with Max and there was a conviction and on the appellate level, and there was no one [willing] to help him."

Peter Acworth, president of fetish studio Kink.com, confirmed Sirkin's take and expanded upon an opinion about Hardcore that is not uncommon within the industry. "If you were to look at Max Hardcore's material...I remember looking at it, and not that I believe that an obscenity prosecution is appropriate or would ever be appropriate, but his material was definitely drawing a line," Acworth said. "And if he wasn't afoul of obscenity, he would have definitely been afoul of OSHA or some other employment law. It depicted people being made to vomit and then eat their vomit. He insinuated the performers were underage. [Kink.com] wouldn't have gone there."

Though Kink.com might not have gone *there*, the company routinely goes plenty of other places. Kink.com lives up to its name, producing ultra-hardcore BDSM material that is available only online. Some of the company's fetish genres include women penetrated by robotic dildos, forced orgasms, male and female humiliation, and intricate erotic rope work. Acworth and his staff are careful not only to document the age- and identity-verification required by federal law, but also video evidence of each performer's consent to participate before *and* immediately after each filming session. The studio has developed a reputation for treating its performers and customers very well, regardless how apparently rough the on-camera action looks.

Although Acworth doesn't deny his company could become a target for obscenity prosecution because the activities it portrays are well outside the mainstream in Middle America, he also feels Kink.com is somewhat insulated because of its physical location.

"Part of what has made [Kink.com] a difficult target is where we are located here in San Francisco," he said. "We are in a very alternative neighborhood in a very alternative city, and there would be local outrage, I'm sure, if we were to be taken down for obscenity for activities which by their very nature are authentic to the BDSM community. There is a very vibrant BDSM community here, and I think we are well placed based upon those factors. In terms of community standards, what we do in this community is very much accepted."

Acworth also noted how some of the challenges Kink.com faced during its early days have transformed into positive opinions. Part of the shift in attitudes, he admitted, is due to his presence in the community and his willingness to engage community members about his business and their concerns. In short, Acworth presents as a good corporate citizen, and endearing oneself to the community is a smart move for any type of business.

"If you look at what has happened over the years at Kink.com—you can actually go back and look through the website's archives and read newspaper articles, and there are videos of all the protests that occurred when we moved into the Armory [a historical landmark in San Francisco that Kink.com purchased in late 2006]," he said. "But I went and stood up at a community hearing and explained that no one was going to be able to know or see what was happening inside, and that only adults would be allowed into the building. I spoke about how we were going to clean up the exterior of the building and what was happening outside. We ended up putting in 24/7 security, and our efforts contributed to the overall neighborhood. We now have a nicer corner in the Mission [district]. It was a seedy part of town, and we changed that."

Anti-Pornography Noise
and Its Effects

"The biggest threat to adult entertainment and human rights is conservatives," Mark Kernes stated unequivocally. "Law or no law, they will find some way to get rid of you, marginalize you, or in any case adversely affect your business."

Many of the adult industry's challenges over the past thirty years have left the industry both vulnerable and powerful. If not for early crusaders like Larry Flynt working vocally and actively against the political establishment, many of the protections that are taken for granted today would never have come about. Still the industry, as a whole, is attacked regularly, and it is personal freedom, not just adult entertainment, that is under fire.

"It was during the 1980s that the feds really decided they wanted to get involved in crackdowns on the adult entertainment industry, and of course, that was under Reagan," Sirkin said. "But that was also during the time when women were really beginning to assert their rights and views towards sex. Women were more open about it and are responsible for opening up the industry."

While political opinions have largely served to promote the anti-pornography movement, it's safe to say that not all individuals who lead the anti-pornography charge are completely religious or conservative in nature, publicity plays a big role.

"When a social group or politician wants to 'crack down' on pornography, usually the first place they go to is the media," Kernes said. "Generally, adult companies aren't great at staying in tune with this. So if there is noise being made somewhere in the country about the industry, it's left up to the adult entertainment company to decide if they still want to service or ship to that particular area."

Additionally, organizations like industry trade group Free Speech Coalition play a significant role in day-to-day challenges against the industry. The FSC encompasses producers, talent, website owners, distributors, retailers, as well as consumers and supporters of the industry. According to its website, the organization undertakes several responsibilities: "One, to be the watchdog for the adult entertainment industry, guarding against unconstitutional and oppressive government intervention; two, to be a voice for the industry, telling the truth about the adult entertainment industry not only in the vital role it plays as an economic contributor, but also in its contribution to quality of life in a healthy society; and finally, to provide business resources for our members to facilitate successful businesses in this ever-changing and challenging business environment."

"I was on the board of directors for the Free Speech Coalition for a very long time, and I have lobbied for the industry both in the state capital and in Washington D.C. to fight legislation that would be harmful," said Joy King, vice president of special projects at Wicked Pictures. "I believe in our right to do what we do, so I am willing to fight for it. What exists out there is a lot of misinformation. And the industry is not always great at putting its best face forward."

Film star Jessica Drake is an industry activist and evangelist, too. "Personally, I am a little disappointed that we still don't [have proper representation in government], and I hope that can change in the future," she said. "I have lobbied on behalf of the industry at the California state capital and have been a member of the Free Speech Coalition for years, and I am always impressed by people who speak on our behalf. What's even more amazing is that when we go and talk to these politicians, the feedback we get is, 'Wow! You're so normal, you're so well spoken, you're so happy.'"

"They have been very successful in California lobbying the state government, but that's unique to California," Sirkin opined. "The California people in the industry need to realize there is a tremendous amount of territory east of the California border, and sometimes I think they don't recognize that. What may work in California could work in other places, but they have to realize it's going to take much longer to get there and the money that is being used on lobbying in the Midwest could be used better. We need to get the issue to everyday people."

Taking the issues to everyday people is easier said than done. FSC is gross underfunded because membership is voluntary, not mandatory. Peter Acworth compares the organization to other trade associations that represent other industries, and finds the adult industry's participation lacking to the point of shamefulness.

"I don't know that [the adult industry] does enough," he said. "The Free Speech Coalition is the industry voice for things like fighting off [the adult-entertainment-specific domain] .XXX [which the adult industry did not want] and obscenity attacks, promoting performer health testing, fighting against mandatory condoms. All of those issues are things the FSC handles, and they are sorely underfunded. Many models are not even members, and the FSC works very hard but with limited resources. Compare that with trade organizations associated with other industries. It's sad.

"The Free Speech Coalition is the closest thing [to a lobbying group] for the adult industry," Acworth added. "I've seen their financials, and the conversation is 'When are we going to host a fundraiser?' But then the discussion turns to doing a party at some bar where people pay twenty bucks at the entrance. They are running the association on a shoestring, and it would certainly be better if the industry took the FSC a little more seriously and supported them."

"We are powerful as an industry. We are incredibly powerful," Drake said. "But I still think there is a lot more the industry could be doing related to social issues now that we are so accepted in everyday life. I wish the adult industry could band together in pursuit of providing a positive influence to some of these issues. Unfortunately, I think there are so many internal issues that many cannot see the forest for the trees."

FSC Executive Director Diane Duke would like to see more involvement, too, but she doesn't fault the industry. However, she wishes the industry were more understanding when the FSC chooses not to engage in some battles. "Members of the industry are fiercely independent," she said. "There is not a culture of 'joiners,' and I knew that coming into the executive director role. However, we do have some very loyal advocates and they might be the same people showing up and helping out each and every time, but this what we have to work with. Ultimately, we are a coalition of small businesses. Some of us might have some impressive profit margins, but we are not big companies under the designation of the federal government. We have to pick our battles carefully."

Part of the problem with an industry of rugged individualists is that, invariably, some individuals unintentionally deliver messages that do more harm than good. In political parlance, they're consistently "off message."

"You have very professional people, and then you have some people who are not opposite of that," King said. "On any day of the week, you have people who might be representing the business who come from either party and who represent everyone whether the rest of us like it or not. When the media or the news decides to talk to someone, they aren't always great at doing their due diligence and don't talk to the person who best represents the industry—they are going to talk to whomever they have access to. That person might not be knowledgeable on the issues that are affecting the industry and it's disappointing, because [members of the industry] do not always come together to fight this.

"Yes, we have the trade association, but not everyone joins and gets the education on the talking points and matters that concern all of us," she continued. "This comes back to the fact that some people treat this like a career and others don't. There isn't a lot of organization." Joy King, on the other hand, is deliberately positive in her perspective. "For the most part, we [in the adult industry] all stick together," she said. "Maybe I'm looking at this from a 'glass half-full' perspective, but I think we have always had a common enemy, which makes it a lot easier to stick together. Of course, there are always going to be wildcards who go out and do their own thing, but the majority of the industry has a willingness to stick together when it really matters." Sirkin agrees the industry needs more internal organization, but he has advice for outside detractors, as well. "The criticism that I have of both sides is that they refuse to sit down and find a middle ground," he said. "You have both sides who say, 'I'm absolutely right and you are absolutely wrong.' What we need to convey to people, and to me the most important thing is, we need to educate people on civility and instill a sense of tolerance. The conservative who believes that pornography is bad has every right to feel that way and to speak about that viewpoint. But there should be an open dialogue with our side. They should listen to us as much as we should listen to them.

"I have gone to speak to these right-wing groups and I hear the common complaint, 'I'm afraid of my child being raped. I'm afraid of my child being assaulted by homosexuals,'" Sirkin continued. "What I have always said to these groups is that I am the father of three daughters. I would go to bed at night when my girls were in college not worrying about if they were going to get raped, because they are confident in themselves and I raised them to be levelheaded. I actually worry about whether or not they are going to continue to live in a free country."

Unlike the adult industry, anti-pornography groups are not only very well organized, but also well-funded. Such groups foment the intolerance to which Sirkin objects and take no prisoners.

Morality in Media, one of the largest anti-pornography organizations in the United States targets pornography in all forms and all mediums. The group challenges pornography on the Internet, cable and satellite television, video/DVD, and adult stores, as well as indecency on radio and TV. Their claims include that pornography and adult content harm children (even though the adult entertainment industry works hard to prevent minors from accessing its content) and adults, contribute to delinquency, hurt marriages and make the divorce rate climb. The organization actively advocates broadening the definition of obscenity to include material the Supreme Court already has decreed protected by the First Amendment. The organization works to restrict supermarkets from placing the magazine *Cosmopolitan* in checkout lanes because of sexual references on the magazine's cover.

"If [a video] has people having sex in it, Morality in Media thinks it should be brought down," Kernes observed. "Thankfully, the Supreme Court disagrees."

Sirkin dismisses arch-conservative anti-porn groups even more bluntly. According to him, what such groups find most irksome is not the material itself, but the constitutional guarantees of free choice and free expression that allow the material to exist in the first place. In their pursuit of core American freedoms that allow their fellow citizens to disagree with them, radical conservative groups grasp at straws. "You can't judge someone and vilify them because they go into an adult bookstore, watch a movie and jack off," Sirkin said. "You can't say they are going to come out and rape someone. Sorry, but I don't know that many guys who can come that quickly twice in a row."

In the final analysis, Sirkin believes adult industry members' attitudes need to evolve in order for the industry to stay ahead of its detractors. Public perception of the industry is drastically different today from what it was even twenty years ago, but some adult entertainment insiders refuse to let go of the maverick posturing that served the industry well in its youth. Those tactics no longer work. According to Sirkin, today's attitudes shouldn't be predicated on social revolution or standing up to anti-pornography zealots.

"The difference between the starlet of today and the ones popular in the 1970s is that the ones during the 70s thought they were making social change, and in the spirit of the Civil Rights marchers, they were fighting in a way that made the battle important. Today, it's just all business, and there is nothing inherently wrong with that. You are out to make a living. But the industry needs to accentuate the people who are ready to be spokespeople for what they do. I wish they designated certain people to speak up and represent the industry."

Feminism: The Adult Entertainment War on Women

Sex trafficking, degrading and exploiting to women, offensive and undignified. These are just a few of the customary objections traditional feminists have to the adult entertainment industry. However, women within the industry feel quite differently about the role their business plays in the lives of women.

"I am a woman, and I am involved in production," said Joy King. "So I support what we do here at Wicked and follow our business plan, which is to create content for women and couples. I am a moderately jaded woman, because I have been in this business a long time, but I can still see passion in a movie and I can still see when people have a true connection and when they don't. I think I understand the female psyche enough to know which scenes a woman would be interested in over what a man would be interested in.

"Not that we don't care about our male consumers, because we do," she quickly added. "But we try to diversify our content to keep that core audience happy."

Bobbi Starr considers herself a pro-sex feminist and works to remind people that pornography is a business that produces a fantasy-based product.

"I am contacted to serve as a speaker at universities," she said. "As a pro-sex feminist businesswoman, I have spoken about building a company based around a person instead of a product. It's not a reality. It's a fantasy. While it may seem like reality, it's not. As much as these girls may seem like what they are like in real life, it's still a fantasy. When that camera is on a viewer may see something that is not happening in a reality-based setting. Just like any other movie," Starr stated.

Starr goes on to point out that even with reality-based pornographers like Brazzers or Reality Kings there is still fictionalization their content as it pertains to the treatment of women. She believes there is as much exploitation and degradation of women in mainstream media—including Hollywood, corporate advertising efforts, and other vehicles—as there is in the adult entertainment industry.

"Just because you might not see it or it's not publicized doesn't mean it doesn't happen," she said. "You can't trust everything you see or what everyone tells you. I always say I can't speak for everyone in the industry, but I have never personally felt degraded when I have been doing my job. I have always known that if I don't like the way a company, a director, or other talent are treating me, I have the option of walking out that door and saying, 'No thank you.'"

She also believes she can do the scenes that she wants to do and is interested in doing, and enjoy them, instead of limiting her options. After all, isn't feminism about women charting their own courses and making the decisions that are best for them?

Jessica Drake has decided that many of the preconceived notions she held about the business before entering it were planted by people who had no point of reference. Even after Drake began her adult career, she was approached by friends and acquaintances in Texas who insisted she was going to be taken advantage of, that she was going to be exploited. Drake's opinion? No one can take advantage of someone who has a choice, and a voice, in what they elect to do.

"Those were just the assumptions that some of my close friends had, and I remember I had to spend a lot of time convincing some of them that I was really okay doing this," she said. "I think people who don't know about the industry like to victimize the performers, but I can honestly say that in my whole time in this business, I have only run into one situation where I felt uncomfortable. It was before I was a Wicked girl, and I was booked for a job. When I got to the set, things were not the way I was told they were going to be. It was supposed to be a condom scene, and I was supposed to be booked with a certain male performer, but the director said he would be performing in the scene and he wouldn't be using a condom. I said, 'No, absolutely not,' and I left. There was never a physical threat; I just politely declined and made sure I never worked with that person again."

Drake is adamant that she has been in charge throughout her career, whether writing her own contract or negotiating her own terms or even telling the director her thoughts about what should be happening on-set. What's more, she understood that her choice to join the adult industry was a permanent one—she had no delusions she could walk away without her time as a porn star following her. She is quick to joke that she got rid of any political aspirations the moment she did her first scene.

The message delivered over and over by women in the industry, both in front of the camera and behind the scenes, is one of empowerment.

"I remember when I first saw a porn, when I became interested in getting involved in the industry, my first thought wasn't 'oh, this is hot,' or 'this is sexy.' No, it was 'look at that woman; look at how powerful she is,'" said Starr.

Traditional feminists may have a love/hate relationship with sex, but within adult entertainment, the relationship is with choice. No woman is forced into the industry, and the ones who ultimately make a career in adult all had one thing to say: "I love what I do."

Presidential Directives and
Sexual McCarthyism

Presidential administrations, whether intentionally or not, often interfere with the adult entertainment industry. Two of the most significant, for vastly different reasons, were those of Lyndon B. Johnson in the late 1960s and Ronald Reagan's in the late 1980s.

The President's Commission on Obscenity and Pornography, a 1968 product of the Johnson administration, stemmed from the Supreme Court's decision in *Stanley*. In that case, the court ruled people could view whatever they wanted in the comfort of their own home. President Johnson subsequently became intent on ordering a study on pornography under the aims of understanding the "Constitutional and definitional problems related to obscenity controls. Traffic in and distribution of obscene and pornographic materials. The effects of such material, particularly on youth, and their relationship to crime and other antisocial conduct."[20]

Interestingly enough, the overall outcome of the Commission was not puritanical or subversive to the adult entertainment industry, nor did it create a stance upon which to preach morality. The Commission instead recommended the implementation of sex education in schools, funded research into the effects of pornography on children while also creating ways to restrict access to children under the age of 18. The Commission did not recommend a restriction for adults and also determined no evidence proved obscenity or pornography harmful to people, and thus recommended the issues not be considered major societal problems. The Commission also found "no evidence to date that exposure to explicit sexual materials plays a significant role in the causation of delinquent or criminal behavior among youths or adults," and there also was "no evidence that exposure to explicit sexual materials adversely affects character or moral attitudes regarding sex and sexual conduct.[21]

Not surprisingly, when the findings were published in 1970 Congress rejected the report, as did then-President Richard Nixon, who was Johnson's successor.

"It's interesting because, there is a huge difference between the Lockhart Commission, which was the 1968 Commission under Johnson, and the Meese Commission [under Reagan in 1986]," Mark Kernes said. "The Lockhart Commission's mission was to find out how sexual material was received across the U.S. and whether or not it was harmful, which was reasonable. And they came out and said, 'Yeah, there seems to be a lot of it around, but no one seems to be too worried about it.'

"The 1986 Meese Commission was specifically designed to list and investigate the harms of sexual material or pornography," Kernes continued. "And they were good at it. They had witnesses coming out the ass who were from right-wing groups who were willing to say anything from 'well, I heard it was bad,' to 'porn ruined my life.' The Meese Commission was happy to hear them. However, the people who came out saying porn was benign or a non-issue were not listened to. And in fact, most of the Meese commissioners were chosen because they were anti-porn to begin with."

The Meese Commission ultimately made 92 recommendations calling for a crackdown on the then $8-billion-a-year adult entertainment industry across federal, state, and local jurisdictions. The final report, which was issued July 9, 1986, stated pornography is "sexually explicit and intended primarily for the purpose of sexual arousal" and pointed out that porn portrayed violence against women, led to anti-social acts like rape and other sexual violence, and needed to be controlled through more stringent anti-obscenity laws. The commission stated pornographic materials were addictive and created obsessive behavior among those who viewed the material, while also damaging the fragile psyche of impressionable youth and creating a breakdown in the innocence of younger generations. Furthermore, the commission stressed that pornography undermines traditional family values and is subversive to marriage, parenthood, and loving relationships between men and women. In conclusion, the commission's report stated that the body's recommendations were not directed toward "sexual repression" but toward "self-preservation."[22]

The commissions significantly differed not only in their findings and takes on pornography and adult entertainment, but also in how they conducted research, the individuals who composed each group, and the sexual politics that defined the era in which each commission operated. Even the published reports of each group were received differently. When the liberal publisher of the 1970 report attempted to create an illustrated version of the commission's findings, he was convicted of obscenity and sentenced to prison under the Nixon administration's definition of anti-obscenity laws. In contrast, the masturbatory and explicit report published by the Meese Commission and printed by the Government Printing Office was comparable to the descriptive text later published about President Bill Clinton's extramarital dalliances in 1998. No one responsible for publishing the Meese findings was prosecuted.[23]

"The guidelines that came along in 1987 with [Meese] made it a new ballgame," Sirkin said. "People who were charged with or had issues regarding obscenity faced going to jail for a really long time."

During the Clinton Administration, obscenity charges took a backseat on the Justice Department's to-do list, even though a series of attempted crackdowns on Internet pornography did occur under Clinton's watch. On February 8, 1996, Clinton signed the Communications Decency Act, the U.S. Congress' first and most prominent attempt to regulate adult material on the Internet. The controversial act laid out strict criminal penalties for any individual or group who "knowingly (a) uses an interactive computer service to send to a specific person or persons under 18 years of age, or (b) uses any interactive computer service to display in a manner available to a person under 18 years of age, any comment, request, suggestion, proposal, image, or other communication that, in context, depicts or describes, in terms patently offensive as measured by contemporary community standards, sexual or excretory activities or organs."[24] Introduced by conservative factions in Congress, the act was meant to provide for the Internet the same sort of regulatory oversight the Federal Communications Commission exercises in regard to indecency on radio and television.

Outrage ensued by civil liberty associations, free speech groups, and the adult entertainment community. Not only did the CDA cover electronic transmission, but it also covered books and printed material that had been scanned into electronic databases and made available to consumers online. It also put significant pressure on medical and scientific communities who shared anatomical and biological information about human sexuality or body processes in an electronic environment.

On June 12, 1996, a group of federal judges worked to effectively limit and block the most controversial portions of the Act under the belief that if enforced it would infringe on the free speech rights of adults over 18. In July of the same year, a U.S. federal court struck down another portion of the Act stating that it was too broad and far reaching in its attempt to restrict children's access or exposure to indecent material or speech. Challenged by Congress, the case went to the Supreme Court in 1997. The Court upheld the decisions made by federal courts, stating that the First Amendment would be infringed upon by portions of the Act, essentially working to "supervise" American children without the influence of the child's actual parents. The Supreme Court believed that the Act did not allow parents to sufficiently choose what their children could or could not have access to, or what was acceptable for their own child to see.

While actions against Internet porn were dramatic in the 1990s, it was during the George W. Bush administration that prosecutors brought up obscenity charges against 361 defendants, doubling what the Clinton administration pursued during the years of 1993-2000.[25] In 2005, under Bush's watch, the Justice Department formed the aforementioned Obscenity Prosecution Task Force. Based on the goal stated on the group's website, its mission followed the lines of "Enforcement is necessary in order to protect citizens from unlawful exposure to obscene materials."[26]

"There was this big movement, and [the Bush Administration] was really going to take it on," stated Sirkin.

The formation of this task force was done so at the urging of a variety of social conservative groups who realized they had the ear of a president who was not only vocal about his "born again" Christian status, but was also a self-professed recovering alcoholic who was dedicated to the moral awakening of the American people.

"There was a time when Bush came into power that I was fairly concerned about obscenity. And [Kink.com] has gone back and forth with certain shooting rules. For a while we allowed certain activities and then disallowed them. Now, we walk a fairly fine line," stated Peter Acworth. "I wouldn't say we were lucky to escape any obscenity issues under Bush, but I do think there are others who have been very unlucky. Evil Angel for instance, was very unlucky, given the quality of their content."

Sirkin recalled that in the aftermath of CDA's remarkable crash-and-burn, the tone of obscenity prosecutions in the U.S. changed— and not for the better. "It was during this time with this task force that prosecutors started to get sneaky and only wanted to show segments of the movies that were in question," he said, noting that the *Miller* Test, still the standard for defining obscenity, requires a work be considered as a whole. "They wanted to isolate scenes for shock value. If you show the entire film, the government is afraid the jury will become desensitized watching the same thing over and over again, and a juror would say 'So what?' Prosecutors felt if they only showed ten minutes of a two-hour movie, they would be able to shock a jury more. The government lawyers argued that if people had to watch a movie in its entirety in an open courtroom, they would be ashamed or embarrassed and more likely to favor with the defense. It's all bullshit really, because anyone would be uncomfortable. Porn isn't made to be watched in a courtroom with people watching you.

"I've had mistrials because a juror would not watch the movie," Sirkin continued. "I had to try a Max Hardcore case in Cincinnati, because in one of the trials a couple jurors wouldn't watch the movies and in another one a few jurors fell asleep. The judge saw it too! One guy slept for forty minutes."

While the Justice Department insisted the task force's goal was to prosecute sellers of hardcore pornography who exposed children to the material, surveys indicated the majority of hardcore or explicit material targeted for prosecution was accessed by consenting adults over the age of 18 who purchased the material through legitimate means. First Amendment and Free Speech proponents called the task force a new form of moral policing. That impression was not helped by the task force's geographical location in rural Montana with a mailing address in the same state—not exactly the most liberal of territories for ordering or receiving shipped adult material.

When President Barack Obama was sworn into office, prosecutors continued to pursue existing obscenity cases, but a halt in new indictments occurred. Additionally, one of the first changes the Justice Department embarked upon was refocusing the task force on child sexual abuse, often called child pornography. The group moved from Montana to New Jersey, a state considerably more liberal, and lenient, towards adult-focused material. In 2009, Obama appointed a new Deputy Attorney General: David Ogden, a law professional who represented Playboy and Penthouse against obscenity charges and other legal challenges. The appointment marked a major victory for the adult entertainment community as the

Number Two law enforcement professional in the country was essentially one of their own.[27]

Sirkin insists that liberal or conservative, government cannot be depended upon to do anything besides interfere with legally operated adult entertainment businesses. He has faith in the ability of the adult industry to counter efforts at moral policing, regardless who is in power. "There is no reason we can't be as loud as [the anti-porn movement] and be more professional," he said. "Stop complaining about these things and get out there and beat them. Kick their asses! When they begin to lose, the anti-porn movement will fall. People have to realize that we are real people too, and we care about what we do."

Industry Efforts to Crack Down on Child Pornography

Anti-porn advocates often attempt to paint the adult industry as some sort of safe haven for child pornography and those who exploit children. After all, in our child-centric culture, rolling out a campaign to protect kids is a good way to get money thrown at your cause.

But in truth, the adult industry is staunchly anti-child pornography. The legitimate industry has zero tolerance for people who sexually abuse or exploit kids. The industry even established a non-profit organization, founded in 1996, called the Association of Sites Advocating Child Protection (ASACP). The non-profit not only works with law enforcement to fight Internet child pornography, but also educates parents and other custodians and helps them ensure their homes and computers are child-friendly and child-safe. ASACP partners with the National Center for Missing & Exploited Children (NCMEC) as well as a variety of child exploitation prevention operations in other countries to help stamp out child pornography. The organization investigates websites, IP addresses, hosting companies, billing systems, and other areas that tie into child pornography rings. What's more, all of this is done without a dime of taxpayer money. ASACP is fully funded by members of the adult entertainment industry. "The one thing I can say is that from the very beginning of my work and representation of the adult entertainment industry, the biggest fear of any adult producer was that there might be a minor in their work, that their product had been sold to a minor, or that a minor might have been in your establishment," Sirkin said. "They were more scared of this than bars were of serving a minor. If you think about it, you get caught serving a minor in a bar, you get a fine and you might lose your liquor license for a week, but if you sold a minor sexually explicit material, you were going to go to jail. No one in the adult industry wanted that."

The adult industry always has been conscious of this very important factor. Although there have been rare cases where a minor slipped through the cracks and ended up on film, i.e. Tracy Lords, the industry is strict about keeping materials out of the hands of children and keeping kids out of the content produced.   The government thinks that creating an onerous record-keeping system like 18 USC 2257 will prevent underage actors from appearing on screen, but many in the adult industry disagree.

"You can have all the 2257s in the world, and the fact is Tracy Lords would have still appeared in the movies because she had a fake passport," Sirkin said.

Young members of the adult industry, like Allison Vivas, president of Pink Visual, support industry efforts to prevent minors from purchasing sexually explicit products or ending up in films. But Vivas also believes that good companies in the industry should do more to fight child pornography, particularly when it comes to holding accountable so-called tube sites and other outlets that pirate content. Adult content producers employ tube sites to promote their legitimate products, but because tube sites also accept uploads from the general public, all sorts of material can, and does, show up on tube site pages. Tube sites are subject to the same laws that constrain all other adult entertainment providers, but too many of the Old Guard in the adult industry distrust law enforcement.

"We have legalese in our corner," Vivas said. "And the young people emerging in this industry, we don't have the same experiences or fears that some of the veterans who survived the crackdowns and prosecutions during the 1980s have. Ultimately, the tube sites are bound by 2257 law, making sure the models are over the age of 18 before filming begins. We will go after these sites; make them produce their documents. This helps reduce piracy and reduce accidental child porn."

All adult entertainment producers are held to the same legal standards. Reputable companies understand the nuances of 2257 law and the extensive recordkeeping that goes into production. What's more, they have the resources to pursue shady or underground organizations and get them to "produce their papers." Vivas is adamant that she is part of a new generation of adult producers who are not afraid of the law and will use it to their advantage.

Any link ever presented between the legitimate adult community and child pornography is strictly fictional and used for demonizing adult producers who are genuinely concerned about the issue and determined to stay on the right side of the law.

The majority of the challenges faced by the adult entertainment industry come down to perception and communication. There isn't a simple solution, but something can be said for positive self-promotion that the adult industry produces content for adults by adults; that everyone has a right to privacy and a freedom of choice. To view porn, or not to view porn...that is the question. The answer *should be* as independent as the individual providing it. Or, as Lou Sirkin says, "The adult industry is a modern-day crusade. It's the last divide between freedom and the alternative."

PART SEVEN

The World Wide Web
Streaming Sex Online

The Internet changed the world. From the adult entertainment industry's perspective, without porn the World Wide Web would be nowhere near as worldly as it is today. The industry long has been known for its ability to bend new technologies to its will. Adult was the first industry to embrace home video distribution and the first to consider how DVDs could reshape business. The Internet provided a vast, fertile new field for monumental innovation, and the adult entertainment industry stepped up to the challenge. But not always without consequence.

"The takeoff of the Internet really had a lot to do with the demise of the DVD business," according to Castle Megastore's Mark Franks. "At the same time, the Internet has helped a lot of guys in the store business, because their profits were down 40 percent [prior to the Web's pervasive presence]."

The Internet irrevocably changed the game for adult content producers. The new technology came with obvious positives: incredible growth, market expansion, new audiences, and additional mainstream acceptance. The positives however came hand-in-hand with negatives, especially for traditional porn producers who had become accustomed to enjoying limited competition. Suddenly, they had to redefine themselves in order to keep up with an ever-increasing gang of upstart competitors.

"When the Internet stated, there were maybe five guys, five major players in the [adult movie] space, and those guys were spending a million a week to make five million a week," KBeech's Kevin Beechum recalled. "Now, I hear those same guys are spending a million to make a million."

John Stagliano has heard the same rumor. "[Evil Angel] didn't jump on the Internet movement as early as we should have. If we did, we would have made more money. But I didn't understand the technology. The Internet was not a significant force for me. As a consumer of porn, until about 2003 the delivery system online was very inferior to a VHS tape or a DVD. This was why I didn't think of [the Internet] as competition."

Ultimately, the Internet redefined the industry and opened it up to new entrepreneurs with a host of revolutionary ideas. But, things also went wrong. Though the Internet is in the middle of its second decade of mainstream existence, the adult community is still learning how to deal with challenges that arise from it. There is never going to be a time when adult content producers can stop worrying about how new technology affects them. Whether they worry about pirated content, supply and demand, industry competition, or anything else that arises directly from the online space, the changing nature of the Internet provides day-to-day schooling to members of the adult industry, for better and for worse.

Opinions are certainly mixed.

"I think the adult industry needs to go through a cultural evaluation," stated Lou Sirkin. "The change in the industry right now says that they have to come together. The Internet really hurt [adult]."

Or, consider the famous last words of Scott Field: "The Internet, in my opinion, will absolutely destroy this world."

So…where do we go from here?

How the Internet Changed Porn

When adult content producers and their customers realized the Internet could deliver sex-on-demand 24/7, a brand new world erupted.   Credit for game-changing advances in graphics, video conferencing, subscription services, monetization strategies, filtering, affiliate marketing, and peer-to-peer sharing properly belong to guys like Ron Levi, Seth Warshavsky, Rob Govlet, and Greg Dumas. Without those largely unsung—at least in the mainstream—pioneers of pornography, much ballyhooed Internet wunderkind like Facebook's Mark Zuckerberg, Napster's Shawn Fanning, and Google's Sergey Brin might not have had the foundations upon which they built tech empires.

"The adult industry, as far as online goes, has always been known as the Wild, Wild West," performer and entrepreneur Sunny Leone said. "We are the first ones to try everything; we are the ones to work out the kinks for the rest of the mainstream world. We were the ones that came up with the innovation."

Porn's rapid advancement of Internet-related technologies not only gave nascent Web giants tools and concepts with which to work, but also helped established tech mainstays like Cisco, Microsoft, and Sun Microsystems expand their businesses in bold—and profitable—new directions.

The Internet strategy created by adult content producers and marketers has been duplicated and emulated. Everything from CNN's citizen journalist initiative to YouTube's streaming videos, Skype's Internet-based telephony and local mom-and-pop operations that employ email marketing or rudimentary e-commerce owes a debt to the adult entertainment industry's exploration and early development efforts. Broadband Internet access, in particular, resulted in large part from the adult industry's eagerness to provide customers with more porn, faster.

Although the Internet presented unprecedented opportunities for the adult industry, it also presented unique, and sometimes vicious, challenges.   In addition to creating a billion-dollar distribution platform, the Internet also opened the field to increased competition as well as piracy. What the World Wide Web giveth, it also taketh away: Web-based adult entertainment entrepreneurs made millions upon millions of dollars in record time…and many of them also lost their newfound fortunes almost overnight.

"It makes me laugh when someone says they want to start an [adult] website," KBeech's Kevin Beechum said. "But I always ask what's going to happen after they open it up? I've seen some great websites, but they end up going broke, going under, because they don't have the money to do it right. They can't get traffic. Most of the guys who have been successful in the Internet space were all Internet guys by trade. Guys like me, guys who had been around VHS and DVD and the manufacturing [end of the business], none of us got rich off the Internet because we didn't jump on board when it was first getting big. We should have, but we didn't."

By early 2012, there between five and six million porn-related websites existed on the Internet.[28] Never before has porn been more accessible to anyone who wants it. And never before have had leaders in the adult industry had to struggle so hard to protect what is theirs: content, brand, and profits. For the first time, power over porn is in the hands of consumers, not creators. The Internet did that.

"I'm pretty adaptable, especially when recognizing new technology and realizing things are changing," Wicked's Joy King said. "I was not afraid to embrace new technology. When computers first started becoming a new medium and everyone was starting websites, I took classes to understand what was going on so I could figure out how to deal with it. If you stop learning, you stop growing, and if you stop growing, you limit the amount of success you can have.

"I think it's important to embrace the new ways and new delivery methods and really understand how people want and are consuming our product," she added. "If you can't stay on the cutting edge of how consumers want to watch your content, then you might as well close up shop."

Greg Dumas, president of GEC Media and marketing director for ICM Registry, the organization responsible for the introduction of the .XXX domain extension, entered the adult entertainment industry in 1995 when he went to work for Hustler as the organization's vice president of marketing. At that time, the Internet was little more than a blip on the radar among the geekiest of geeks. Although a few adult computer bulletin board services (BBSes) were migrating to the new medium from scattered host computers connected to the outside world by armies of modems that could handle one connection per incoming telephone line, the World Wide Web certainly hadn't begun to register as a primary resource for commercial porn. Still, Dumas suspected that in order to fulfill his role at Hustler, he needed to encourage founder Larry Flynt to buy into the new technology.

"[Hustler's management] thought the Internet was a fad and initially were against making any investment in it," Dumas said. "They wanted to see how it would develop."

At the time, Hustler was "dabbling, at best," with a BBS, according to Dumas. At Dumas' insistence, the company launched two rudimentary websites, one free and one membership-based. Hustler's membership site was one of the first such destinations offering adult entertainment.

"Larry [Flynt] wanted proof there was going to be a viable business model behind [the website]," Dumas revealed. "Hustler was a publishing company, an old-school publishing company, not a tech company. They were still doing paper memos; there was no email. It was a different time."

Dumas, a fan of anything "geeky," had to fight for every step forward at Hustler, but he immediately saw the money-making opportunity of the Internet. At the same time, he was well aware the new technology represented a relative crap shoot.

"There were times during [the early days] when I would go into the bathroom and throw water on my face and ask 'Am I doing the right thing here?'" he recalled. "I was really putting my career on the line with this. I just believed in it so much; I knew we had to do this. I sold it to Larry [Flynt] through the idea that we are taking the magazine and making it electronic."

Joy King, on the other hand, approached the newfangled Internet from a completely different perspective at Wicked Pictures.

"I didn't have any fear," she said. "If you think back to '95, the Internet was all about this 'free information highway' and having the ability for people to find out about you. People weren't watching content on the Internet yet; it was about delivering information. It was about keeping things free so you could expand your reach into the marketplace, to let people know who you are. That's how I looked at it. I was excited about it. I had no idea that we had something to fear."

For many adult entertainment Internet pioneers, the Internet business model was a "shoot first, ask questions later" proposition. And many pioneers, including Dumas, found freedom in that notion. Reveling in the mostly unregulated online world, they likened themselves to cowboys with a gunslinger mentality.

Though somewhat moderated over the years, the cowboy personality remains alive and well in the adult online space. Over time, it has been adopted by other, more mainstream companies and movements, as well. Facebook is an excellent example: Zuckerburg's company changes privacy controls, data gathering and other sensitive features at the drop of a hat. Initially, the moves offend a lot of people, but eventually most users give in and accept a new way of interacting. While the mainstream media typically gives credit for developing the "shoot first" business model to social media mavens, the truth is, Dumas and his contemporaries approached business from that direction from the very beginning.

"We used to operate under the idea of 'ask forgiveness, not permission,'" Dumas said. "We figured if people didn't say anything about what we were doing, then we were okay."

While people like Dumas spent their time attempting to convince established adult companies of the need to be online, small start-ups sneaked in under the radar. According to Allison Vivas, president of upstart Pink Visual, the Internet removed much of the advantage from the Old Guard because everyone had to learn the new technology from scratch.

"If companies like Hustler and Vivid and Wicked had moved into the Internet space early on, there probably wouldn't have been room for people like us and companies like Reality Kings," Vivas said. "Our success comes from fifty percent of traditional adult companies not capitalizing on what the Internet could do, and the other 50 percent comes from the fact that online porn start-ups didn't have anything to compare their revenue to. If a start-up made $100,000 a month off the bat, that was great, but to a big company like Hustler or Vivid, that doesn't seem like much. They delayed because it didn't seem significant, it wasn't worth it, and to the start-ups it was."

One thing hasn't changed about the industry, even in the instant-information Internet Age: The adult entertainment business thrives on misinformation, drama, and mystique. Although several books, movies, and magazine articles have attempted to shed light on the explosive early days of the adult Web, most of the efforts have encompassed more fantasy than reality.

One of the most recent such efforts, *Middle Men* (Paramount Pictures/Oxymoron Entertainment, 2009), was promoted to viewers as "based on a true story," but industry insiders saw little they recognized on the screen. At best, the movie trivialized the origins of online porn; at worst, the story engaged in wholesale fabrication.

"The only thing true about that movie was maybe the first three minutes," Dumas groused. "None of [the rest of it] happened, none of that ever went down, and that's not how the business developed. I knew [the guys upon whom the movie's characters were based] when they had a little office in Woodland Hills, California, and they were always just a billing company. They never had their own sites, never had their own content.

"It was crazy guys like us who began the online industry," he continued. "I remember back in 1996, when Congress was trying to get one of the first online decency acts passed, and Senator [Jon] Kyl from Arizona held up a printout of the home page of Hustler.com. The image was featured on the cover of *TIME Magazine*. I was like a proud parent."

For all the success the industry has experienced, the road has been fraught with challenges and roadblocks. While the adult entertainment industry was at the forefront in the early days, in the mid-2000s it encountered a tipping point at which innovation began to slow, and then almost halted. Coupled with a decrease in DVD sales, money stopped flowing.

"I'm not sure if there was this 'ah-ha' moment where we realized we were losing money," Wicked's Joy King recalled. "It was a gradual thing where [traditional] sales were dipping, but the Internet sales weren't rising as much as DVD sales were slowing. It was a gradual realization. Around 2000, everyone was making tons of money on the Internet—and then the bubble burst. It wasn't until about 2006 that we all started saying, 'DVD sales aren't recovering and the [Internet sales] aren't going anywhere.' It was a realization that these sales might not ever come back, so we had to go into the mode of 'What can we do to remain a profitable production company?' It has been a long road to examining the process and making sure we are implementing the strategy where we are profitable and smart."

Wicked CEO Steve Orenstein agreed. "I was a slow mover, like many of the established guys in the industry were. But I also didn't think the Internet was going to be the death of [Wicked]. Inevitably, it became another method to get our product out there, but the people who were getting rich were the ones who were scamming people. Wicked wasn't going to do that, so we took a hit when our DVD sales decreased, but we have survived. As a company, you have to continually look at your model and say, 'How do we compete?'"

It's a continual reassessment process. And Dumas has his own opinion on the topic. "There is a certain point in the adult business where they went from innovating, to following. The industry began to stagnate. And what happened was we lost a bunch of great talent. We weren't developing, we weren't in the leading edge.

"Think of some of the great things that have come out of mainstream markets—Groupon, for instance," he continued. "The adult world hasn't done anything like that in a long time. That's what frustrates me. The adult business was founded on the cowboy mentality, and that's not there anymore."

Bringing Adult Entertainment to
Life on a Computer

As public interest in the Internet grew, so did the adult industry's realization that in order to be successful online, one had to mix business savvy with creative urges.

From a design standpoint, creating an adult website requires much more than simply posting pictures online and calling it a day. Internet pioneers quickly realized that in order to generate significant revenue, they first had to generate traffic by offering an attractive, easy-to-use online presentation.

"Once Hustler got onboard with the Internet, the magazine design team really took to mentoring me with layouts, how to tell a story with photos," Dumas said. "We were taking photo sets that were in the magazine, for instance, highlighting seven pictures to whet the appetite of a magazine reader, and putting twenty on the website. We were focused on cross-promotion, stating, 'Hey if you like these in the magazine, go to Hustler online and get more.' Keep in mind there was a different mentality in the business at that time; magazines were not doing this."

Dumas left Hustler in 1996 after realizing some of the management team didn't share his vision. Regardless whether the membership site showed a profit, old school factions within the publishing giant saw the online project as a threat to tried-and-true aspects of Hustler's business and wanted the website killed.

Dumas coupled the experience he'd gained with his native ingenuity and started his own company. He went all in, first setting up the website ClubLove.com and then founding Interactive Gallery Inc. The Internet was the future of adult entertainment, he figured, and he was determined to be a part of it.

iGallery sold memberships that allowed consumers to access content from a variety of adult entertainment sites—a practice that became standard operating procedure in the ensuing years. The company also sold and distributed content to thousands of adult websites owned by others.

While established companies like Wicked were figuring out how to change their business models to incorporate the new distribution medium offered by the Web, individuals like Dumas were scouting for fertile ground and untapped markets that were ripe for new business ventures.

"Initially, I was much more on the business side of it, I knew about traffic and how to get memberships to flow, but I didn't understand the creative [aspects]," Dumas said. "I partnered with Scott Schalin, who had been the creative director for Hustler. He had the ability to take my business thoughts and put them into a creative format that worked. We developed a very dynamic team. That is what made iGallery attractive to New Frontier Media, who we sold the company to in 1999."

At the time of the sale, iGallery's revenue exceeded $21 million dollars annually. Though iGallery broke new ground in many areas, creating one of the first true giants in the Internet space, Dumas and Schalin found their new lifestyle was anything but worry-free.

"We had days when we would sit back and wonder, 'Where are all of these customers coming from?'" Dumas revealed. "We were convinced we were doing something wrong, that something was messed up in our billing system and we were committing fraud.

"We were scared of being arrested," he continued. "We were scared to put assets in our names. The content, the billing, this was all attached to us. This was not long after the [obscenity] prosecutions in the 1980s, and it was fresh in our minds because we were still talking to the people who had gone through that."

And Dumas and Schalin weren't alone in their fears. Dumas remembers a friend who carried $5,000 in his pocket on Fridays: In case he got arrested over the weekend, he wanted to be able to bail himself out of jail. The marketing director for another large operation, Cybererotica, routinely wore tens of thousands of dollars in diamonds and gold for the same reason. The practice was not without merit. Although Dumas was never arrested, as the registered owner of iGallery he was charged in absentia when the German government prosecuted iGallery for obscenity.

"My lawyer told me, 'You probably shouldn't travel to Germany right now,'" Dumas recalled. "I was like, 'Are you kidding me? I don't even get parking tickets!' It scared the shit out of me. We ended up having to hire legal counsel in Germany to defend us. There was nudity—not anything hardcore, just topless nudity. It's one thing to have the police knock on your door; it's another to have someone say, 'Hey, what's this letter from the German government?' Even after I was cleared, I was still nervous about flying to Germany, the EU." iGallery never produced content; Dumas and his partners only bought or leased material for redistribution. Because they had worked with many domestic and international freelance photographers, the iGallery staff was able to sign deals for original content that was not being seen or accessed anywhere else.

In the days before video was available online, "it was very much about [the amount of still-image] content, and not quality content necessarily," Dumas said. "We would buy the content, and I thought it was really good stuff. We would format all of this material in such a way where it might resemble a *Maxim* magazine spread. We were really witty, sarcastic with all of it. We all came from the Hustler world, which was trucker mentality, and so we wanted to be somewhere between *Hustler* and *Penthouse*. That was the attitude we took as we did our sites."

During the explosive growth of the early days, iGallery and other companies that embraced the new Internet with a vengeance made a lot of money. Not surprisingly, a few enterprising types saw value in attempting to consolidate distribution across a variety of platforms. Founded in 1995, New Frontier Media, which is now publically held, was among the first to begin attempting consolidation of the then $1-billion adult entertainment industry into a conglomerate of pay-per-view and subscription services via cable and satellite television, and the Internet. The company's acquisition of iGallery was big news, although Dumas now admits buyout generated mixed feelings within the iGallery ranks. The money was nice, but watching his brainchild transformed from Wild West buckaroo into staid corporate citizen hurt, he said.

Sexy Tech Entrepreneurs:
No Longer Business as Usual

When Allison Vivas graduated from the University of Arizona in 2001, she knew she wanted to work in an Internet-related field. She also knew she was entering the job market at the end of the dot-com boom, so she wasn't altogether surprised when she didn't receive much response to the resumes she sent out *en masse*. Then one day, lighting struck, and she received a call inviting her to interview for a job in Internet marketing. Little did she know the call would lead her into a career she never saw coming.

"The ad I responded to was pretty general; it was a position for an Internet marketing coordinator," Vivas said. "I applied via email, and then I got a response detailing what the company did. They stated they were a member of the adult entertainment industry, but they were a responsible, professional organization. That got me interested and more curious about it. My fiancé at the time was excited about it." She laughed as she added, "He was thinking free passwords and stuff like that."

The company was TopBucks, which specialized in affiliate marketing and advertising for the adult entertainment industry.

"I went to the interview, and it was in a nice office building— lots of computers set up," Vivas recalled. "I was in my little 'power suit' and probably very overdressed, but the meeting went well and it was a quick decision on the spot for me. I liked that there was no bureaucracy. I had been to other interviews where there were three and four meetings and a lengthy waiting process. It seemed like some of those corporations didn't know what they wanted. I liked that TopBucks just seemed to know."

The next day she became the company's seventh employee. And she realized she had to break the news to her parents, well aware of the stigma surrounding the industry.

"At first I attempted to hide it from my parents," she said. "I was only 21 at the time, so I was still in that transition period over 'Am I an adult?' and 'Does what my mom and dad think matter?' I waited for about a week before I told them what TopBucks did.

"My dad was very comfortable with it, kind of had a laugh about it," Vivas recalled. "My mom was okay with it. She made the comment, 'Well, this is okay for now, but someday you will find a real job.'"

Vivas and her mother now laugh about her mother's initial response. By the time the company reorganized in 2004—consolidating its Internet, broadcast and DVD-distribution divisions, plus a new content-production operation, under the name Pink Visual—Vivas had worked her way up to marketing director. In 2006, she was named president.

"My mother ended up moving to help me out with my two children," Vivas revealed. "She is now exposed to the fact that there is real business going on. She overhears conversations about legal matters, copyright infringement, employee, or [human resources] matters, so I think she is much more aware as to what is going on. Plus, she understands now that sexuality is very normal. We just happened to make a business around that."

Under Vivas' leadership, Pink Visual has established a reputation as an innovative, tech-savvy brand. Though the transition from small Internet firm to large multi-platform conglomerate was relatively painless, Vivas said the company still experienced growing pains.

"We had a few challenges off the bat [managing production, when that division was new]," she said. "The filmmaking process is so involved, detailed, with so many moving parts, and we didn't have that before. We would set deadlines for ourselves, stating, 'Okay, this all has to be in by Monday, and it has to be processed by Wednesday so it can be up on twenty-eight different sites by Friday,' and sometimes that wouldn't happen. Sometimes we had to have a kill [live] feed because a performer didn't show up, or we had a corrupt video and it had to be re-encoded—all sort of different things. Maybe the [talent] agency had to replace someone at the last moment. Early on we even had an HIV scare, so we had to shut down production for a while. We didn't come to terms with all of this and learn to work with it until about three years ago."

The year 2008 was a breaking point for much of the industry, including Pink Visual. Until then, the company had subscribed to an operating structure found in many mainstream corporations. Pink Visual even implemented Six Sigma, a business management strategy first created by Motorola in 1996. The process seeks to improve the quality of business outputs through the identification of errors and roadblocks. Through the assignation of identified process experts within an organization, the theory goes that Six Sigma should help improve efficiencies and instill quality management methods to the workforce. For Pink Visual, the implementation of the Six Sigma process was a spectacular bust.

But in 2008, free amateur content, piracy of commercial content, and the proliferation of so-called tube sites reached critical mass. Faced with a faltering industry, a worldwide economic recession and the overhead associated with 100 employees, Pink Visual's management knew a general downsizing was imminent if the company didn't make some drastic changes.

"We tried to implement [Six Sigma], and it was probably our worst two years in terms of morale and treating people like human beings," Vivas said. "We tried to implement things that mainstream companies had done to be successful, and it didn't work for us. We came up with all of these arbitrary deadlines. Why not get rid of that? Maybe we deliver the product five days past when we said we would have it done, but maybe it's a better product."

By then down to 60 employees, the staff was nervous, just like the rest of the American workforce. The company's core was shaken, management changes were occurring, new directives were laid out, and uncertainty reigned.

"We had this structure and everyone had to follow it," Vivas recalled. "We would have a project planning meeting and then an initial project meeting. We had another rule that said you had to instant message someone before you went by their office, instead of just having a casual stop by [to brainstorm]. Our employees had to get approval from their manager, who had to get approval from another manager before they went inter-department with an idea. All of this was prohibiting innovation. We had the feeling of 'Are we going to keep all these rules in place, or are we going to allow our employees to showcase their talents?' It was then that we became a flat organization."

Pink Visual threw the traditional corporate mentality out the window.

Almost immediately, the bottom line perked up. Happy employees within a less-structured environment were more creative and productive.

"We had gone through a two-year period of consistent decline, month after month after month," Vivas said. "And when you are looking at those charts, it's pretty scary. You begin to think 'We only have another year and a half left at this point.' We not only got rid of the corporate feel of the company, [but we also] refocused our imaginations. We needed to redefine ourselves. What we decided to do was reflect our unique corporate personality, and the personalities of our staff, in our work. This included being more innovative, and really having fun with technology. We got turned on to the mobile market and focused on delivering great mobile products to the end consumer. We saw results almost immediately."

Pink Visual reached a point of stability within three months, ending their period of decline. Within nine months, the company began to see profitable growth, which has remained steady.

The change in gears led to a complete revamping of Pink Visual's internal corporate culture, and Vivas thinks the fun-yet-focused atmosphere led to Pink Visual's widespread recognition as a pioneer in new technology. She believes having employees who buy into a culture that is invested in creative vision produces better results than forcing employees to follow rules or procedures they don't understand or subscribe to.

Ultimately, Vivas learned she cannot judge the success of a project based solely on revenue; instead, she believes return on investment also must be measured in terms of a project's ability to support a creative environment that will produce future successes. The mindset is not uncommon among people of Vivas' generation—the first to have Internet access in college classes and dorm rooms. Couple her strong belief in the power of the Internet to change business models with a departure from traditional corporate rules and a devotion to freeing employees from dependence on geography, and it's no longer business as usual.

"Since the Internet boom, some of the largest adult companies are no longer in L.A.," Vivas said. "They are in Montreal, Miami, Phoenix, New York, overseas, and this has completely changed the dynamic of the industry. Because there are so many moving parts to an adult company, there is no reason it has to be in California. Maybe studios need to be in Los Angeles, but when you have the website and the other parts, it makes more sense to be somewhere else because you no longer have to pay the overhead that comes with operating in California. That is where your competitive advantage lies."

Vivas also believes that to keep reaping rewards at Pink Visual, she can never get too comfortable, lest she sink into a level of complacency and the "next big thing" passes the company by. "Otherwise you make the same mistake that the big adult studios did [with the Internet] in 1999 and 2000," she said.

Bondage Goes Tech

For Kink.com owner Peter Acworth, combining his fetish for bondage with his love of all things technology-based has made his career.

Originally from England, Acworth migrated to the U.S. to pursue a PhD at Columbia University in New York. At the time, he saw himself making a career in finance or the academic world. Then he became entranced by the power of the Internet and its potential for those who, like him, were equally entranced by an alternative lifestyle.

"The Internet was sort of this untapped, new thing that people were doing," Acworth said. "I jumped ship and brought together my interest in the Internet at this very early stage with my fascination with BDSM."

Acworth recalls that when he first began exploring the niche, he frequented BDSM clubs, usually located in dark alleys, in the middle of the night. At the time, this didn't seem strange to him. There was no other public forum offering a way for fetish enthusiasts to connect.

"Everyone had a stage name because they were so freaked out that someone would find out about this supposedly dirty activity," he recalled. "When I started thinking about [Kink.com], I figured there was no reason for it to be that way."

It was this thought that created Kink.com in 1997. Acworth was committed to fashioning a place online that brought alternative sexuality to light in order to get rid of the stereotype surrounding the niche. Acworth didn't think consensual BDSM was something to be ashamed of or kept hidden.

Today, Kink.com operates its production efforts and a host of websites within one of the most historic and visible landmarks in San Francisco: the Armory in the Mission district. Acworth and his staff welcome interaction with the public, especially those who can't quite wrap their heads around exactly what safe, sane BDSM encompasses.

"We have an open-door policy," he said. "We book tours for the public; anyone can come in and tour the Armory. We did this to demystify what we are doing, in an effort to become transparent."

Acworth also incorporated mainstream operating policies into Kink.com's mission, based on those in use by the mainstream companies that were taking over Silicon Valley when Kink.com was founded.

"Kink.com is a company I admire," reflected Bobbi Starr, who regularly performs in and directs content for the Kink.com website. "Growing up in the Bay Area, I saw a lot of tech start-ups. The way Kink.com runs their company has a tech company feel, which is different than other companies in the adult entertainment industry. They run their company very efficiently."

Acworth's business model plays off the personal interests of his employees. As the business has grown, Acworth has asked his employees to play a part in the development of content for new sites. Much as a similar approach did at Pink Visual, employee investment in the product has contributed fresh ideas about what to create. Acworth tasked his employees with ownership of the content they produce and the sites they run, delivering in return a commission on revenue. More traffic equals more money, and the employees who buy into the vision of growth promoted by Acworth reap the rewards. This content specificity on the Kink.com websites serves the interests of the customers who frequent the sites, promoting long-term subscriber behavior.

"Part of our success has been based on how specific our sites are, instead of being a shopping mall, so to speak," Acworth said. "That has been because of the good people we hire."

Kink.com currently employs more than 100 people who are well served by the Fortune 500 benefit structure installed by senior management. Still, because of the niche in which Kink.com operates, Acworth said it has not always been easy to attract high quality employees.

"I'm sure mainstream businesses have it easier when it comes to hiring professionals, for instance a Chief Technology or Marketing person," he said. "When we grew to be a certain size and moved into the Armory that upped the attractiveness of the company to a variety of people. We have always offered full benefits, we pay competitively, and we try to maintain a culture that makes Kink.com a fun place to work, where there is a sense of community. We are also opening a bar across the street, somewhere the employees can go when they are done with work. What we provide is an alternative to working at a bank or a corporation or somewhere of that nature. I don't care if someone is gay or transgendered or if they want to paint their hair red. That's all fine, as long as they get their job done."

Many of the practices employed at Kink.com mirror the values and missions of mainstream companies featured in publications like *Fast Money* and *Inc.* While Acworth wouldn't mind a phone call from a publication that wants to spotlight his company, he said he does what he does simply because treating employees and customers well is good business.   In turn, Kink.com's policies encourage greater acceptance of the company by mainstream markets.

Kink.com has always stayed on the Internet side of things, thus simplifying the business and reducing its legal exposure: Being strictly Web-based, the company doesn't have to negotiate DVD distribution or send physical products across state lines.   In terms of the "community standards" prong of the Miller Test for obscenity, Acworth feels the network of websites is relatively safe in San Francisco, where the BDSM community long has been an accepted part of the larger society.

"We did toy with the idea of doing some DVDs that didn't involve bondage, and we tried to sell [that kind of content], but our brand wasn't known for it," Acworth said. "We have always been known as Kink.com and not just Kink, and our studies show that once someone starts consuming the product on the Internet, they stop buying DVDs.   So people probably saw our videos in a store and just didn't know who we were."

Instead, Kink.com focuses on technology, adhering to a "tech company feel" and working to stay abreast of changes in the online community.   Currently, the company is looking into how changing trends on the Internet can help it compete against or even partner with amateurs or other companies that are able to produce and publish content while incurring less overhead than large brick-and-mortar studios.

"We have been concerned for a long time over the future of recorded content," Acworth said. "We seem to have weathered the storm pretty well, and now our sales are stable.   Having said that, we are now interested in recoding our publishing system such that you could be anywhere and publish material.   This would help us go after the amateurs or people who can publish at lower costs, and have them work through our system with their own website.   We see that as a key to success.   "So, if you are interested in producing content from home, you could sign up for a Kink.com website account and you would be able to upload material directly to a publishing system and have a site that looks very much like one of our existing sites. And then we would pay out a commission, minus the affiliate costs, to those producers—who could be anywhere."

Acworth believes that through this sort of "franchise system" for his brand, not only will recognition of the Kink.com name be increased, but also overhead costs will be controlled and less studio space will be required in the long run, which will assist in promoting longevity.

Acworth also wants to make sure Kink.com is known in the marketplace as an ahead-of-the-curve company when it comes to bringing consumers live and interactive feeds of reality-based content. The Kink.com staff is developing a social networking aspect for their products, allowing users to interact with the models online. Acworth likes the initiative because live content and social networking applications can't be pirated, making both unique experiences for the user.

Regardless where the future takes Kink.com, Acworth believes that through continued good business practices, both inside and outside the Armory, the longevity of the company will be protected by loyal customers. "We don't have the broad appeal that some of the other adult companies like Bang Brothers or Reality Kings might have," he said. "We operate in a relatively tight niche and we serve a small customer base, but ultimately we serve them very well."

Revolutionizing Revenue:
The Recurring Business Model

What would any adult entertainment site be without the ability to bill for memberships?   Probably a loaded question there, considering the industry's current issues with piracy and free content.

"The Internet really opened things up and made the business more prolific, but people were really distrustful of the Internet model at first," Castle Megastore's Mark Franks observed. "You didn't want to give your credit card information because you weren't sure what someone was going to do with it. The technology wasn't there to protect people at first. When I started with Castle in 2003, the Internet was not a trusted place to go buy adult products. It wasn't a strong vehicle for commerce. There were some people doing okay, but it was only starting to hit its stride."

The Internet did more for porn than increase the market and audience size. The World Wide Web presented the opportunity for creative billing and accounting systems that allowed website operators to charge customers' credit cards on a recurring, month-to-month basis. Until about 2007, the success of the adult online industry was a billing game, relying more on convincing customers to part with their credit card numbers than on providing quality content. The public couldn't seem to get enough of online porn, and the cash piled up.

The automatically recurring billing model originated in the phone sex industry.

"A lot of the technology that went into the first adult sites came from the phone sex industry," Dumas said. "Billing was part of that. The first entrepreneurs in the Internet age didn't know how to bill, but the phone sex guys knew how to do this, from a virtual standpoint.   When I first started in that area, [phone sex professionals] didn't communicate with us regarding the technology associated with the Internet; rather they schooled us in the technology we would be using [to bill]."

The phone sex industry's success, in large part, derived from consumers punching in their credit card numbers on the dial pad of their phones. While phone sex did not bill on a monthly basis, it did bill on a minute-by-minute basis. All that was required to make the transition between phone and Internet was an adjustment to the billing cycle.

In the early days of the Internet, Hustler charged approximately ten dollars per month for an automatically recurring subscription. The company raked in between $150,000 and $200,000 monthly in recurring revenue. Not huge numbers for an established company, but the volume excited Dumas.

"At the time, that [amount] was really significant," he said, attributing the monthly revenue to the low price of a Hustler.com membership.

The billing procedures that adult websites operated off piggybacked from the Helms Amendment, which was a phone sex law enacted that stated that if a purchaser used a credit card to buy adult content, the owner of the site, or the person or company selling the content, was able to operate under the assumption that the purchaser was in fact of legal age.

It was at the dawning of the new millennium that adult websites decided that they needed to get "creative" in their billing procedures, much of this had to do with a new realization that there was a huge amount of adult content available, both for free and at a charge, available online, and many were beginning to feel the pinch from the competition. Dumas, for instance, realized that you could lure a customer in based on a "five days free" model. Interpreted from a billing standpoint, that just meant they got "re-billed" on the thirty-fifth day. The customer got charged up front, and received longer access during the first month. No harm, no foul, after all, they did get five days free, it just came at the end.

"We made a lot of money, like millions. Then the FTC clamped down on that and we had to change that business model. However, the funny thing is that was the business model we were using when New Frontier got interested in us. They looked at us, and said, 'Wow, these guys are making a lot of money.' But being the cowboys that we were, we just dealt with the changes. So when we had to take down the five days free model, we looked around and said, 'Okay, what's next?'"

Domain Names as Strategic Geography

Have you ever thought about the money represented by domain names directly associated with the adult entertainment industry? Ever considered how owning a keyword-focused Internet addresses could affect your bank account?   Adult entertainment Internet moguls have. Just as 900 numbers like 1-900-HOT-SEXX had the ability to rake in the dough during the height of the phone-sex era, virtual real estate on the Internet can fatten the owners bank account…but not without a price.

Early adult entertainment Internet entrepreneurs considered domain names the same way they would any other piece of property. They could build something at the address, hoping the result eventually would be worth much more than the investment. They could rent the vacant property to someone else who wanted to plant a business on it, or they could allow the land to lie fallow, as devoid of life as a weed-infested parking lot, until the neighborhood developed around it. Greg Dumas was an early investor in all three types of adult domain names.

"One of the things I learned days from the phone sex guys back in the Hustler was the value of vanity phone numbers—typing in 1-900-WET-BUSH, etc.," he said. "When we started iGallery in 1996, there was the need to register, or even buy [from someone else], domain names just like they did in the phone sex business. One popular domain name we registered for $35 back in 1996. In 1998, we were able to buy another direct hit dotcom for $1.2 million. People thought we were crazy. I even had to try to sell [the $1.2 million buy] internally, to justify it. But we were making money, and we were able to make our money back on that domain name in fifteen months."

Dumas said many domain-name deals were negotiated entirely over AOL Instant Messenger. He didn't balk at dealing with people he'd never met; he simply wanted to get the deal done by any means, and as quickly as possible.

iGallery's portfolio of domain names became so valuable that when New Frontier Media bought the company, part of the settlement included conveying ownership of certain domains to iGallery's founders. In other cases, the founders are contractually able to regain ownership in the future.

"I am very knowledgeable about the domain world, and the problem with the adult business is that very few large companies are domain owners," Dumas revealed. "They might own CindysWetCrotch.com, but they won't own Crotch.com. Some of the most valuable adult domain names are owned by non-adult companies. For instance, Sex.com has never been owned by an adult company. Porn.com was not purchased by an adult company until 2007 or so. Porno.com is owned by a big domainer, or rather an online speculator who engages in the practice of identifying, registering and acquiring Internet domain names with the intent of selling them later. Domainers who work in this practice are regularly called "cybersquatters."

"The point is, the adult business is good at being renters, not owners," he continued. "They want traffic, but they didn't see things the way the phone-sex guys did as to owning the traffic. Back in the iGallery days, we wanted to own our traffic; that was our point in wanting ownership over the domains. We never wanted to be held hostage by some affiliate coming to us and telling us their terms."

Pink Visual's Allison Vivas agrees traffic is a big thing, especially to an Internet-based company, but she also sees thorns among the roses. The domain game has changed the business environment, making it easy for someone with a little money to buy a series of domain names, post content that may be stolen, and create a revenue stream. A significant black market for domain names exists in the adult entertainment industry, so domain owners like Pink Visual must be ever-vigilant to protect their intellectual property.

"The online world provided a level of anonymity that in the early days Larry Flynt and Steve Hirsch [of Vivid] didn't have," Vivas said. "And now there are these online companies for which no one knows the ownership. You can look up the ownership of the domain and find fake names or corporations. When it's a matter of copyright infringement, it's a challenge to enter into litigation."

Ownership of domains and their collateral is on the minds of many in the adult sphere—so much so that Dumas and others have staked out new territory as part of the now-infamous adult-content-specific .xxx.

.xxx: Revenue Regeneration or an Attempt to Put Porn in the Corner?

Does the emergence of the .xxx extension signal the development of a virtual red light district? Is it a springboard for potential online censorship?   Could it promote better parental controls and online responsibility? Or is it a monumental cash grab perpetrated by ICM Registry? The company stands to make an estimated $200 million per year from the domain registry contract from the Internet Corporation for Assigned Names and Numbers.

The idea of .xxx was proposed to ICANN by ICM Registry in 2000. ICANN initially rejected the application because the group's board of directors believed the sTLD was not sufficiently backed by the adult entertainment community. ICM resubmitted its application in 2003 and in 2005 preliminary approval was granted after several rounds of public input, the preliminary approval was revoked in 2006.   Several years, a complete change in ICANN's board of directors, and an arbitration panel's ruling in ICM Registry's favor later, .xxx received approval. ICM Registry launched the domain space in mid-2011.

The very notion of an X-rated sTLD caused all hell to break loose from the start.   The Free Speech Coalition, representing the adult entertainment industry, blatantly expressed blatant outrage, stating the development would place undue cost and an extra level of bureaucracy on top of an industry already facing challenges.   The trade association also expressed the fear that a .xxx extension could "wall off" adult entertainment from the rest of the Web. The FSC went so far as to compare the potential landscape to a ghetto.[29]

"My fear with .xxx is that it is going to label [adult websites] as being different; put them outside of the mainstream," observed attorney Lou Sirkin. "And just like with the strip clubs, there will be this new level of zoning regulations on the Internet, so people know right away that they are different and they are dirty and they are regulated. The same thing that happened with the rating system for movies will be what happens here. If you can't get rated, then you have no outlet for your product."

The Free Speech Coalition offered a litany of complaints. Not only would the .xxx extension force websites designed for adults into "the corner," per se, but the domain space also would force increased overhead on adult website operators: Based on the complexity and extent of existing website networks, registering .xxx websites to correspond with all the sites they already owned in other spaces could cost some individuals and companies tens of thousands, if not hundreds of thousands, of dollars per year. Potential legal battles over cybersquatting loomed huge.[30]

Today the FSC is headed by Executive Director Diane Duke, who has been none too shy about her thoughts on .xxx, ICM Registry, and the the International Foundation for Online Responsibility (IFFOR), a non-profit regulatory body established by ICM to monitor .xxx sites. In early 2011, Duke and the FSC organized a boycott of the extension.

"We are concerned on an advocacy level that it will be much easier to censor adult content—not just on a government level, but with many anti-industry organizations who would use [.xxx] as a tool of harassment," Duke said. "And from the business perspective, the cost associated with .xxx, during a time when the industry is hurting, is prohibitive to the business itself. It inhibits any type of growth."

Even more than the potential for censorship, the cost factor—a minimum of $99 per domain per year at retail—enrages a significant segment of the adult entertainment industry. From their perspective, ICM Registry is the contemporary epitome of a carpetbagger: An outsider that bullied its way into a financially strapped area with the sole intention of enriching itself at the expense of people it considers beneath contempt. A large number of .xxx opponents resent feeling forced to purchase expensive .xxx domains they'll never use simply to protect their trademarks and service marks, or to ensure cybersquatters don't homestead .xxx domains similar to profitable existing properties in other spaces.

"I don't think that .xxx is going to do too much for the adult industry," Vivas said. "We [Pink Visual] are not planning on registering a .xxx domain. I feel that we get more out of .com, and there are plenty of .com names available. There is noise that [.xxx] is going to take down the industry and bring on all kinds of copyright-infringement issues, but we aren't the type of company to act like the sky is falling. We don't feel that it would be an intelligent move for someone to try to register PinkVisual.xxx, because since we do use the law and we do sue people and if someone [registers a name copyrighted by Pink Visual], they will definitely be sued."

Peter Acworth of Kink.com said .xxx has the ability to impede a business he and his team have been passionate about over many years.

"I have been against .xxx [from the beginning]," he said. "We have spent many years building up the Kink.com brand as well as various .com domains corresponding to our websites. The approval of .xxx means we now have to go out and buy the .xxx version of all our domains, plus all the misspellings, simply to protect our brands against those who buy domains purely to leech off existing brands. Generally speaking, we feel it is going to cost us money without providing any benefit."

"I don't think consumers are going to want to go to .xxx sites, and I don't think [.xxx] is ever going to be required [by the government]," Vivas said. "I'm not going to buy the .xxx for Pink Visual, so I don't have to agree to the terms and conditions [of IFFOR] and endorse .xxx. I'm not going to buy into [ICM's] money-making strategy—not right now. Maybe if they can deliver what they promise, then maybe I will change my mind. Right now they haven't proven that .xxx is any more valuable than a .com, and the onus is on them to do that."

Dumas agrees, to a point, about the relative value of .com. "Dot com's are still going to be valuable, the gold standard. That's not going to change and as a .com owner, I don't worry that this is going to replace my existing domains. But I do think that third-tier domains like .org, .biz, and .info could suffer."

Not every adult entrepreneur is anti-.xxx. Performer Sunny Leone, who owns several .com domains and runs her own websites, found .xxx "intriguing" enough to convince her to invest in .xxx domains related to her brand. Still, she admitted, she doesn't know what the future of .xxx might look like or how it will affect the industry.

"It will be really interesting to see what happens; whether they'll be able to get better rankings than what can be experienced in .com," she said. "Fortunately for me, I will own the .xxx as well as the .com.

"It's about money at this point," she added. "Obviously, if you own hundreds of domain names, it is going to cost you a little bit of money. But if you are a large company and you are making money, it's just another expense. Yes, it is a hassle, it is a pain in the ass, but the world is changing and you have to deal with it. You can't fight it. It's not like you can stop [.xxx] from happening."

The jury remains out on .xxx, but attorney Lou Sirkin doesn't expect that to last.

"If this takes off, [ICM Registry] is going to become their own censorship board," he said. "Where does it stop? We already know censorship of any kind is lie cancer. If [ICM Registry] starts to censor, there is going to be someone else who doesn't like something, and it just spreads. Once you allow it, there is no way to stop it."

The Problem with Pirates

People get bored easily. They also like free stuff. If they didn't, piracy probably wouldn't be an issue within the adult entertainment industry.

By the time the adult industry became a major target for content thieves, the music industry already had been through the ringer and come out the other side—battered, but not broken. Napster and its clones, a primary focus of the music industry's ire, had been brought to heel. At that time video piracy was in its infancy, but in no time at all, video pirates proved to be a much tougher foe.

During the music industry's battle with Napster, *et al*, about five big companies dominated the commercial music scene. By comparison, the adult industry is composed of thousands of content producers of all sizes, from one-person operations to multinational corporations.   The music producers banded together to fight a handful of foes. Not only did the adult industry have more foes to fight, thanks to the rapid evolution of sharing technologies and so-called tube sites, but asking a group of rebels to band together to do anything is like trying to herd cats.

That the adult industry has always been at the forefront of emerging technology has worked against the business as often as for it since the advent of the Internet Age. Rapid deployment of new technologies in the service of widespread distribution increased demand for a product that no longer hid in the shadows. Even worse, adult producers were slow to adopt technologies like watermarking, digital rights management, and digital fingerprinting, because they wanted their material to be as easy to consume as possible. The industry's greatest strengths became its greatest weaknesses as pirates turned digital tools on their creators.

According to Paul Fishbein, founder and former publisher of adult industry trade magazine *AVN*, "The very technology that helped bring the [adult] business into the 21st Century is also killing it. It's hard to sell what consumers can get for free."[31]

Although his company's streaming video model safeguards the vast majority of the content AEBN distributes, founder Scott Coffman has seen the effect of digital piracy on other companies' revenues. The piracy problem is epidemic, he said, and for the time being, it appears to be unstoppable. "Anybody down in a basement somewhere can buy ten DVDs, rip them, create a website and upload the content, and then find someone to buy advertising [on the site], and it's done," he explained.

At the heart of the problem is a change in consumer mindset: As a matter of principle, some consumers refuse to pay for anything online, while others delight in out-cowboying the cowboys. As a result, the cowboys have been left reeling.

"There used to be value associated with online porn," Pink Visual's Allison Vivas said. "For forty dollars a month, people thought a [porn site] subscription was worth something. Now, that value to many is zero. If you were to post something online about the cost of porn, you would have a hundred responses that say, 'Who buys porn anymore? I get my porn for free from these ten websites.' That is what has been the hardest, most disappointing thing. Few industries have ever had to go through this, where their product went from being highly valued to free, and having to get back to the point where people think the product is worth something. I don't know if the adult industry can do that."

Needless to say, anger and frustration abound.

"Like everyone else, [Kink.com] has been affected deeply by piracy," said founder Peter Acworth. "There used to be at time when the sky was the limit [for revenues]. We would just continue to add websites and generate more revenue, and there didn't seem to be any end to it. But we aren't doing any new sites right now. We're just trying to maintain the pay sites we have."

There's also a certain amount of hopelessness.

"I was lucky to enter [the adult entertainment industry] when I did," said performer and website owner Jessica Drake. "There was a very Old Hollywood feel about everything, and the glamour and excitement was there. Online piracy has really been a huge factor in sinking our ship. It spreads like wildfire."

But the industry has no time to wallow in its misery, Vivas said. Hers is one of the strongest voices urging the adult industry to work together. She believes that's the only way anyone will weather the piracy storm. "[Piracy] is beyond frustrating, but all of that anger makes us weak," she said. "We need to take ownership of the problem."

Over the past few years, several of the largest companies in the industry have done exactly that. Every one of them now believes there is strength in cooperating with their peers.

"Piracy has been a huge, huge problem for the [adult] industry, just like it was for the music industry," said Wicked's Joy King. "But the industry has come together to determine a strategy for combating this, and companies have brought lawsuits jointly in order to fight the problem. Although every company has to look out for itself, I do believe there is a lot of value in working together."

Adult performer Barrett Blade agrees, "People say to me, 'You pick music and porn, the two industries that have the most problems with giving away free stuff.' There needs to be laws mandated on the Internet and, of course, that is going to take a minute to happen."

He anticipates that through the creation of good product and if there is an industry-wide movement away from the production of low quality content, porn will see a renewal. On the flip side, many production companies have been cutting their budgets, tightening up. This process improvement and focus on lean principles has allowed many companies to "cut the fat" and get rid of overhead that doesn't contribute to profitability. Blade also believes that better technology will facilitate change within the adult entertainment community as this has always been an industry attribute that has allowed for profitability.

"People have to band together on this, across the entertainment community, porn or mainstream. Especially if we are going to get better."

Though she admits industry players cooperate much more frequently now than they did even five years ago, Vivas is convinced even more cohesive efforts are possible if industry insiders will let go of old prejudices. "Napster happened in 2001," she said. "There was piracy happening in adult in 2001, as well, but people didn't do anything about it for numerous reasons. For one, the money was still flowing. It wasn't until the money began slowing down that people started getting frustrated. And two, the adult entertainment industry is somewhat afraid of the law. They think it is somehow going to backfire. At Pink Visual, we disagree with that because we feel we are a responsible adult entertainment company, and because of that we can have the law on our side. Finally, there is the cost of the litigation. Some people have lost so much of their revenue that litigation is just not feasible; it's too [financially] risky."

Evil Angel's Christian Mann is inclined to agree, but he carries the argument even further. In Mann's mind, the adult entertainment industry is giving up too easily. After all, adult isn't the first industry to suffer a global setback due to forces that seem all but insurmountable. Someday, the survivors will look back on the period of rampant piracy and wonder how they could have thought the sky was falling.

"I like to use this analogy when discussing piracy: Pretend McDonald's decided to give away free hamburgers," he said. "Do you think a move like that would impact the restaurant industry? Absolutely it would. But eventually, people will go back to paying $20 for a steak, because they want the quality and the experience."

Porn 2.0: The Tube Sites

The adult entertainment industry only thought it had problems when pirates were scattered islands of irritation. The problems increased exponentially when the pirates organized. Enter the tube sites.

The tube site phenomenon saw its genesis with YouTube, a wildly popular website that allows end-users to upload their own videos that others can view for free. The concept caught on immediately, allowing anyone with a video camera to become an amateur filmmaker. Commercial entities even learned to embrace YouTube and its numerous clones as innovative marketing channels. By posting funny or otherwise engaging videos about their brands, they could reach an entirely new audience within a highly sought demographic: primarily young, tech-savvy folks with the disposable income to afford video-capable computer equipment and broadband Internet access.

Mainstream tube sites have had their share of trouble with pirated content showing up on their pages, but for the most part, Hollywood and Big Music have little to fear. The average consumer is not going to be satisfied with a few minutes culled from the latest Hollywood blockbuster, and music videos are promotional material to begin with.

The same is not true of porn video content. One of modern porn's primary roles is as masturbatory fodder—and a few minutes is all it takes. While some adult content fans have favorite performers and scenarios, there's an interchangeability factor in porn that makes one brief scene almost as good as another. Thus, when an army of adult tube sites arose, allowing anonymous end-users the unfettered ability to share not only their homemade porn but also their commercial adult movie collections, the adult entertainment industry couldn't help viewing the development as a financial sinkhole of enormous proportions.

"I think a lot of the boom in free-content sites came about because [consumers] were getting burned out on the billing games that were being played by a lot of adult sites," said Greg Dumas. "People were going crazy on the billing side of the business." Tube sites offered not only a free alternative, but also a way for consumers to get back at adult companies they felt had abused their trust.

It is this threat which most concerns traditional adult studios. According to an article published by *Forbes* in 2009, Steve Hirsch, co-chairman and president of Vivid, revealed that while one in 200-400 individuals who search for Vivid videos using search engines is willing to pay for what they find, only one in 8,000 to 10,000 people who search for Vivid content on tube sites is willing to pay. Combine that with an assertion from Digital Playground founder Ali Joone that as much as 99 percent of the material found on the tube sites is pirated—and usually uploaded by the sites' owners, not end-users—and the enormity of the problem becomes inescapable.[32]

And it's not just the loss of revenue from the content that plagues studios and other producers. While the Digital Millennium Copyright Act (DMCA) provides some recourse for victims of content theft, it puts the entire onus for enforcement on the content owner. Hirsch told *USA Today* that "Vivid fires off more than several hundred takedown notices a month to sites that illegally show its content."[33] The company employs monitors that constantly troll the Internet looking for pirated material. When a cease-and-desist letter is issued, the offending site has 72 hours to take the material down, so the monitors must visit the site again to ensure the target complied. All of that manpower, time, effort, and legal consultation adds to a producer's overhead.

And that's only the tip of the proverbial iceberg. Much like the mythical 12-headed Hydra grew a new head when one was cut off, tube sites and their users have an astonishing capacity to regenerate. As soon as stolen content is taken down from one place, it emerges somewhere else.

Ironically, adult tube sites saw their genesis within the adult entertainment industry. Video-on-demand giant AEBN launched the first-ever adult tube as a means of generating traffic for AEBN's online pay-per-view network. Owner Scott Coffman looks back on the decision with more than a little chagrin.

"We were the first company to ever put a tube site out there, to cross over into the tube world," he said, adding the traffic generated by the product "wasn't great." These days, "we try to do deals with companies that are proactive about keeping their material off the tubes. If the companies aren't protecting their content, it's very hard for us to do anything with their movies because it is out there for free somewhere else."

Having seen the tube-site issue from both sides, Coffman understands better than most how difficult it is to fight a fair battle with someone whose business model isn't fair to begin with. "Pick whatever product you are selling and if there is someone else out there who has no cost and is just going to give it away, there's no way you can win; there's no way you can compete," he said. "If you have to pick one thing that has killed the adult industry, it's the tube sites. You can blame it on the economy, but really, that is cyclical. An industry will always have the ability to come out of a natural downturn, but there's no way to combat free content."

Steve Hirsch can attest to that. In 2009, Vivid experienced a 20-percent decrease in DVD sales, the worst drop Hirsch has seen "in 25 years."[34] Hirsch says, "I try not to think about the failures. You can't be around for 28 years without having some hard times here and there. At this point I feel that we have the tube site issue under control. What I worry about most is the underground network of people who can't be controlled; you can put your arms around that side of things whether they are going after content that is adult or mainstream. As far as the Manwin guys who own the majority of tube sites, they will take your stuff down if you ask them. They don't want to put your stuff up there if you don't want them to."

"When the tube sites first came on board, adult businesses online were still making money," Greg Dumas said. "Looking at my business from 2007 to [2011], revenue is probably down 75 percent. It wasn't just free content that changed the business. Google changed, there was a thing called 'domain parking.' With all of these other factors combined, that's when people started saying, 'Okay, these [tube sites] are evil.'"

As with anything else, there are some within the adult community who believe the worry over tube sites is nothing more than scapegoating. Stephen Yagielowicz, managing editor at trade magazine *XBiz*, believes people who frequent porn tube sites are the type who isn't willing to pay for porn under any circumstances. Yagielowicz said tube sites are not sustainable entities. The bandwidth alone for a single tube site can cost hundreds of thousands of dollars monthly. That kind of overhead is difficult to recoup via click-through ads and affiliate marketing.

Dumas isn't so sure that perspective is valid.

Tube sites "make huge sums of money, because they have traffic [they can sell]," he said. "They make money from advertising. If you go to a tube site and you want to watch a video, they will direct you to a different site so you can watch, and they are making money off that click-through. The moral of the story is it doesn't matter what your billing model is; it doesn't matter what your site looks like. If you don't have traffic, you don't have shit."

Performer and web entrepreneur Sunny Leone has yet another perspective. She doesn't like the effect the tube sites have had on some companies, but she's found a way to use them to her advantage.

"They have traffic," she said. "You have to work with them to get that traffic. You can be partners. We give them updated clips, and they send traffic back to my site. Now they are making money instead of just pirating content. They direct someone to my site who signs up, the tube site makes money, and I make money."

Leone's partnerships didn't happen overnight, and the road to profitability wasn't always smooth. She employed a team of web professionals to look for pirated content. When they found it, they presented the tube site owner with a choice: either send traffic back to the copyrighted material's original location, or take the content down and possibly face legal action in the process. The choice, for the majority, was easy.

"The only people we couldn't trust are those weird people who live in another country in a basement and are crazy hackers," Leone observed. "You can't find them. Most people, you can tell them what to do—you just have to present it attractively. Yes, it's hard, it's difficult, but when you own an adult company, these things happen. You just have to put the right people in place who can think creatively to make it not happen. When we approach someone who is running a tube we say, 'Look, you have all this traffic. If you send it back to me, you could be making three, four, five thousand a month.' And that's more money than they are making at their regular job, because they are doing this hacking business at night."

Coffman believes it is almost necessary to subscribe to Pink Visual's concept of litigation first, friends later in order to deal with the Tube sites successfully. While it is one thing to partner to benefit from the traffic, Coffman said tube-site owners need to be dealt with using a heavy hand. He lays a lot of the blame for that on the DMCA.

"The DMCA is the worst law ever put in place," he said. "I can contact a tube site and tell them to take my content down, and it's their responsibility to do so. But, if someone in the next hour uploads [the same material] to the site, then I have to call again and have the same conversation. [The pirates] can have one person sitting there all day continually uploading content, and [the studios] are expected to police this activity. It would be more effective if the owner of the tube site was responsible for policing it. In pawn stores, for example, there is a responsibility not to resell stolen products. If the DMCA worked the same way, it would be a different story for the industry."

The Free Speech Coalition's Anti-Piracy Action Program is trying to make a dent in the problem.   According to Executive Director Diane Duke, among the program's main goals are to educate the adult industry and to act against the tube sites and individual pirates.

"[FSC] put together a seminar during which people from mainstream Hollywood spoke about the efforts taken on that side of the industry to protect their material," Duke revealed. "Universal and MGM came, and we spoke about how to pursue copyright litigation and digital fingerprinting. We found that there needed to be better organization regarding the technology in order to be effective, as it is really cost-prohibitive to the individual distributor or manufacturer. However, as a trade association, we were able to work some deals that might be able to help the industry band together better to fight this major issue. Ultimately, we will fight tube technology with better technology."

As usual, Pink Visual was among the first to prove the fingerprinting technology can be an effective deterrent.

"Like most of the industry, [Pink Visual] complained about piracy for years and years, blaming piracy for everything," said Allison Vivas. "Then we decided to some stop complaining and do something about it. We hired an in-house attorney. She showed us how copyright law works; that it is very strict about infringement. So we decided to take on one of the tube sites, and we came up with a solution that would help us prevent copyright infringement in the future.

"We now employ digital fingerprint technology," she continued. "When a user goes to upload content, this technology works to match the 'fingerprint' of the uploaded content to the 'fingerprint' that is in the database. If the fingerprints don't match, the material can't be uploaded. We have had success with this, and now our content can't be found in places where it shouldn't be."

208 *The Unexpected Story*

The Evolution of Video-On-Demand
in the Deep South

Calling North Carolina a mecca for the adult entertainment industry probably would cause most people to do a double-take. But, it's a fact. The Southern state, smack in the middle of the Bible Belt, is home not only to Adam & Eve, one of the world's largest adult products retailers, but also to the leader in online video-on-demand programming, Adult Entertainment Broadcast Network (AEBN).

Founded by Scott Coffman in 1999, AEBN set up shop in Charlotte, North Carolina, as an offshoot of Coffman's now-defunct magazine called *Vivid*. Initially, the operation was the epitome of stereotypical geek culture: It was headquartered in Coffman's garage. All of the company's assets are online: a network of websites comprising an extensive distribution platform that showcases the work of adult producers including Vivid, Wicked, Evil Angel, Jules Jordan Productions, and a host of others.

"In the beginning, I didn't know anything about adult," Coffman said. "[The magazine *Vivid*] actually outlined where all the strip clubs and adult video stores in North and South Carolina were located. Before that, I had never worked in anything related to adult."

Coffman had tried his hand as an entrepreneur in several different industries prior to launching AEBN; he ran a restaurant, a bar, and a video store. He came upon the idea of launching an adult business when he realized the local entertainment paper, *Creative Loafing*, would not run ads from adult businesses. After Coffman's magazine got off to a promising start, a business associate approached him with an idea about how the newfangled thing called "the Internet" was loaded with potential for marketing adult entertainment.

"I looked into the Internet in early 1998," Coffman recalled. "There weren't a lot of people making money on the Internet in the adult category, unless they had a lot of money to invest right off the bat. So I looked at the concept of selling videos online. I was already in Charlotte, so I set up shop here. I was really isolated from the rest of the industry."

With inventory stored in his garage, it didn't take long for the local press to sniff out a story—one that was sure to anger local conservatives angry: A pornographer living among the God-fearing Christians of the Carolinas.

Okay, maybe not a pornographer, but Coffman was selling sex.

"One day I noticed a van sitting across the street from my house," Coffman said. "I didn't think much of it until a guy got out and came across the street to knock on my door. When I answered, he said he was referred by one of my friends and he wanted to buy a couple of videos because he didn't have an Internet connection and was embarrassed to go to an adult bookstore. So I told him no problem and invited him in.

"It turned out he was a reporter for the local news channel, and later that night they did a big exposé about how this person in a neighborhood in [Charlotte suburb] Matthews was selling porn," Coffman continued. "They had me on TV, and suddenly none of my neighbors would talk to me and they wouldn't allow their kids to trick or treat at my house anymore. For a while, it was bad. Investigators were sent to my house; the police would come and sniff around to see if I was doing anything wrong, neighbors would complain about everything I did. So I decided I needed to move, get out of Matthews."

Charlotte wasn't Coffman's first choice as a location for what would become the AEBN Empire. However, in the years since, the company has grown to more than 250 employees, several attracted from Fortune 500 companies like Bank of America and Wachovia (now Wells Fargo). Coffman believes the benefit and pay structure AEBN offers are among reasons the once-ostracized adult company has taken firm root in Charlotte, especially as mounting criticism and deep layoffs have gutted the titans of finance in Charlotte.

"I was one of Scott [Coffman's] very first vendors at Video Team," Christian Mann recalled. "That country bumpkin is a visionary with AEBN. What he provides, that kind of third-party aggregate—and his model where you can pay for [porn] by the minute, by the scene, by the movie, whether you want to download it or watch it streaming—what he provides is just going to grow as [digital device] convergence becomes common in all households."

Coffman remains humble, saying he understands the local community's initial reluctance to embrace his business. But like a good Christian, he turned the other cheek to criticism.

"It took a bit of time to get to where we are today," he said. "When we were first looking for office space, most places wouldn't even rent to me. We were working to grow, but running into issues just getting office space."

He admits he could have relocated AEBN to a more adult-friendly place like California's San Fernando Valley, but he didn't want to move away from his roots—even if staying close to home meant learning the adult business long-distance.

"The thing about Charlotte was the amount of people that were available to hire," Coffman said. "I've been out to L.A., and in [Charlotte] you have a benefit because of the cost of living, the pool you can hire from, even though 90 out of 100 would never come to work for me. It was hard, at first, because they would come in and say, 'Yeah, it's Charlotte, it's adult, I can't put this on my resume, I can't tell my wife where I work,' so it was a pure numbers game in the early days. I need quality employees just like any other business. So I have to be more aggressive than other companies. At the same time, we were very isolated, very far away from the heart of the industry."

As the business grew and the quality of technology the company dealt with improved, it became easier for AEBN to attract the kind of employees Coffman sought. Bible Belt residents with preconceived notions about what an adult entertainment company's office might resemble were pleasantly surprised to discover AEBN's digs are as nondescript as any other corporation in America. There are no pictures of naked women in provocative poses on the walls, and Coffman said anyone who walks in would never know the company deals in adult content. All explicit material is kept in the basement of the facility, where it is encoded for use online.

Coffman admits he still has a hurdle to surmount when it comes to gender balance in the workforce, however: approximately 80 percent of AEBN's employees are male.

Working for AEBN is "an easy sell [for men]," Coffman said. "Consider the fact that in my coding department, the main job is simply to look at porn all day, every day. A guy will tell his friends he has the best job in the world. However, I do have more women in higher or more advanced positions. They serve as project managers, in sales, and finance."

The women who work for the company have "strong personalities," according to Coffman, who believes that is almost a requirement for working within the industry in any capacity.   He doesn't think a woman can be a shrinking violet and compete in what historically has been a male-centric business.

"You have to have a dominant personality, because they [women] are dealing with guys like us," he said.   "There is already the idea that you are [not offended by] the material if you are working in this world. There is also an implicit level of understanding: a woman knows what she is doing if she is already operating in this space."

At the time of AEBN's inception, the concept of Internet-based video-on-demand was slow to catch on, as people were just starting to grasp the concept of actually buying a video or DVD online instead of having to go venture into a brick-and-mortar store.   Plus, while the VOD option was present, the support technology, specifically Internet connectivity, did not provide the best experience when watching adult content online.   Remember this was the day of dial-up and 56K modems. The company experienced a decrease in profit right off the bat, which is to be expected until consumers have the ability to catch up with technology or understand the options that are available to them.

"We saw gradual growth, but it wasn't huge to begin with. Yes, we would grow 100 percent each month, but it would be 100 percent growth on five grand or ten grand in business. I could have retained the other side of the business with the videos, but I shut that down completely, I would have remained profitable there, but it was too much overhead to deal with," stated Coffman.

During the first seven months of operating the Video-on-Demand platform, AEBN through the direction of Coffman ended up going through all of the money that had been provided through investors. They had to go back to basics and reexamine the business model, ultimately deciding if they were going to put more money into the platform, or simply close up shop with the idea that "this didn't make it."

Coffman believes that there is little choice in the fact that companies who work in streaming video or any type of dominant and ever changing technology must remain fluid in their ability to morph and modify their business plan and their mode of operations. In fact, if you don't Coffman states that you will be pushed out of the space, and quickly.

"When we first started, we worked in Windows Real Player, that's how early on this was. That was more prevalent that Windows

Media at the time. Well you can see what happened there. So you not only have to evaluate your business at all times on what your customer wants or the buying decisions they make, but also how you are going to deliver that product to the end user," commented Coffman.

At the same time, Coffman has been tasked with establishing himself in the adult entertainment industry. As well as educating industry mavens on the benefits of streaming video. He is quick to recall that when he went to some of his first manufacturer events and trade shows, he would walk up to established companies in the adult space, hold out his hand and say, "I want to stream your movies." They would first look at him and say, "Well what is streaming and who are you?"

When Coffman first began the business, he was heavily focused on understanding the algorithms that online search engines operated by. He was intent on learning how a search engine pulled information and how he could ensure that the AEBN site would be at the top of search returns. He realized then that instead of starting from scratch, it might make more sense to go to the places that already had traffic, such as Caris and First Movers, and ask them to show or advertise his site on theirs. This was indeed where the money was at and this is one of the reasons that the business struggled during the first seven months of operations. Coffman had not realized that there was an entire industry out there that he could either build upon or partner with, and this turned out to be a viable alternative as opposed to starting from scratch and recreating the wheel. Industry veterans bought into his model, becoming affiliates of the company and directing business his way.

"AEBN is one of the biggest VOD companies out there, and it's cheaper to send traffic their way and get paid on it, over doing it yourself. It's really a time consuming business and very costly," stated Kevin Beechum.

"When I realized that we could do business with all of [the existing industry], that is when the business really took off, because we were doing something that no one else was doing," Coffman said. "It was a natural fit for [other companies] to send traffic to AEBN and let their users watch the movies that were featured on our site."

Once the company was able to wrangle the traffic it needed to be profitable, the goal became devising a delivery method that was flexible for the end user. AEBN currently allows users to access streaming video for certain amounts of time or forever, or a purchaser can also download movies to own permanently. Coffman said the streaming method is the most popular, because not only can a streaming movie be accessed from anywhere, but also because streaming leaves behind no evidence…meaning nothing for a wife or partner to find.

"Our vision is no different from the music industry's," he said. "We see everything cloud-based. There doesn't need to be tons of storage on someone's computer or iPad these days. Everything should be on a cloud so you can access it from anywhere.

"When material is cloud based, you can access it on whatever device you are using and from any location," he continued. "It's much easier to create brand loyalty when you have this setup, because it provides for ease of use."

Coffman believes everybody benefits from cloud-based material, as opposed to increasing the storage size available on computers or trying to keep downloadable formats relevant. He thinks the majority of industries that produce electronic content will migrate to cloud storage and delivery. As bandwidth and Internet connectively continue to evolve and improve, cloud-based computing will allow for a significant reduction in buffering (the time it takes for material to load on the consumer's end).

Of course, cloud computing puts the entire storage onus on the delivery company's network, and in AEBN's case, that's an enormous burden. The company's servers house, on average, 125,000 available movies. The selection changes based on monthly, quarterly, and annual reports about which titles perform.

AEBN stays in constant contact with its clients, asking to be provided with the newest content as soon as it's ready for release. This allows the team to encode the material and get it online for purchase as quickly as possible. AEBN is willing work with any studio, even though some, like content-protective Digital Playground, decline the offer. Although some studio's prefer not to partner with his company, Coffman believes anyone in the adult business can benefit from a distribution agreement with his company, especially if they're willing to release new material online before, or at the same time as, the content debuts on DVD. The industry-wide decline in DVD sales has bolstered AEBN's value, Coffman said.

"Going forward in 2012, our business plan involves [the film] first being released on the web, only to go to DVD after its initial release," noted. "The web is where we get the numbers, so it's coming full circle that if you are a manufacturer and you are not playing in [the online] market, you are going to go out of business because the profitability is just no longer in mass DVD production."

He also said AEBN's and studios' statistics indicate releasing a film as streaming video before sending it to DVD results in greater profitability per title. Capturing video streams is difficult, which lowers the risk new material will be pirated before recouping at least part of the producer's investment.

As AEBN moves into the future, Coffman believes there is a chance for a certain level of revival to take place within the industry, at least for companies who refuse to get too comfortable with antiquated distribution methods.

"I am encouraged by the idea of the technology that is out there, the convergence of computers and TVs," he said. "When we get there, we'll expand our market further because we'll be back in the entertainment center of the home, and our sole focus won't be on computers."

Additionally, AEBN is working to cross over into the world of manufacturing. As he put the concept, it's one thing to distribute other company's films and quite another to own content that belongs specifically to AEBN. The company recently acquired two gay adult studios, Ranging Stallion and Falcon, which operate as a content-production division. Coffman labeled the move the "HBO principle," after the mainstream cable giant revolutionized its own business model by starting a production company. Both HBO and AEBN now can dictate how original product is is used.

"I have come to the belief that you have to own some type [of content], otherwise it's easy to get lost in what you are doing," Coffman said, adding that companies tend to fail when they decline to diversity. "I am looking forward to moving towards more of an HBO-style operations policy that allows for marketing of original work. Ultimately, you have to think about adult movies the same way you think about mainstream movies: Any channel or company can show them. The stuff on Starz isn't that different from the movies on HBO. What makes HBO different is the fact that they show *Boardwalk Empire* or *Hung*, their original programming. That's why consumers opt for HBO over competitor channels."

AEBN is branching out in order to stay relevant and building upon past success.

"I am proud of AEBN's ability to be the first in pay-per-minute and VOD," Coffman said. "We did stuff first—five years before mainstream ever figured our policies out. "The whole business now is about working to stay ahead and figuring out new ways of delivering or creating.

"We watch trends, we watch studios and stars that are popular, and we analyze that," he added. "We want to give all people what they want, no matter the genre or niche."

Making Online Sex an
Interactive Experience

The live video-chat industry is a huge departure from traditional adult entertainment online, and one piece of the business that has changed the landscape of the Internet drastically since porn went digital. Greg Clayman, the president of Video Secrets, is a pioneer in this segment of the industry. He and his partner, Constantine "Chuck" Tsiamis, founded their brand when the idea of online video-chat was new.

Clayman and Tsiamis have known each other since the third grade, and their relationship progressed into the corporate world when both graduated from business school. While working at financial giant New York Life, Clayman started to brainstorm better ways for his clients to communicate with trusted advisors like their lawyers, accountants, insurance agents, and financial planners, especially when time is of the essence and face-to-face communication is desired. Clayman was convinced more business could get done faster and easier if all parties could meet in a virtual setting.

"I said, 'Wouldn't it be a great idea if we could create a business called the Cyber Advisors Network, where we can make sure we are able to have the lawyer on the screen, the client is present, the accountant is on the screen, and everyone can talk at once? And when an agreement is made, the contract is printed out and the deal is closed,'" Clayman recalled. "[Tsiamis] thought it was a good idea, and so we started talking to people who had technical expertise in that area."

But there were roadblocks. Every person to whom the pair talked said the endeavor would be expensive to develop. Even afterward, building a network of willing and open-minded participants would be no foregone conclusion. That's when Clayman and Tsiamis realized an industry usually eager to jump on new technologies already existed—especially if the technologies meant attracting new customers. The adult entertainment industry seemed a custom-made proving ground for the idea.

"One night we were on the Internet—this was probably 1995—
and we were watching live adult video conferencing," Clayman
recalled. "We watched the show for about ten minutes and we were
pretty impressed. But then we looked at each other and said, 'We can
do this better.' We both wound down our financial careers and
gathered all the resources needed to start the company, and in 1996
the company was founded in Stoughton, Massachusetts."

Although the pair thought the medium and the model were
fantastic, they found the overall the experience mediocre, at best.
The good news was, with the right adjustments, the platform would
be able to duplicate an experience second only to meeting someone
in person. Clayman and Tsiamis set a goal: to create the best
platform for live adult entertainment video conferencing in the
world.

Now in its sixteenth year in business, Video Secrets has never
sidetracked from the original mission. Unlike competitors, Video
Secrets has succeeded because Clayman and Tsiamis decline to chase
whatever is hot instead of following their core business model.

"Instead of staying true to the business model that mainstream
businesses follow, living by their mission statement—which I
understand has to remain flexible and fluid depending on what is
happening in the marketplace—other companies veer off," Clayman
said. "[Video Secrets] has always stayed true to our corporate
business model."

Clayman attributes much of his company's success to his and
Tsiamis' corporate business background. The rest comes from their
status as relative outsiders to the industry, at least in the beginning.
Because they were not immersed in a traditional adult industry
mindset, they didn't possess many of the Internet-related fears that
plagued the industry.

"In this business, I believe there are two kinds of people,"
Clayman said. "There are people who live adult entertainment and try
to make a living, and then there are people who work to provide a
good product, and who think of it like a business. The latter are the
ones who succeed."

That's not to say Video Secrets keeps the industry at arm's
length. Clayman readily admits the company's success has been based
on learning from mistakes while also partnering with knowledgeable
adult entertainment entrepreneurs. Instead of trying to do everything
themselves, Clayman and Tsiamis incorporated their Fortune 500

background into the day-to-day operation of the company and left marketing to affiliates.

"Before we even got off the ground, we went to a show called NetProfits that took place in Vegas right around the same time as another major show, Adult Interactive 2000," Clayman said. "We went to both shows, and we found something very special. It was the *Audio Text Affiliate Handbook*, which was a book of all the names and addresses of everyone in the audio text industry. We said 'the natural next step here is video text. Why don't we call everyone in this book and get them to make the jump?' So we split the book down the middle and started calling."

Initially, Video Secrets managed all aspects of broadcasting in-house, maintaining studios at corporate headquarters and treating the on-camera models, or "broadcasters," as employees. As the company grew, though, that method of operating became unwieldy. In addition, consumer demand for interaction with the women and men on-screen eventually outpaced the supply of local talent.

"In 1998 we hit a critical point in the company where we were doing pretty well, and we made a decision that in order to thrive we needed to be somewhere between Silicon Valley and Silicone Valley," Clayman said, chuckling. "When we moved to Southern California, we began to outsource [the role of the broadcasters] so we could focus on our core competencies, and that turned out to be the best thing that we ever did."

Outsourcing to independent contractors allowed Clayman and Tsiamis to focus on the technology behind video conferencing. At the time, the majority of adult video conferencing companies used a system called "point-to-point." The technology required consumers to download and install an application that facilitated online chatting. People didn't mind, because viruses and other issues were not yet a perceived threat; as long as there was a perceived value to the download, most users were amenable. Even though Video Secrets started out with a client download product and gained momentum on the platform, Clayman believed unveiling a video streaming product that allowed the user to view a live feed directly through the web browser would increase the company's cachet. He was right.

"We had thousands of competitors who had thousands of clients who were using a download product that charged $6 a minute," he said. "At the time we started, because of the learning curve we had to go through, we weren't so invested in this older way of doing things. Video streaming allowed many people to see one model at the same time. We saw this as a gigantic opportunity. This was our window to really make a push to lead the video streaming side of the industry, where others were more hesitant to move in this direction because they already had all of these clients who had the downloadable software and were using it. They were afraid to move into streaming because they were afraid they were going to lose customers, even though the software we were using was less expensive.

"We almost immediately changed everything to streaming and got our major push there," Clayman continued. "Then, when our competitors finally switched over, it was almost too late for them; they couldn't catch up. iGallery and Babenet, who had downloadable products, had this mindset that 'if it's not broke, don't fix it,' but we wanted to be the best. Even though we had to take a pay cut in doing it, we knew this was the future."

Video Secrets changed its technology very quickly, so by the time viruses and other computer issues became a big issue, customers already were using the new technology. Because of the technology's immunity to an emerging threat, the company converted competitors' customers and generated its own new business. Unlike competitors, Video Secrets never gave consumers an option to choose between downloadable software and video streaming, so once the company made the changeover to the new product, it had to support only one product...thereby reducing another cost.

Clayman compares the adult entertainment industry's take on converting from a downloadable product to video streaming to what AOL went through when making the transition from dial-up to broadband: Both entities scoffed the new technology, calling it unnecessary and destined for failure due to lack of interest. Both entities turned out to be wrong.

Today, Video Secrets operates a host of websites devoted to a variety of niches. A consumer is able to go on a site like Flirt4Free.com, for instance, buy credits that never expire, and browse a gallery of broadcasters who are online at that moment. Consumers interact with broadcasters through a chat room interface before deciding whether they want to pay for a private. Once in private mode, the user is able to direct the broadcaster's action. Interactions can be unidirectional or bidirectional, depending upon whether the consumer wants to be seen, as well. Broadcasters may record their private sessions with customers for later access. Anytime a private session is accessed, either live or recorded, the broadcaster and Video Secrets make money.

"What's even better is that after you are done watching the show you just directed, you will get an email link to the show so you can watch it [again] whenever you want," Clayman said. "You can create a library, virtually, of shows you have watched in the past."

Most of the broadcasters on the sites are amateurs, not professional performers. Occasionally an established name like Tera Patrick appears on the site, but Clayman said a poll of Video Secrets customers revealed people are less interested in seeing known adult entertainers than they are in interacting with women who could live right down the street.

"The mentality of consumers is 'the [porn star] is great, but we prefer the girl next door broadcaster because she is attainable,'" Clayman revealed. "We don't use the feature girls as much as we used to; instead, we have drilled down into the broadcasters we have by niche, so a customer can see what squirters are currently online, which big-boob girls are online, which couples, etc."

Video Secrets remains upbeat about the state of the adult entertainment industry, mostly because their service offers an ever-growing revenue opportunity to the broadcasters and affiliate marketers. Clayman believes his company is a great spot, considering these days everyone believes they have what it takes to be a porn star.

He's also excited about what developments in mainstream technology mean for his business, especially the convergence of video, television, and the Internet.

"When you can watch a video on your TV in your bedroom, living room, or hotel room, or when you are able to direct your own film and upload it to your TV, that's when our business will change," Clayman said. "Some may say the adult industry is no longer innovating, but I think we are just getting started. The level of innovation doesn't stop. We are in a perfect position for the next phase."

PART EIGHT

The Mainstreaming of the Industry

There is something mildly reassuring about the idea that pornography is no longer a taboo subject. While adult material may not be mainstream in all circles, it certainly is part of pop culture, and that designation normalizes the industry. In large part, the mainstreaming of porn is a testament to the dedication and openness of the people who work in front of and behind the cameras. No longer do they evade the public spotlight or avoid talking about what they do for a living. They no longer feel that approach is necessary. Adult entertainment has been humanized. It's not just about the sex.

A former researcher on the Human Genome Project. A Rutgers graduate with a degree in English Literature. A classically trained musician with a focus on the oboe. A humanitarian adventurer who lectures on safe sex. A passionate lawyer dedicated to the protection of free speech and human dignity. This is not the sort of group most people envision when the term "adult entertainment" comes up, is it? But these are the people who make up the industry. Adult entertainment professionals are not pariahs who exist on the fringes of society. Instead, they are focused, determined and avid professionals, each fantastic in their field and dedicated to their craft.

If they ran a Fortune 500 company—and some of them could—no one would think twice about their qualifications.

Steve Hirsch, president of Vivid Entertainment, reflects on the first time the industry was highlighted in the mainstream press. "The first article that had ever been written on the business of the industry was after [Vivid] sent out a press kit, which had never been done before, and it was picked up by *The Economist*. The article wasn't some crazy story about some crazy girl, it was about the fact that suddenly, adult videos were being placed in mainstream stores and that the marketing surrounding the videos was the same type of strategy that Hollywood used," said Hirsch. "We wanted people to look at us as a movie studio, so we did things that had never been done before. We hired a mainstream New York publicist, which was another first, and we pursued advertising on billboards, mainstream magazines, music videos. Vivid was intent on becoming a household name."

Opinions are mixed about whether the mainstreaming of porn has been good or bad for the industry, and indeed, just as with anything else, the good comes with the bad. For instance, former performer Sasha Grey, who was able to break into the mainstream by way of a guest appearance on HBO's *Entourage* was lambasted for reading to elementary-age children in the L.A. public schools. She defended herself, saying she had been invited—and besides, the kids didn't know who she was. The L.A. public schools offered an apology to parents.

On the flip side of this sort of public outrage, it's important for me to help you, the reader, understand that porn has come a long way, and not just in terms of professional recognition or through desensitization in the public eye.

At the same time, an adult entertainment connection can help mainstream celebrities increase their visibility in the mainstream media and Hollywood. Leaked sex tapes are almost *de rigueur* (thank you, Paris Hilton), being caught with a porn star usually is more amusing than embarrassing (ahem, Charlie Sheen and Tiger Woods).

"I think the mainstreaming of the industry has helped because one, it brought more people, including women, into the industry, making them aware of what was out there," Scott Coffman of AEBN said. "And society has changed so much. Nothing is shocking anymore; it's a natural thing. People aren't shocked by porn stars, who are just as big of celebrities as many of the people you see in the tabloids. Look at [Kim] Kardashian! The only reason she's famous is because she made a sex tape."

Castle Megastores' Mark Franks concurred. "I think that there is something positive about the mainstreaming of the industry. If you go into some drugstore and buy a sexual enhancement item, it could lead a consumer to wondering what else is out there. This opens up the market even further to us. All of these businesses who used to look at us like we were scum have latched onto our business model. You see the trends hitting CVS and Target—they carry their own brand of lube. Look at Victoria's Secret. That store has never been sexier."

Teresa Flynt, however, worries about the trending of adult material at mainstream stores. "The Trojan [condoms] brand has introduced some adult toys such as finger vibrators which are sold at places like CVS, right next to the baby food and the tampons. If this type of drugstore market continues to grow, Hustler Hollywood can't compete with your local CVS. We are going to be edged out," stated Flynt.

Changes within the industry have been even more pervasive. In the old days, the entire industry was controlled by a small group of people. Those people made the money, and they also created the myth that clings to adult entertainment to this day. By operating behind closed doors, in the dark, they fed the public perception that pornography was seedy, something to be loathed and feared. In turn, that perception fed adult's coffers.

"The shadiness of the industry [before the Internet] was actually the driving force that made all of the money," Coffman said. "If you went and asked the original manufacturers if they could go back fifteen years before the advent of the Internet, all of them would say yes. Back then you had more control, and it was the Internet that changed everything and thrust the industry into the mainstream. Now anyone can see [our product], whereas before you had to go somewhere in order to buy it or see it. Even here at AEBN, while I have made a lot of money, I would still go back to the days when I just owned a few video stores. The technology has killed the industry, even though it has helped us, too."

Jessica Drake also believes the mainstreaming of the industry is a mixed blessing. In her view, as sex has become more normalized and accepted, the taboo that used to be associated with adult entertainment has disappeared.

"Sex in general has lost much of the taboo," she said. "Porn became a lot more accepted in the mainstream, and that was cool to a certain extent, but then it also started to hurt us."

Part of the problem, according to Drake, is that as the market has expanded via the Internet, so too has the ability of the average citizen to create his or her own porn. With little more than a camera-enabled smartphone and a willing partner, anyone can be an online porn producer.

"The mainstreaming of the industry is slightly ironic," said Kink.com's Peter Acworth. "We, as an industry, have seemed to succeeded in gaining acceptance because there is so much material out there, but that flood of material [on the Internet] is a result of anyone and everyone thinking they can do what pros do. There is a lot of truth to the idea that normalcy breeds complacency."

Drake argues that the mainstreaming of the industry has diluted the mystique that prevailed when she debuted in 1999. Business was better when there was more mystery associated with the product.

"I'm not talking about taboo that says 'this is really bad and shameful,'" she said. "I'm talking about the taboo that says 'this is really hush-hush and sexy and mysterious.' Porn is relatively less sexy when the people on camera live a couple blocks away from you. It was more desired when there was still a taboo surrounding it."

Coffman believes there is very little left that shocks consumers. He also thinks not much differentiates porn stars like Jessica Drake and Sunny Leone from their non-professional counterparts. Those counterparts can be anyone from a college student with a video camera at a frat party to the middle-aged MILF next door. In fact, Coffman has a favorite analogy: Porn stars are like tattoos. "It used to be that a girl with a tattoo was a rarity," he said. "Now if you meet a girl and she doesn't have a tattoo, you immediately think she's lived a sheltered life." Coffman also believes the only thing separating a porn star from any other woman is a pair of elevator pumps with clear acrylic heels. That is one fashion accessory associated with pornography that hasn't made it into the mainstream.

Evil Angel's Christian Mann offered another perspective. "I think the upside of media attention is greater acceptance of or tolerance for adult entertainment and adult content," he said. "It might not be your cup of tea. I might not like adult material, but I do like freedom. Everyone has the right not to look, or to look. The downside is that the media likes to create a story that is salacious and that gets attention and attracts viewers. When they start yelling about things like an AIDS epidemic in the adult entertainment industry, it's simply not true. They are creating headlines just to create headlines.

"Mainstream media feigns shock and awe at the adult industry even while they love to show it and comment on it over and over and over," he added. "I laugh at the irony, because I feel that mainstream markets, media, are just as much pornographers as we are. I just want to say, 'Hey guys, welcome to the gutter.'"

A gossip mogul and expert on the world of celebrity sex tapes, Kevin Blatt, compares the industry's modern problems to the uptick in obscenity prosecutions during the 1980s, as VHS tapes emerged and opened up the market.

"The mainstreaming of the industry is actually the reason behind its decline," Blatt said. "You had all of these people flaunting wealth, had magazines saying how much money the industry was making, everything was over-the-top, and inevitably, that's what brought the negative attention to it. This is where the prosecution of people like Max Hardcore and [John] Stagliano came from. This is why people were getting sued left and right. There is an old saying that goes, 'The only time a whale gets harpooned is when it comes up to spout,' and essentially the minute that we started spouting as an industry is the moment we got harpooned."

The situation is not all doom and gloom, though. Even though he was "harpooned" by the feds, Stagliano believes mainstreaming has been a positive thing, for the most part.

"It's a positive, natural development that each generation is more tolerant towards pornography," he said. "The young people today are so much different from the people in the '80s. Back then, we had to step outside of society and be outcasts. It took a lot of courage back then. That's not to say it doesn't take courage today, but there are fewer people today who will condemn you for what you do. Every year it seems to be getting better."

Steve Orenstein, who owns the company that made Jenna Jameson a larger-than-life celebrity, said he can't argue with mainstreaming, since Jameson's career had a positive impact on Wicked. "That was the goal, to mainstream our business, and it has led to comfort with people not only talking about the soft and pretty things we did, but also the hardcore stuff. That's progress."

Crossing into the Mainstream:
Can it be done?

An urban myth spouted in the halls of L.A. adult talent agencies hold that a new adult film inductee still has mainstream options in front of him or her even after appearing in porn. Considering how normal and accepted the majority of the industry has become—as evidenced by the success of performers like Jenna Jameson—it's easy to underestimate or completely overlook the consequences of an adult industry career. Stars do cross into mainstream roles, but more often they don't.

When Joy King reflects back on her time with Jameson, she remembers not only the success that came from building the Jenna Jameson brand, but also the hard work involved.

"It was a year of pounding the phones," King said. "This was way before email. It was pure persistence and probably being annoying until people finally said okay. I must have called and sent at least a dozen [press] packages to *The Howard Stern Show* before they finally called me. It was a constant effort, and it paid off."

Orenstein has similar memories. "We had Jenna autograph and send personalized pictures to each of the [*Howard Stern Show*] cast members so it made her appear to be a fan of the show," he said. "Then we sent some other beautiful pictures that had been taken for a toy line, along with a silly picture of her making a funny face with a dildo in between her boobs, and it worked. That's when they called us."

Jameson's appearance on *Stern* was the key to jumpstarting her career.

"What we did with Jenna was a big deal," Orenstein recalled. "We kept putting her out there in places where an adult performer had never been before. *Howard Stern* back then didn't have porn stars on every day—he had Hollywood people on. But Howard became enamored with Jenna, and that's when everything started happening."

More recently, Sasha Grey has shown crossover potential after landing a role as herself on the HBO series *Entourage*. While film credits like *Anal Cavity Search 6* may predominate on her current resume, she also can claim roles in Academy-Award-winning director

Steven Soderbergh's *The Girlfriend Experience* and in *I Melt with You*. She has co-starred with Hollywood mainstays like Rob Lowe and Jeremy Piven.

"What [Sasha Grey] has done is incredible," said adult industry performer-director Bobbi Starr. "Everyone knows that transitioning from adult to mainstream is not an easy task. She's done it and maintained a very authentic brand throughout it. She doesn't work in adult anymore, but it's not as if she is ashamed of her adult career or acts as if she only used pornography as a stepping stone. She has kept her integrity.

"I don't have an interest in becoming a mainstream actress," Starr continued. "My creativity stems from my writing. I would love to transition into making mainstream films as a director, maybe one day write a book and continue playing music. That's where I see myself going as far as mainstream goes. I believe the adult industry can be somewhat limiting, and I don't want to always be making a product that is designed for the sheer purpose of masturbation. Eventually I want to have kids, start a family, and I would prefer my writing, not my face, be in the public eye."

Starr's attitude about mainstream work is common among performers. In fact, it's a common misconception that those who work in adult do so only with the intent of one day crossing over into Hollywood. That's not always the case, according to Drake.

"I do a bit of mainstream work on the side when it is offered to me, but it's not something that I actively seek out," she said. "For instance, I did the Lady Gaga/Beyoncé [Knowles] video for 'Telephone.' That's because they called us and wanted me to come down and audition for it. That stuff is fun for me. I also did the Fox TV pilot for *Skin* and a feature-length movie called *Barry Monday*."

Drake also has dabbled in reality and daytime TV, if only to open minds about what actually happens in the daily life of a porn star.

"I did *The Tyra Banks Show*, and I was really nervous about it because she is scandalous," Drake said. "But in between takes she would look at me and say, 'Wow, you are not what I thought you would be.' In doing her show that day and inviting her camera crew to follow me around for 24 hours, which I had never done before because I feel that reality TV shows are intrusive, I felt that I could show people an accurate representation of what a day in my life looks like."

Nick Manning is an actor who might be well-known in the adult industry, but coming from a mainstream career and taking some time to gain notoriety in adult allowed him the opportunity to, interestingly enough, alternate between doing an adult magazine spread or movie one day, and the next day, flying off to another location to fulfill a mainstream contract.

Manning stated, "I always said that it took me five years to become an overnight sensation, so I could go on and do mainstream work and no one knew who I was. So I would do a magazine shoot and then I would go back to Miami and do Disney commercials."

Indeed, Manning gained much exposure as a male porn star via his time spent on *Howard Stern*. This in turn made people realize that he had been doing mainstream work prior to being in adult movies and allowed him more exposure in mainstream markets, growing his popularity. Manning is an interesting case, he went from mainstream, to porn, back to mainstream and has ultimately, settled on porn.

Sunny Leone, for as many mainstream opportunities she has had both in the U.S. and her native India, cannot picture herself ever leaving the adult entertainment industry. She thinks adult entertainment will always be part of who she is and whatever business in which she happens to be engaged.

"I have been in this industry since 2001," she said. "That's a long time. I know so much about my world that I don't see myself stopping what I am doing and pursuing another career. If an opportunity comes my way, I will consider it. [Mainstream work] is something I enjoy and a whole world that I think is fantastic. But I would not stop doing what I am doing to pursue it. There hasn't been a mainstream opportunity that would make or break my career.

"I've been on *Howard Stern*, VH1, MTV," Leone continued. "I was just in a sizeable film called *The Virginity Hit*. I had a cameo spot in *Middlemen* and *The Girl Next Door*. I have received so many mainstream offers even just over the past couple of months. There are some deals in the works right now, so knock on wood, the world might be watching me on mainstream television, and in India, too."

Even when a performer's career in adult isn't an issue, other factors can represent hurdles to crossing into mainstream work. Some Hollywood companies want to work with adult stars, but they want the women to use their birth names instead of the stage names around which they've built brands. In other cases, adult studios may place limitations on contract stars or their stage names.

The latter is the case with Digital Playground's Jesse Jane. Digital Playground owns the trademark "Jesse Jane," so the actress who is known by that moniker had to use her real name, Cindy Taylor, when she founded a mainstream tequila company by the name of Diosa, which means goddess in Spanish. Leone and Drake own their names, so they do not face the same challenge.

"If a mainstream job comes along and they don't like my name and want me to change it, that is not going to happen," Leone said. "My name is attached to my image, and people are going to know right away that the person on-screen is Sunny but there is a different name in the credits."

Imitation is the Sincerest Form of Flattery: Celebrity Sex Tapes

The private bedroom moments of Hollywood stars broadcast for the world to see. Oh the injustice! What an invasion of privacy!

Or is it?

After all, how can privacy be invaded if you broker the deal yourself?

Where would any number of celebutantes be without the release of their sex tape?

The first celebrity sex tape to really cause a stir in the mainstream press and in the industry was the Pamela Anderson and Tommy Lee sex tape. While it set off a media and consumer frenzy, certain industry professionals saw a potential goldmine in a brand new market segment.

"It was a whole new genre that was going to just be huge, and really, it was the beginning of the celebrity sex tape craze," Kevin Blatt, a celebrity gossip monger and sex tape broker said. "When the [Anderson-Lee tape] came out, people were still working on 28K modems. They would go to bed at night downloading this video, and when they woke up in the morning, a 30-second clip would be on their computer. I remember seeing it for the first time and thinking, 'Wow, this is something that we aren't supposed to see.' That tape changed the landscape on how we viewed celebrities and what we thought we had a right to see or access," Blatt added.

As the story goes, the Anderson-Lee sex tape had been stolen by a construction worker contracted to remodel the couple's house while they were away on vacation. The disreputable worker posted the pilfered goods on the Internet. Vivid Entertainment then acquired and marketed the video without permission from Anderson or Lee, sparking an epic legal battle Anderson and Lee eventually abandoned without acquiring the royalties they sought.

Rights to this tape started a phenomenon and in the intervening years Vivid can lay legitimate claim to the lion's share of celebrity sex tapes distributed in the United States.

Steven Hirsch of Vivid comments on his company's foray into the world of celebrity sex tapes. "Have all of the celebrity sex tapes that we marketed been profitable? No. Have certain ones? Yes. Ultimately, if we make an offer for a tape, we do it based on what we think we can generate off of it."

At the same time, celebrity sex tapes have also served as the launch pad for more than one star's career.

"None of us knew who the hell Paris Hilton was," Blatt recalled.

David Joseph, co-owner of Red Light District, was originally approached by a friend, who knew Rick Saloman. Apparently Salomon had indicated that he had a sex tape involving Paris Hilton, who he was involved with at the time.

"This was at about the same time that Rick [Salomon] had gone on *Entertainment Tonight* and said that he had a sex tape involving Paris Hilton," said Joseph. "He came to me and we had a discussion at my office. He wasn't sure what he was going to do with the footage, if anything at all. He wondered if there was a market for material like this and if so, would Red Light District be interested in doing a deal. I told him I was.

"I'm not sure how cool Paris [Hilton] was with the tape. Most movies do require [releases]," said Joseph. "I think she was nobody before the tape and I believe she became somebody because of [that tape]. It was an accident. Rick Salomon was looking at it from a financial point of view and also he liked that by [putting the tape out there] he could say, 'Look at me, I'm with Paris Hilton.'"

Joseph states that there is always a lot of careful preparation with a deal like this because at the end of the day, you "don't have the power or the money to fight with a family like the Hilton's."

He says that there is also a big risk/reward factor that is incorporated into the promotion of tapes like this.

One Night in Paris was the first foray into celebrity sex tapes for Joseph and Red Light District. But Joseph believes that it was also the first tape with an individual in it who was not a celebrity at the time, but who had the potential to be a celebrity because of the name they were associated with.

"When we got that deal and announced it after the contracts were signed, it was an overnight sensation, a phenomenon really. We did a press release and immediately after that we were in every single tabloid magazine and it was talked about on *Entertainment Tonight* and *Access Hollywood* and MTV. It was all over the world overnight."

Joseph says that by today's figures, it is reasonable to say that the Paris Hilton sex tape has sold over a million pieces since its release. He says that Internet piracy ultimately led to the tape's demise, but even so, the tape, as a whole, was an incredible success story for Red Light District and Joseph's career. Not to mention Paris Hilton's career.

As both a manufacturer and distributor, Kevin Beechum reflects on the celebrity sex tape business and how marketing these tapes set certain production houses apart from their competitors.

"[Vivid co-chairman Steve] Hirsch's best niche is getting the celebrity sex tapes," Beechum said. "I was offered the Pam and Tommy tape and the [Kim] Kardashian tape before it went to Vivid, and I turned them both down. I remember saying, 'Who the hell is Kardashian?' But [Hirsch] has carefully structured his company around both the acquisitions and promotions of celebrity tapes.

Steve Hirsch agrees that Kim Kardashian was relatively unknown when her tape came out, but that as a celebrity, or potential celebrity, Kardashian did have certain things going for her.

"People might not have known who Kim [Kardashian] was personally, but there was an interest in her father, Robert Kardashian, and his role in the O.J. Simpson trial," said Hirsch. "There was the Bruce Jenner connection. There was the Paris Hilton connection. There were all of these little connections that she had which were really touch-points for people. This gave the media something to ask about or speculate about. Even her mother, Kris Jenner, was out there a little bit. Obviously not like now. But the family was out there in a much quieter way. Then of course, there was Ray J. who she was in the video with and his sister was the singer Brandy. So we looked at all of these things when we were considering the tape."

Joseph goes on to state that if it wouldn't have been for Paris Hilton's sex tape, "there's no way that Kim Kardashian would have ever permitted her tape to come out. But she saw Hilton's success. If Paris would have been shunned by society and judged and never worked again because she did a sex tape, Kim would not have done it, and no one else would have done it. But the businessperson in Kim Kardashian looked at it as a business and examined how Paris' career catapulted out of that experience, and you can't argue that it didn't help her career. The same goes with Kim's career. That sex tape launched her career."

Hirsch states, "For the most part the [celebrity] comes to us because we know what we are doing and understand the exact process that we have to take with it. And I think that on the few occasions where the tape has not been marketed by [Vivid], there hasn't been as much success."

Personally, Blatt believes the glory days of celebrity sex tapes are over. According to him, people are more interested in seeing "what Lindsay Lohan had for breakfast that morning on *TMZ*, as opposed to watching Tila Tequila get banged by one of her girlfriends."

Alternatively Joseph believes that the celebrity sex tape business is a form of tabloid journalism, and in his estimation, is far from being over. Simply put, our society thrives on scandals and tabloids, and the fascination with what celebrities do behind closed doors will always be present.

"Sex sells," said Joseph. "It's always going to be popular with consumers because people have a fascination with celebrities."

According to Blatt, both men and women flocked to view Hilton's escapades. Men watched because they wanted to get off; women wanted to know if they could learn anything from her technique, or to check out the faces she made during sex. Even more interesting: Blatt said women checked out the tape to see what Hilton was wearing.

"There was a pair of boots that [Hilton] was wearing in the tape—they came up to her knee," he said. "The place in Hollywood that carried those boots sold out of them a week after the tape came out. And then [women] were checking out the bedspread, and they wanted to know if Paris shopped where they shopped. Well, the bedspread was courtesy of the Four Seasons [Hotel], so bedspreads weren't up in sales the next week.

The celebrity sex tape market has changed drastically since Pamela Anderson and Tommy Lee ignited a trend, however if there is one thing we have learned from the many celeb tapes on the market is that this market sector is a far cry from being accidental

Adult Technology in the Mainstream Markets

Technology is more prevalent in our lives than ever before, and mainstream businesses, just like adult businesses, depend on a variety of virtual platforms for staying in touch with clients and selling products.

It's not a coincidence that since the 1980s, the annual Adult Entertainment Expo (AEE) in Las Vegas overlapped with the Consumer Electronic Show (CES). In fact, the AEE was originally a part of the CES, with porn producers exhibited at the event until their own industry expo was created. Until 2012, the two immense trade shows shared space and a love of gadgetry, often cross-pollinating their respective markets and resulting in surprising tech adaptations in both realms.

In a 2008 *PCWorld* article, writer Dan Tynan outlined some of the technological innovations that arose in the adult industry, where according to Tynan developers weren't "hobbled by common sense, good taste, or bureaucracy." Tynan gave credit to the adult entertainment world for kick-starting the development of online payment systems, streaming content, live chat, traffic optimization, 3G mobile services and even broadband networks. At the same time, porn techies also can be blamed for more dubious innovations like spam-driven business (between 2001 and 2002, adult-oriented email marketing campaigns increased by 450 percent), malware, pop-up ads, and browser and domain-name hijacking.[35]

Neither all areas nor all members of the adult industry are tech-savvy, but the majority is astute enough to realize porn consumers are early adopters of new technology. Particularly insightful industry newcomers like Greg Clayman, Allison Vivas, and Greg Dumas were able to introduce technology to a stodgy giant, improve upon existing platforms, and then deliver their creations into the hands of mainstream business. Veterans like John Stagliano have mixed feelings about that.

"The competition that new technology [has brought to the industry] is something I did not feel prepared to deal with, because I have no skill set in that area," Stagliano said. Yet Stagliano eventually came to realize the industry's new tech-savvy blood brought as many opportunities as it did challenges—and since the adult industry in many cases got the jump on mainstream interests, adult businesses got to exploit the financial benefits first.

Clayman makes no secret of Video Secrets' mainstream ambitions. He sees a good fit between his company's sophisticated video-chat platform and mainstream's need for a human interface in the digital world. "There is not a business out there that cannot benefit from having their sales team interact face-to-face with their customer base," he said.

"We debuted our technology in the mainstream market by rolling out a new website called Psychics Live at the Affiliate Summit in New York City in July 2011. Currently, the psychic audio text industry is a $2 billion dollar industry, but on the Internet it is currently only $1-2 million, at most. It's untapped," commented Clayman. "We have taken everything we have learned and developed over the course of sixteen years in adult and interjected it into mainstream markets."

Video Secrets sees significant opportunity in mainstream markets, and it has nothing to do with psychic ability. Clayman and company think their technology is applicable in a variety of industries, although no one will comment about the specifics. Clayman does note that video streaming and conferencing technology would be of great use in the education and medical fields.

"Live video conferencing is not going anywhere," he said. "It's one of the most popular things to do online, and not just in the adult entertainment space. Think of Skype. If it weren't for what Video Secrets developed, that platform wouldn't have the traction it has today."

And it's not just videoconferencing that has gained leverage in mainstream markets after original development in the adult space. According to AEBN's Scott Coffman, the adult industry historically has been more accepting of and eager to work with radical, unproven technologies in order to sell products. "The [industry] has been at the forefront in figuring out how to work with VCRs, verifying credit cards online, affiliate marketing on the Web, Flash video technology. We are the ones who took these technologies and decided how to implement them in business. Once we did that, then mainstream companies decided to take what we did and inject it into their business models."

Because the adult industry has always been shunned by mainstream society, it's always developed its own solutions, many times by trial and error. Industry professionals understand they can't depend on traditional venues for answers. "This is where we are cowboys," Dumas said. "We figure it out for ourselves. Moreover, we have flexibility when we introduce a new product or tech service. Mainstream companies don't have that because they are slaves to market feedback."

Christian Mann agrees with Dumas' assessment. "I don't think we have some of the same constraints mainstream tech companies have, because if they roll something out and it backfires, they have to deal with the opinions from their shareholders and the public. [The adult industry] doesn't have that issue, because we can just change direction. We don't have to worry about public opinion."

From the Outside Looking in:
A Photographer's Look at the Industry

If the business of the industry has taught us anything, it's that just as much goes on behind the lens of a camera as happens in front of it. At the same time the industry is "mainstreaming" itself to gain wider respect and acceptance; mainstream professionals are looking to the industry for artistic inspiration.

Michael Grecco, a celebrity photographer who has worked for Apple, the Walt Disney Company, and *Time* and *People* magazines and has photographed Mel Brooks, Ben Stiller, and Steve Martin, became interested in the adult entertainment industry when he decided to publish a coffee table book and produce and direct a full-length movie entitled *Naked Ambition*. The 2007 book and film took an intimate look at 200 actors, filmmakers, and other personalities associated with the adult entertainment industry.

"For me, there was definitely a hook in looking at what might have some popular interest, and adult, whether it is agreed upon publically or not, generates huge interest," Grecco said. "There are a lot of people buying it and it's popular, regardless if people will come out and say they are interested in the industry itself. As a photographer, you need to do personal projects that go outside of commercial shoots and other assignments, so I thought [*Naked Ambition*] would be a great first independent project."

In 2002, Grecco received his first invitation to the AVN Awards show, which he compared to a Fellini movie because of the fantasy and outrageousness.

"What first struck me as a portraitist was this vast array of characters and people, and shooting those individuals who are all a part of the industry," he recalled. "The primary drive was artistic, but of course with any marketable project, you must consider the amount of people who would be interested in the final project."

Grecco already was familiar with many of the important players in the industry, as his wife worked in television and part of her focus lay in adult programming. Therefore, Grecco felt somewhat aware of the business side of pornography. But even with his exposure to and knowledge about the industry, he still received considerable pushback from individuals associated with the project.

"My book publisher [didn't really get the concept]," Grecco said. "They felt I either needed to be really hard core with my work or keep it really clean. They felt [the work] wasn't erotic enough and it wasn't vanilla enough. They didn't understand the concept I had because it was in the middle. It was edgy, but not so much so that it would offend. And maybe this strategy is where I went wrong."

The publisher's lack of understanding about Grecco's artistic perspective ultimately limited the finished product in both distribution and sales.

"[The book] was in-between," Grecco lamented. "It wasn't a book of erotic photography, but if I put an image of a naked transsexual in the book, then we are going to be met with pushback from the bookstores. Borders wouldn't carry it, but Barnes and Noble would."

Grecco's book emerged in a format that didn't suit the content. The images bore too hard an edge to make the product suitable as a traditional, mass-market coffee table book, and the coffee-table-book size of the volume made it unwieldy for a harder-core audience. True art connoisseurs and those who consider themselves social libertines would have no problem with Grecco's content. However, that group makes up a small market and does not constitute enough people to provide for mass market appeal.

"It was my first coffee table book, and ego was involved there," Grecco now says. "Maybe we should have made a more pocket-sized book, something that would not have been for display purposes, and maybe then it would have sold better. But I thought a coffee table book would ultimately assist in legitimizing the industry; that it wasn't just about pornography."

Even with confusion on behalf of the book publisher, Grecco did feel well received by the industry. The people he looked to partner with or photograph "got it." New Frontier Media, one of the few publically traded adult companies, sponsored the book shoot itself. Moreover, when Grecco started filming the performers in the comfort of his suite at the Adult Entertainment Expo, he realized many of his preconceptions about what adult industry professionals were flawed.

"[The performers] are a kind of dichotomy, and impressions are not formed at the exact moment you are working with someone," he said. "The one thing you realize is that these girls are competitive; they want to win. The other aspect is that these people have no inhibitions, meaning we would start a shoot not wanting anything sexual, but still, they would drop their clothes. We had to explain that was not what we were looking for."

Grecco said the individuals who seemed to get the concept were the ones who saw the bigger picture: They understood the book would be featured in the art section of Barnes and Noble, and it wasn't a foray into the world of erotica or sexuality. This realization, Grecco noted, was significant for many because performers are accustomed to being marginalized by society based specifically on sex.

"There were several people who were really a joy to work with, both on the promotion of the book and the film, and it's because they were such professionals," Grecco commented. "Sunny Leone and Joanna Angel were two of those people. Sunny went on *Howard Stern* with me, and Joanna is just a smart, strategic businesswoman. She got involved in the marketing of the book and the movie."

Although adult industry pros embraced the project, mainstream businesses remained confused.

"The ad agency we hired to promote the movie and the book really missed the mark," Grecco said. "I think that was because the person in charge of the account couldn't wrap his head around the subject matter. Pornography polarizes people, and the account manager insisted on debuting this material in the New York Review of Books and other art forums that are equally as polarizing. Maybe it made him feel better to promote the material this way, making it so highbrow that it was out of touch with the normal consumer. It did nothing to get this material to the buying public."

Grecco believes the industry is more mainstream than ever before, but the mainstream won't let go of outdated taboos. The everyday consumer is inured to porn stars and sex, and the adult industry as a whole is happy to work in mainstream markets, but traditional publishers, ad agencies and marketing firms struggle to be comfortable when marketing sex.

"The companies within the [adult] industry, I think, are much more well-adjusted and comfortable in their skin than many mainstream companies," Grecco said. "And it's not about being shameless; it's about saying, 'This is my company. I work in adult. I am driven, I am competitive, and I am going to sell my wares to you.

The interesting thing is, even with this mindset, the industry is struggling to survive. They have to figure out their own business model and figure out how to make people pay for their product again."

And that is The Eternal Question. Even as comfortable as contemporary adult businesses are with what they do, and taking into account how mainstream the industry has become, the question remains: How does an industry—historically a proud maverick—maintain its relevancy when it's no longer the black sheep? Where does the industry go from here? Onward and upward? Or is it time to go back to the drawing board?

PART NINE

Onward and Upward?
The Future of Adult Entertainment

So what's next? Where does the adult industry go from here? Does it have a future now that people are desensitized to sex in general? And if so, how will the future look?

I'm not sure there are any easy answers to these questions, especially now, in a time when the industry is losing money each and every day and the consumer can find nearly anything they want on the Internet for free. At the same time, it's a fact that the industry will never go away.

"The good news is people are still buying porn," said producer-director-performer Joanna Angel. "Porn can't end. But I think [adult industry companies] need to band together. We are trying to stay ahead of the curve. [Burning Angel] promotes quality, we engage the community, we have started live shows. We stay in touch with the members, asking what they like, what they don't like. We really try to do everything we can do to make our paying members happy; make a membership to our site something that is enjoyable."

Cheerleading about where the industry may be going is ceaseless, especially among the movers and the shakers, yet it doesn't exist in a vacuum. Underlying all the positive chatter is a current of unease and apathy, not least about the adult industry's ability to seize a leadership role in technological innovation once again. Some attribute the mixed feelings to a lack of community and an expanding gulf of mistrust between industry players.

"There was a time when we were all friends," said adult Internet pioneer Greg Dumas. "We might have been competitors, but we sat around and shared. Maybe you didn't share the tweaks you were doing, but you still didn't want to see anyone go down, because that would bring scrutiny to all of us. It's not that way now; it's all very cutthroat. That's a sign of the times. Back then, we were making big money and people were happier. Now people aren't making that kind of money, and they are a little more desperate."

There is a significant debate about what happens next, especially as the industry moves into the future. In the 1990s the industry was all about moving, morphing, and changing. New ideas abounded, and the opportunity within the industry seemed limitless. But times have changed.

"One of the main problems is that adult doesn't buy into innovation anymore, because mainstream has bought into the technology and they can push the envelope," observed AEBN's Scott Coffman. "And now with the Internet, it's hard to be first in anything anymore. Somewhere, the industry stopped trying to be better. An employee mentality was adopted."

Indeed, there are obviously some murky waters to navigate, but fresh ideas remain. Opportunity exists—one just has to know where to look.

"I think there is still promise," said performer Jessica Drake. "I have to believe that an industry as big as adult entertainment also has the ability to sustain itself in the future. As a whole, we just need to keep injecting new ideas into our business model."

Drake is right, and new ideas come from many avenues, addressing a variety of new delivery methods, piracy prevention, and the convergence of devices. While some industry pros sound cautious and doubtful in their analysis of the future, there's no denying a whole lot of brainstorming, creating, and developing is going on.

Steve Hirsch of Vivid Entertainment states, "When I look at the business going forward, there is so much opportunity. It's about the convergence of technology and how we are able to use it. Whether it's about making a TV a 24/7 video store or live models talking to you through your TV, there's a lot to be excited about. And Vivid is an 'acceptable' porn brand. People understand what they are dealing with when they decide to buy from Vivid. And people who don't buy into the new opportunity won't survive."

Porn Goes Mobile

If the Internet reshaped the world of the adult entertainment industry, the advent of the mobile generation sent it into a space race. The Internet changed the way people access information, and mobile devices such as smartphones and tablets have allowed even greater connectivity, putting the Internet in the pocket of 87 percent of the world's total population.[36] Juniper Research Group estimated in 2011 that adult content sold on mobile devices accounted for $3.3 billion worth of mobile sales. This is out of a total of $77 billion generated by the entertainment industry as a whole.[37]

However, if the adult community thought greater connectivity would lead to greater profits, it was mistaken. Some mobile technology companies are doing their darnedest to keep porn off their networks and devices.

It's no pop culture myth that Apple has been staunchly against its devices accessing any type of pornography. The late Steve Jobs, former CEO of Apple, pulled no punches about his desire to have the iPhone and iPad "porn-free."

Ever since the first iPhone debuted, adult entertainment purveyors have salivated over the idea of launching their own applications, or apps, on the lucrative and innovative handheld moneymaker. Alas, Apple banned porn apps from the wildly popular iTunes store—and tried to ban porn apps from the Apple platform altogether. Sneaky app developers who found a way for their products to gain access to the app store were smoked out and banished by the company, leaving adult producers standing on the outside looking in, wondering how they might someday, somehow be a part of the Apple juggernaut.

Jobs made no secret of his desire to create a family-friendly environment on Apple's ubiquitous software platform, but adult industry insiders decry the policy as hypocritical. After all, Apple's app store features games that promote guns, destruction, and violence, as well as apps that instruct about the *Kama Sutra* and sex positions. The iTunes store sells sexually explicit music. So, is Apple is really trying to be smut-free, or are Apple's in-house censors simply idiosyncratic in their moral policing?

"Maybe Apple will change their stance, now that my beloved Steve Jobs is no longer with us," lamented Dumas. "But then again, Apple is Apple. They have more money than Jesus, so who knows what's going to happen?"

Regardless the anti-porn stance taken by Apple, the company remains greatly admired by many within the adult community, as much for its innovation and technology as for the functionality the organization introduced to a new generation of consumers.

"Apple has done a great job," Dumas said. "I would buy anything they make. And they have changed how people think about music, about books. This is the type of innovation the adult industry has to follow."

Pink Visual CEO Allison Vivas agrees. "What I like about [Apple's] business model is that they have made their products about more than just a product. [Apple's products] are cool, they are fun, and that is what [Pink Visual] wants to achieve with our products. We are about more than just porn; there is an experience and innovation around what we do. The customer feels good about being a part of Pink Visual. But this is a long road; Apple didn't achieve what they did in a year."

While porn apps might be banned from the app store, Apple has no way to prevent a user from accessing an adult Internet site using his device's browser. And it is here where adult content producers have focused their efforts to attract mobile users.

Vivas encourages her group to champion innovation efforts that have broken the Apple barrier. Pink Visual frequently is highlighted in mainstream and adult media and trade shows as a visible, vocal agent of change. The company understands not only its own products and marketing goals, but also the products and marketing goals of companies like Apple, upon whose products Pink Visual relies for revenue.

"Any time there is a new communication or entertainment technology that comes out, we want to be the very first, if possible, to make our content available,"[38] said Quentin Boyer, Pink Visual's director of public relations.

Pink Visual didn't let Apple's porn ban stymie its development of mobile applications. The company figured out how to launch an app-style website dedicated to seamlessly delivering adult content for use on Apple devices. What's more, Pink Visual had an iPad-dedicated website ready to go exactly three days before Apple launched the iPad in 2010.

"We looked up all the developers' specs, and the programmer who was assigned to the project said, 'Yeah, I don't think there's a problem with getting this done. I can have this at 99 percent, and then the day the iPad comes out, we just have to get one so I can test it,'" Vivas revealed. "So we had someone pick up an iPad the day it came out, and on that Saturday, a few people came to the office, fixed a few things, and that was it. We launched it."

Pink Visual may have been first to develop a workaround for the Apple porn ban, but since the advent of the iPad many adult content producers have followed Pink Visual's lead. "Mobilized" websites specifically designed for use on the iPhone, iPad and other mobile devices are now an adult industry standard. The Pink Visual mobile website even offers an icon that can be placed on a mobile device's home screen, making the connection process look and perform very much like an app. Except it isn't.

"We have done this for all of our most popular websites," Vivas said.

Regardless, products like Pink Visual's branded PinkVisualPad.com are considered the way of the future in the adult industry. Results speak for themselves.

"We saw results right away," Vivas said. "As soon as Pink Visual Pad was released, I think we had over 15,000 visitors to the site on Day One. And it has continued to trend upward. Right now, we have over 200,000 visitors to the site on a daily basis."

Vivas also said the company was able to get some softer content into the iTunes app store before Apple tightened its restrictions and outlawed even mildly pornographic material.

"We could probably build an app very quickly and get it put in the app store, but that's quite an investment, and there is a lot of time involved in that process only to have the app discovered and removed after three or four months," she said. "We choose to make mobile-friendly websites instead until Apple revises its policy on adult applications."

But it must be stated, that just because some type of technology is new and different, doesn't mean it is going to contribute to the bottom line in terms of growth. Despite Pink Visual's success with mobile content delivery, Vivas is quick point out that not all new technologies contribute to an adult company's bottom line.

"We tried to do the same thing we did with the iPad to the Google TV product," she said. "[That effort] didn't have much bite. We should have asked around to determine popularity. You can ask who has an iPad, and people raise their hands. You can ask who has Google TV, and you get nothing. But then again, sometimes products surprise us."

Statistics indicate one-third of iPhone users regularly spend $100 more than other cell phone users on ancillary phone and data charges monthly. These numbers continue to rise, meaning the more products and services available to iPhone users; the more likely they will open their wallets.[39] Ultimately, mobile device users are proven purchasers. They regularly buy subscriptions and pay for applications and other account-focused services that enable them greater connectivity on their devices. Mobile users typically comprise the antithesis of traditional online porn consumers, who know how easily they can access a variety of material for free on their desktops and laptops. Mobile users understand—and even more important, accept—that in order to get the experience they desire, they are going to have to pay.

Castle Megastore's Mark Franks observed this trend in the brick-and-mortar novelty business, as well. "There are a ton of trends in retail markets that cross over into adult. The idea of packaging your materials for use on mobile platforms is big. Being able to scan bar codes and see if your pricing is competitive with industry-wide standards is very big right now."

At the same time Apple is staunchly anti-porn, rival devices based on Google's Android operating system aren't. Consequently, the Android porn app market is growing.

"Android is really starting to pick up a lot of the Apple market share," said Dumas. "The Android system is an open system, so in reality, you can do whatever you want. You can go download whatever porn app you desire. What's more, for developers who have a background in HTML5, the applications can be built quite easily. I have a lot of people who come to me who want to build these apps, to partner in new adult businesses around these products."

Pink Visual has developed an Android app that is available through the MiKandi Marketplace, an adult-themed online shopping destination that is censorship-free. The marketplace provides a platform for developers and distributors alike to publish and promote their wares, and tech industry analysts predict the platform will continue to grow and be profitable, at least until Apple drops its objections to porn apps.

"The mobile adult market has a ton of possibility, and as data access and connectivity continue to get cheaper and the networks get faster, the market will continue to grow and gain users, which only provides more revenue-generating opportunity for the adult industry," Dumas said. "I think this is one area where adult content producers and tech experts continue to be innovative. I think more mobile products are going to come out, along with advances in mobile billing. I see good things going on in the mobile porn market."

Preventing Piracy: Virtual DNA and Spidering Technology

While there may be some hand-wringing over online piracy, there is also a very proactive, and growing, group of industry pros who stand strong against those who would exploit or steal proprietary content. And they are making use of new technology to protect the material that rightfully belongs to them and others.

Virtual DNA, sometimes called digital fingerprinting, doesn't change the original content by inserting additional features like watermarks. Instead, virtual DNA uses software to identify, extract, and then compress individual characteristics of a video, thereby creating a unique digital fingerprint that can be used to identify the video should it be posted online without permission. The technology has proven highly effective, especially in combination with spidering.

Spidering technology employs software to track digital fingerprints and other markers in order to uncover copyright infringement and other content violations on websites and tube sites and in cyberlockers. Both types of software are supported by the Free Speech Coalition's Anti-Piracy Action Program (APAP), an effort to create an industry standard for combating online piracy, detecting violators and preparing lawsuits against those groups or individuals who would steal protected content.

"Virtual DNA and spidering technology will make online piracy that much easier to detect, stop, and prosecute," said Christian Mann. "It will make it that much harder for Tube sites and free sites to provide safe harbor to those individuals who would steal our products. These sites will no longer be able to hide behind their users and use the excuse 'we didn't know it was pirated.' Providing this data, this fingerprint, to the entire Internet community with the warning that if someone tries to upload content with this particular fingerprint on it that we will, as an industry, come after them" should make potential content reconsider whether content theft is worth the effort.

The technology has been particularly useful against copyright infringement on so-called tube sites—sites similar to YouTube, to which users upload content that is viewable by everyone. Most such sites are protected by "safe harbor" provisions in laws like the Digital Millennium Copyright Act, meaning site owners and administrators cannot be prosecuted for users' illegal behavior except in rare instances. Adult content producers estimate they lose millions of dollars each year to tube sites. Mann goes on to credit fingerprinting and spidering technology in bringing owners of tube and other file sharing websites together with legitimate adult businesses in ways that not only have kept the tube sites out of litigation, but also have produced new revenue streams for people on both sides of the equation. Typically, the tube sites receive affiliate revenue from the content producers, and the content producers benefit from the enormous amount of Internet traffic tubes sites circulate. Although not every tube site user makes a purchase after viewing a video clip, enough do that the relationship is reasonably beneficial for everyone involved.

The adult industry's APAP program makes it easy for tube site owners to comply with the letter and spirit of applicable law. First, APAP gives tube site owners free access to the digital fingerprinting databases, which allows them to monitor user-generated content without added expense. Second, APAP allows tube site owners to earn a percentage of sales when they replace infringing content with approved promotional material provided by the adult content producer whose work was pirated. And finally, partnership with APAP ensures compliance and minimizes the chances of being sued. This ultimate partnership between the APAP and tube site owners is one that assists adult producers and allows for greater efficiency through a standardized software system and protocol for dealing with pirated content.

"We pulled together some of the top performers in the industry," stated Diane Duke, "and we realized that a lot of the major players didn't know how to protect their content, or they couldn't afford the cost of purchasing [digital fingerprint and spidering] technology. So as a trade association, FSC went out there and negotiated a deal on behalf of the industry to bring this technology to adult content producers and distributors. We made it cost-effective for big and large studios."

On the mobile side, tech-forward companies like Digital Playground and Pink Visual have partnered with mainstream content identification platform developer Vobile, which also addresses piracy issues for Hollywood Studios and the Chinese Government. Vobile protects copyrighted mobile content by inserting portable, customizable code that works across device platforms.

Piracy is not likely to stop being an issue for the adult entertainment industry, but adopting a proactive line of defense and controlling technology and legal costs is certainly an organized step in the right direction. And that can only stand to benefit the industry in the future.

Making Money via Micro-billing

As the DVD market continues to shrink, adult producers continually seek new ways to make money, and many have looked to the iTunes model as a way to make online billing systems more appealing to Internet-savvy consumers' new mindset. iTunes revolutionized the way consumers purchase content by taking a dim sum approach to online sales: offer a wide variety of tiny products at tiny prices.

Micro-billing isn't a new concept, but it represented a sea change for the adult industry, which was accustomed to charging premium rates and delivering content according its needs and desires, not those of consumers. As micro-billing began to grow in mainstream markets, adult producers were forced to give more credence to an uncomfortable new approach.

"I think the iTunes model is going to replace [website] memberships," Dumas said. "People are getting tired of going to a website and spending forty bucks [a month] on porn, just as people were tired of buying an album to listen to one song."

The music industry gets the credit for starting the trend. When music trade association ASCAP (American Society of Composers, Authors and Publishers) wrestled Napster to the ground and then worked with the file sharing giant to create a way for artists to receive income from Napster users, the micro-billing revenue model bore fruit. Suddenly, consumers were able to pay a reasonable amount for their favorite song on a CD instead of buying the whole package at a price they felt unnecessarily high.

Of course, while this method provided an opportunity for money to be made within the music industry, it also dramatically decreased revenue of performers could expect to receive. Compared to what a music artist had been making when fans were required to buy the entire $18 CD, they now faced with a new reality: In order to make reasonable incomes at 99 cents per song, performers needed to produce more songs for which consumers were willing to pay. Their margins are much slimmer than ever before, the days of $18.00 full CD profitability are over.

AEBN was one of the first companies to incorporate micro-billing methods into their business platform, and Coffman states that he is quick to laugh when other industries become excited over new electronic or micro-product lines. For instance, a great example of this is the publishing industry's move towards eBook readers. He says sure the money is piling up right now, but there is going to come a time when publishers realize that the good old days are truly over.

"When an industry goes strictly electronic they do make money, but their profits decrease because of the lower overhead costs of the new technology mean a lot more people can enter the market," he said. "The profitability continues to decrease, because someone is going to figure out a way to charge even less for the product, or make it free all together. I want to say…you are going to be sorry!

"When [AEBN] started in micro-billing, my whole principle was pay by the minute," Coffman continued. "Our whole model starting out in [online video on demand] was 10 cents a minute. Consumers bought credits in bulk, and then spent them in micro-installments. That's where we made our money, and that's what other people started to copy. The adult movie model says most guys only watch for seven to ten minutes, so our thought was, 'okay, pay us 70 cents, instead of buying the entire movie for $14.95.' We built the entire company in micro-billing."

Christian Mann takes his assessment one step further, saying micro-billing is a byproduct of Internet culture, which is increasingly afflicted with attention deficit disorder.

"The video clip model promoted by Evil Angel is based on an ADD mindset," Mann said. "If you are sitting at your computer looking at porn, you probably aren't interested in watching an entire feature; you're looking for a quick fix. The gonzo material we tend to produce falls in naturally with the mindset and the micro-billing payment method."

Video distributors like Scott Field are not as enchanted with micro-billing, because the model which has significantly impacted his core business, video distribution.

"The micro-billing model isn't taxed. It needs to be, everything on the Internet needs to be taxed. What's more is that content producers started off charging too little. Instead of charging five dollars a minute, they started off charging five cents. There is no wriggle room here, there's no way anyone can charge more, so how do you create more value?" Field questions.

Micro-billing is indeed growing in popularity right now, but again, this could easily change as other technology rolls itself out, such as the convergence of technology. When adult entertainment is conducive across delivery platforms, will it grant new popularity to full-length features, or create an intensified ADD environment where consumers can easily access a variety of material, still a pennies for minute, on any device they currently own?

Deliverability across Platforms

No longer is adult content constrained to a single format. Today's consumers can get their porn fixes on DVDs, websites, mobile devices, and a wide range of direct-to-television platforms.

"There is no standard platform anymore, the way it was when people were watching a VHS tape on a TV," Coffman said. "Now you really have to be able to encode your movie in such a way that one click delivers it to any device, and that takes special programming."

Perhaps the best-known company to approach the multi-platform successfully is Netflix, which delivers Hollywood movies not only through the mail on DVD, but also via Internet streaming video to TVs, desktop and laptop computers, Xboxes, PlayStations and other so-called set-top devices. Netflix does not allow adult content producers to use its platform, nor will it promote adult material. This meant adult entertainment techies had to reinvent the wheel in order to give end-users the same sort of easy access to porn.

Many adult industry insiders see the continuing convergence of television and the Web as the biggest beacon of hope for the future. Obviously, the adult industry has had a home on both TVs and the Web for quite some time, but the Internet, with its vast array of programming, displaces more of the traditional audience for DVDs and pay-per-view TV every year. Most consumers now watch their porn on a computer, and that initially presented a bit of a conundrum: Who wants to sit at a desk to watch adult movies when it's so much more comfortable to lounge on a sofa or a bed and observe the action on a larger screen with better resolution?

The emergence of Internet-enabled television sets could represent another boon for the adult industry. Hooking a TV up to the World Wide Web offers the best of both worlds: the comfort and privacy of the bedroom TV and the vast selection available on the home computer. Come home from a day at the office, flip on CNN, check your email, and then surf over to your favorite subscription site like Pink Visual, AEBN, or Wicked and relax while your favorite performers...perform. Compatibility issues solved: The TV is the computer and the computer is the TV.

"When TVs and computers are the same thing across the board, you are going to see some revival in the adult marketplace," predicted Coffman. "Everything will be on-demand. There should never be a question about whether something is available to watch in either adult or mainstream programming. HBO already has gone the on-demand route; so have plenty of other networks. The whole TV world will go to an on-demand platform eventually.

"For the adult world, the convergence of TV and Internet is fantastic, especially from a marketing perspective," he added. "We get off the computer and we are back in the bedrooms. That's where this industry belongs."

Maybe so, but does that mean there is no downside to TV-computer convergence? What about the tube-site phenomenon that wrought havoc in the Internet space? When TVs and computers become one, won't tube sites and other free porn take an even bigger bite out of an industry already groaning under the strain of content piracy? What role will digital video recorders play in this brave new world?

Coffman believes consumers will record and store adult material on DVRs in the same way and for the same reasons they record and store mainstream programming now. The difference, though, is that in order to record the material in the first place, they will have had to purchase it at least once.

"You can record a movie that you get off pay-per-view and the distributor of that movie doesn't care, as long as they got their initial $8.99 from the purchase," he said. "The same goes with the adult industry. If you pay me for a $7.99 movie, I don't care if you record it and watch it forever. The important thing is making that first $7.99 sale."

The TV is still considered the entertainment center of the house and a variety of companies are trying to predict what the convergence of TVs and computers may look like when it finally happens. All of them want to be sure they're in the right place to capitalize on whatever develops.

"The Evil Angel marketing model is probably going to have to change when convergence happens, especially since our model revolves around clips," said Christian Mann. "It will be a game-changer really, because the feature companies will become more attractive, as their products are meant to be watched on a TV in the comfort of your living room or bedroom. So if you can access that through online means and watch it and be comfortable, there is going to be new profitability there."

Mann thinks there is a downside to convergence, at least where piracy is concerned, but he also believes the majority of the product produced by the adult entertainment industry is better viewed on a TV. Convergence will offer opportunities, but there are trade-offs at every turn: Production costs will go down because the DVD market will die, but profits may not rise because barriers to entry will shrink, allowing more players on the field. More consumers will be able to access adult content more conveniently than ever before, but free online porn and pirated content will be easier to access, too.

John Stagliano, though, sees reasons to hope. "Companies like AEBN are coming up with such spectacular ways to deliver content to consumers and I'm sure they'll figure everything out. My focus has always been on producing great material, and I just have to believe [AEBN] is going to continue to come up with innovative approaches for getting this material to consumers [profitably]."

Ultimately, TV-Internet convergence may provide a breath of fresh air to the adult industry. It offers the ability to create new products that not only appeal to computer and mobile users, but also a platform that allows for greater consumer interaction and comfort in the home. Moreover, convergence may provide the biggest economic opportunity the adult industry has seen in more than a decade, whether that comes in the form of new consumers, returning customers who can't resist the lure of better viewing, or greater mainstream acceptance.

Virtual Sex: Becoming Part of Porn

Many technology mavens within the industry believe the future is based on providing an interactive or virtual experience to the end user. Several companies are investigating ways to involve consumers in what so far has been the passive experience provided by commercial pornography. The most successful endeavors to date involve virtual sex toys and 3D or live-action products.

Steve Hirsch of Vivid Entertainment believes until mainstream technology develops glasses-free 3D presentation, there won't be any "significant adoption of the technology by the adult entertainment industry. When people watch adult movies, they want to take their glasses off, not put glasses on."[40] Indeed, the consensus is that when one is multi-tasking, it's hard to deal with accessories.

At the same time, Scott Coffman thinks content production costs play a role in the adult industry's hesitancy to adopt 3D technology: The majority of adult content producers simply do not have the budgets found in mainstream Hollywood.

"There is this idea that 3D is going to be huge in adult, but I don't think so," AEBN's Coffman said. "It might be the way mainstream movies are going, but really, adult companies don't have the multi-million dollar budgets required to shoot this level of film. It's tougher for them to shoot like this, even if the end user has the technology to watch it at home."

Pink Visual's Allison Vivas sees another problem: "The 3D aspect of pornography highlights certain areas of the male anatomy, that, at least from the perspective of a male viewer, viewers do not necessarily want to focus on when engaging adult content."

Instead of attempting to surmount 3D's limitations, AEBN has devoted resources to other areas where virtual products could find a footing with traditional porn consumers. Coffman and his crew believe there are other areas in which they can create an interactive environment without requiring hefty consumer investments in expensive technology like 3D home-viewing equipment.

AEBN's RealTouch product is part of that innovation. A virtual sex device for men, the product plugs into an AC power supply and a computer's USB port. Through a masturbatory sleeve triggered by special coding embedded in a video, RealTouch allows a male user to feel what is happening on the screen, replicating the sensations of sex. While RealTouch wasn't the first such device of its kind in the industry, AEBN's budget for marketing the product was much larger than other industry competitors.

"The concept of our RealTouch product is exciting to me," Coffman said. "It's interactive and takes that level of collaboration with the person on the screen up a notch. Now we are also developing these dildos for the cam girls to use so there is a two-way interaction. That is our big push. That is the way the industry is going: creating a live experience, because live cannot be substituted."

Susan Colvin of California Exotic Novelties agrees, "Technology has allowed us to make a more personalized experience. We can promote green technology through solar powered or USB devices. The amount of material that we ultimately use and how it is produced is so much better and it's being well-received by consumers."

Indeed, live products compose one of the areas with which the entire industry hopes to generate an economic turnaround. Live video streams cannot be pirated, and one-on-one interaction with consumers provides brand loyalty and encourages users to return for an experience that cannot be found anywhere else.

"[Kink.com] has focused a lot of time, energy, and money on the development of live products and other types of social networks to attract customers and also to prevent piracy," founder Peter Acworth said. "We are doing this because we are concerned about the long-term viability of recorded content."

Other companies, like Pink Visual, have even launched their own versions of sex simulation games during which users can play out fantasies with animated 3D men and women. The companies hope to expand their market shares by engaging traditional "game geeks," combining their love of video games with their love of porn. Erotic games allow users to become the director and star of their own sex scenes. Pink Visual's initial virtual sex game is free to enjoy; the company makes money by encouraging users to buy virtual accessories like outfits and body enhancements, or adding sexual positions or a kink module. Think of it as a kind of Dungeons and Dragons or Second Life, with sex. The game, a perfect fit for Pink Visual's motto "We innovate, you masturbate," is still a regular attendee of the Consumer Electronics Show and Vivas thinks that a focus on new and emerging technology into a symbiotic partner for porn.

Looking Ahead: The Insider's Opinion on the Future

Opinions vary widely about where the industry is headed and what may develop next. While some industry veterans mourn the good old days, newbies eagerly anticipate the next big thing. On one thing there is consensus: Nothing is certain anymore. Yet hope for the future isn't dead.

"It's hard to say where Wicked will be in the future," Vice President of Special Operations Joy King said. "Sometimes you think things will move quickly, but then they move slowly. I think we will continue to experience this gradual shift in how consumers see our content, and more of our business will go online. But at the end of the day, our core audience will continue to grow because we consider the female consumer to be incredibly important. And I think that idea is going to continue to serve us well into the future."

Wicked has long been considered one of the industry powerhouses, but whether the studio continues to thrive, only the future can tell. Studio owner Steve Orenstein thinks Wicked will grow, possibly even further into mainstream markets through a new personal care line that includes lingerie, lotions, lubricants, and other merchandise to be available in drug stores and other mainstream retail outlets.

"We have gone the sex toy route, and that did more harm to the brand than it did to help what we do," Orenstein said. "In order to be successful in the novelty space you need revolutionary ideas along the lines of We-Vibe, but we didn't have those ideas. But the personal care line we are getting ready to launch is designed to stand out. We understand that with DVDs going the route they are, we need to do something that still appeals to our base consumer: women and couples. This is a product line that makes economic sense, because I can purchase products made in the United States; I don't have to outsource to China."

Young guns like Allison Vivas believe a more defined fragmentation of the industry into small, relatively distinct segments are a positive thing, allowing sectors to band together with their contemporaries in order to address the challenges they all share instead of trying to get every adult company to march to the beat of the same drum.

"I wonder if there needs to be a redistribution of the industry, almost like the difference between Hollywood and television," Vivas said. "If there is an emergence of that type of distinction, where there are two markets—the TV market of porn, which might include Pink Visual productions, and then the Hollywood level of the market, which would have the big features put out by Digital Playground and Wicked—I think the consumer would be able to see the difference between the factions. I think this separation would help the industry address the problems that face us."

As an industry veteran, Susan Colvin believes that there is still plenty to look forward to and be excited about as it relates to the business of adult entertainment. "It's such a fun industry, it's an enjoyable business to be in, but a lot of that has to do with the consumers that we serve and the people who are on my team. I like coming to work and I feel a tremendous responsibility to the people who buy into my vision, and the customers who believe in what we do. Yes, the industry has been going through major changes in recent years, some changes may be viewed as negative, but there is also much positive change as well."

Colvin believes that the novelty industry itself will continue to evolve as technology improves while also continuing to address the need to deliver quality products to consumers.

Colvin states, "Technology is always going to allow us to present new options to consumers, but we also must earn the trust of customers. There was a time when products were not what they are today. Consumer confidence has been restored as novelty companies offer the quality and the assurance that mainstream companies deliver. For instance, offering a warranty and a guarantee on our products contributes to the customer experience."

Larry Flynt, as another veteran, feels as if he has seen it all and the future doesn't necessarily scare him. He said, "It's all going to be digital. Hustler publishing, I give it another two to five years, and it will be done. With our presence on the Internet, I feel that we can continue to be successful. It's important to perpetuate this in order to protect the brand. Just because we aren't making it on the newsstand, doesn't mean it's over. We have the retail stores, the broadcast division, and the online portion of our brand. Technology is changing everything and I saw that happening in the late 1980s and that is why I started to diversify."

On the other hand, veterans like John Stagliano worry the industry is losing its edge as technology changes and veterans themselves age. "I think my business model is vulnerable," he said. "I am getting older and frankly, I'm not as motivated to look at as much porn. What type of business has the ability to continue when the majority of the business owners are not driven to look at their product? They don't view it; they don't get off on the porn their studio makes. This is probably 80 or 90 percent of people on the traditional studio side of the business. For the time being, I am still a consumer of my product—some of it, but not all of it." As for managing the Evil Angel brand into the future, "It's not something I can do. Maybe I will find someone who is able to take it over. I have other projects and other things I am interested in."

In addition to the "graying of porn," social factors continue to shift, threatening the industry and shaping the landscape within which it operates.

HIV and other sexually transmitted diseases are always a hot-button topic. While regular monthly testing is a fact of life for the majority of performers within the industry, some outside the industry believe performers are playing Russian roulette with their health. That has become the latest battleground. In January 2012, based on a public controversy ignited by a highly vocal health-advocacy organization some say is politically motivated, Los Angeles Mayor Antonio Villaraigosa signed a historic law mandating male adult performers wear condoms while working on any project that requires a city film permit. Based on its apparent success in L.A., the health-advocacy group, AIDS Healthcare Foundation, vowed to take its condoms-required initiative statewide, lobbying California's Occupational Safety and Health Administration to strengthen its regulations. AHF already is considering a nationwide campaign.

At the time of this writing, California and New Hampshire are the only two states that specifically allow the production of sexually explicit material, and industry insiders wonder what will happen if Los Angeles—which encompasses the San Fernando Valley, home to the majority of adult film productions in the U.S.—embarks on a program of caving to special-interest groups and outlawing the adult industry bit by bit. As soon as the condoms-required law became effective, studios began contemplating moving somewhere else. An exodus could harm Southern California's fragile economy, but a bigger issue exists: If famously liberal California begins cracking down on the adult entertainment industry, to where would it relocate? After three decades in plain sight, the industry might be forced back underground.

"This is a case where CalOSHA is ultimately becoming a victim of the AIDS Healthcare Foundation, which is just a political group; the group doesn't combat HIV/AIDS," opined Evil Angel's Christian Mann. "It's a political organization parading itself around as a human welfare organization. CalOSHA doesn't want anything to do with this battle, if we are being honest, but they have been dragged into it by the AHF because of the complaints the organization made. Worker protections need to be in place, of course, but most regulatory schemes end up not achieving that ambition, creating other problems which are detrimental to business.

Here's a situation where you *do not* have the workers crying out for protection," he continued. "This is a case where the workers themselves are saying, 'We know what we are doing. Leave us the fuck alone.' Hysteria is being created about some very isolated cases [of HIV infection that could not be traced to the adult industry], and suddenly we're talking about a group of sexually active people having their behavior regulated—and not regulated privately."

According to Mann, condoms-required legislation could kill the industry. For the same reasons people watch blood-and-guts Hollywood fare—to serve fantasy and imagination—many pornography watchers prefer to see adult actors have sex "in the raw." Facing yet another hit to already dangerously sluggish revenues, adult entertainment producers might abandon long-embraced, voluntary codes of conduct that protect performers.

"Watch the business produce a product the public doesn't want, watch revenues decline further, and watch it be harder to enforce mandatory testing when certain facets of the industry go overseas [where current American industry best practices do not exist] or operate in secret," Mann said. "That will put everyone more at risk and hurt the industry as a whole."

Orenstein is not convinced the condom requirement is a deal-breaker for the industry. Wicked Pictures always has been a condoms-only company, and the studio has been successful since its inception in 1993. Still, he opposes condoms-required legislation.

"I know people don't go into stores looking for the 'condom section' when they are searching for an adult DVD, so I don't know if we have sold less movies because we do have that policy," Orenstein said. "I just don't think this can be regulated, though. It might put us in a better financial situation if everyone had to subscribe to this kind of regulation, but I don't think the government should have any role in regulating what our industry does. They have no idea how our business is run."

Social issues aside, adult entertainment always will be a controversial subject. Industry professionals have no desire to run roughshod over the rest of society, but they would like their opinions about social issues and economic factors that directly affect them to be heard and considered before politicians rush to install regulations based more on emotion than on fact. The results, they say, not only could be disastrous for the industry, but also could invoke the law of unintended consequences on a broader scale.

As things stand now, a perfect storm of outside influences has many inside the industry weighing their options.

"My work can stop any day now, especially with the recession the industry has experienced during the last few years, but I feel like I have always had one foot outside the door, looking for the next step," performer and director Bobbi Starr said. "If my work stops, if my DVD sales go down, if my website doesn't produce, what is my next step? I have a certain level of calm about my role in the industry because I know it's not my only option. And I really think that has had a lot to do with my longevity. I am not stressed about where my work is coming from or how I am going to earn money. I have peace of mind, which allows me to get along with people on-set and affords me a positive attitude."

Bruce Murison of We-Vibe, too, remains positive, embracing confidence about his company's future. Partially, that's because We-Vibe continues to solidify itself in markets outside the adult space. Planning is the key to long-term longevity, he believes.

"I think the sky is the limit for [We-Vibe]," he said. "We are going to continue our mainstream focus and produce high-quality toys. The world has responded to what we have done. And we are going to continue on our path."

His compatriot in the novelty business, JimmyJane's Ethan Imboden, also subscribes to the vision that either business model accommodate changes in the industry and the economic environment, or they don't. Attitude and adaptability affect companies' ability to thrive.

"I believe the people who understand their business and their audience is going to be the ones who are around in the future, just like in any other industry," Imboden said. "Those people who can't adjust or who are unable to realize times are changing and modify their businesses accordingly will go away. Adult business or mainstream company, if you can't jump on board with new delivery methods and ways of getting in touch with your customers, you will go out of business."

Whatever evolution takes place socially or technologically, the adult industry, in some form, always will be a part of the commercial landscape. Perhaps by subscribing to both traditional and industry-generated business models will allow adult entertainment to remain true to its maverick roots while continuing to mature. Indeed, today's adult industry does seem to be able to throw on a business suit in the morning, even if that suit is paired with clear acrylic heels.

"I think the industry will always be the black sheep," Free Speech Coalition Executive Director Diane Duke said. "We will be the rebel, and I think that is appealing to the majority of people who choose to work in adult, on all levels—in front of the camera, behind it, in the studios. But the industry has grown up; we work on a much different level than we did even ten years ago. I think you will continue to see a level playing field develop between the industry and big mainstream businesses. But we will keep our originality and all of those factors that make us unique."

On a broader scale than the layer cake analogy employed earlier indicated, the adult industry could be considered a buffet: full of flavor, full of variety and with the promise there is always more where the tastiest bits came from. Composed of people who believe in what they do and in the product they produce, individuals who believe in the staying power of sexual consumerism, the role that the industry is responsible for in the defense of free speech, a bounty of opportunity will continue to be found in adult entertainment.

"The adult industry isn't going anywhere," said Sunny Leone. "We are changing, and I think the people who are going to matter in this industry are getting smarter. There is a realization you can't do the same things that have worked in the past in order to get new or improved results. The average consumer might think we are just about sex, but there is a lot of brainpower present in the industry as well."

"For so long, it was difficult to get people to accept [adult] as a real business," stated Steve Hirsch. "Acceptance was hard and getting people to understand that we weren't a bunch of guys in gold chains sitting around smoking cigars and taking advantage of girls was tough. But progress has been made and we are now viewed, primarily, as something normal and an industry to be reckoned with. And that is positive to me. Vivid is going to stay focused and continue to run a clean, honest business."

Pornography, broken down to basics, is simply the business of sex, satisfaction, aesthetics, and fantasy. It has been present throughout human history and continues to develop in modern times. The product is part of pop culture and has social meaning, appealing to our most basic biological urges. But the industry itself is a multi-dimensional economic engine that creates jobs, generates profit, and "thinks outside the box." Non-conformity is as important to the future as an ability to appeal to mainstream markets.

As much as adult entertainment is like any other business, it is also different. The differences drive progress and attract consumer attention, for better or worse. Both the similarities and the differences influence how well adult entertainment, as a viable commercial endeavor, will stand the test of time.

After all, sex—in a surprising variety of ways, shapes, and forms—is one thing that will always interest people. They can't stop thinking or talking about it. Sex sells, it entices, excites, and fascinates. There's no way around it.

Afterword

Where We Go From Here

It's a bittersweet thing, the way I think about the adult entertainment industry. On one hand, I have a distinct appreciation for the business and the people who work within it. On the other hand, it's impossible not to worry about the future, no matter how much promise I feel the industry has.

I hope this book has proven many things, first and foremost that the business of sex is a business, and it's about much more than something as simple as sex on a screen. Moreover, it has been my desire to illustrate that the people who work in this business are the utmost professionals, with distinct ambitions and goals that so many times are not highlighted by the mainstream media. I not only believe the people who were interviewed for this book are incredibly savvy and fantastic at what they do, but I also have the highest regard for the way they conduct business and the personal and professional dedication they exhibit each and every day.

I must thank those who gave their time and provided their unique points of view to this text. During my tenure in the adult entertainment industry, I was able to call the people featured in this book business colleagues, and more importantly, friends. I am very proud of the relationships I formed.

Of course, as much as I am thankful for the unique insight expressed on these pages, I also am aware that not all of it is positive.

As diverse as my feelings are about the adult business, I knew before I started that I would get a variety of feedback from the interviews. But I think what is on these pages is very honest.

The adult entertainment industry has a colorful and complicated past, and I have no doubt about its future, as well, even though I also understand that the future of the business is incredibly uncertain.

The late Steve Jobs once said, "You can't connect the dots looking forward; you can only connect them looking backwards. So you have to trust that the dots will somehow connect in your future. You have to trust in something—your gut, destiny, life, karma, whatever." I think those words fit the adult entertainment industry quite well.

There is no real way to predict what will happen in and to the adult industry, although there might be some models with potential relevance. Just like any other business, it's impossible to say "this is what will happen tomorrow." You simply have to hope that the business decisions which are made today pay off tomorrow.

I think the adult industry faces more threats than other businesses, both internally and externally. Under fire by social and advocacy groups as well as state and federal governments, the industry has not only regulation to worry about, but also the impact that changing technology and an ever expanding market have on the business. What's more, while the consumer base has continued to grow and the belief that "porn will never go away" has stayed strong, the mixed blessing of technology has taken a once valuable commodity and decreased the price tag to nil.

Adult entertainment has been a benefactor of technology, there's no denying that. Because of human demand for the material it produces, the industry often has been at the forefront in technology development. But somewhere along the way, technology accelerated. As we have discussed, the explosion of the Internet affected, and continues to affect, the adult entertainment industry in ways nobody could have predicted based on technological developments of the past. The way things look now, technology may continue to go faster and faster, causing more profound change in the adult entertainment industry and mainstream markets.

Ray Kurzweil's Law of Accelerating Returns states that the rate of change in evolutionary systems, including that of technology, increases exponentially. Essentially, once progress commences, the speed at which it continues accelerates. Therefore, if a barrier to one form of technology is presented, a new technology will be invented that will breach or eliminate that barrier—and the breach or elimination likely will arise more quickly than the barrier did.

It's interesting to think about this theory as it relates to where the adult entertainment industry is headed. Kurzweil believes the Law of Accelerating Returns has been in place since the beginning of time, adding untold layers of complexity as life forms evolved. The more complex an entity becomes, the faster it morphs in order to increase efficiency and ability.

Kurzweil also believes we are headed towards a form of technological singularity, which he predicts will occur before the end of the 21st century. "An analysis of the history of technology shows that technological change is exponential, contrary to the common sense 'intuitive linear' view," he wrote in 2001. "So we won't experience 100 years of progress in the 21st century—it will be more like 20,000 years of progress (at today's rate). The 'returns,' such as chip speed and cost-effectiveness, also increase exponentially. There's even exponential growth in the rate of exponential growth. Within a few decades, machine intelligence will surpass human intelligence, leading to the Singularity—technological change so rapid and profound it represents a rupture in the fabric of human history. The implications include the merger of biological and non-biological intelligence, immortal software-based humans, and ultra-high levels of intelligence that expand outwards in the universe at the speed of light."[41]

Now, you probably are wondering how I tie this back to the adult industry. Essentially, technology has progressed so rapidly within the adult space in the past thirty years or so, and even faster if we consider the last ten years as technological advances have taken root. Now consider the roadblocks that have appeared and the solutions presented not just to keep up, but to forge ahead. I believe the advances in the adult entertainment industry in coming years are being developed today, both within and outside of the industry. And of course, while there is a lot of hypothesizing over what may come next, I feel we don't have the technology today to build the sexual devices and pleasure systems of the future, but the plans to develop and create that technology are in the works. If we apply the principles of the Law of Accelerating Returns, we are able to predict, on some level, what the future may hold for the industry, as the barriers that are faced today will have solutions presented to crest those walls tomorrow.

As you can see, I am a big believer in the power exhibited by the information technology field, and I am an even bigger believer in the adult industry's ability to succeed through the use of these remarkable tools. While technology might require the industry to be open to constant morphing and evolving as a community, I feel like this is good for business. It forces us, as a whole, to get better, even while making some individuals and companies fall by the wayside as changes are applied.

Exponential growth in the technology arena will continue to impact the industry. Just look at the technological changes that have happened in adult entertainment over the past twenty years. We have travelled from adult movie theaters to the convenience of VHS in our bedrooms; from interactive DVDs to live, one-on-one chats via streaming video on our computers. The change is revolutionary, and it continues to become more and more personal. It's not farfetched to think that eventually, the experience provided by adult entertainment someday will become even more "at one" with consumers: a type of direct synergy or cross-pollination of adult content or stimulation with humankind. It might sound like science fiction, but I think the reality of an adult entertainment computer chip will become a reality, at least within the next 25 years. Imagine a nanocomputer in your bloodstream that allows a type of sexual stimulation not even conceivable today.

Nanotechnology is already in the works. The biomedical community, as well as other industries, is interested in discovering how conditions like disease, genetic mutation, old age, and other debilitating conditions could be re-programmed and eliminated from the lives of humans. It is only natural to think that if this type of technology could be used for the sake of science, medicine, and human longevity, it also could be used for sex and pleasure. After all, there are few things more biologically basic than the sexual urge, so why wouldn't the industry be involved in this type of technological advancement? Although sexual nanobots might sound like something out of a sci-fi movie or novel, if you consider what an orgasm is, how it is triggered, and how the brain and nervous system respond to sexual activity, it's not that far-fetched to think responses could be manufactured and custom tailored to fit the needs or desires of a consumer.

All in all, I think the "means to an end" that is achieved through current adult entertainment will continue—it's just going to continue to become more technologically focused. Instead of being visually driven, adult entertainment might be bio-centric. I suppose you can call me a futurist.

There is still so much promise within the adult entertainment industry. I am one of those people who always has been intrigued by what technology can provide to the industry, and I am optimistic enough to believe there is limitless opportunity for continued expansion and ingenuity when the adult community sees technology as an opportunity for advancement, instead of a challenge, barrier, or roadblock. What's more, I am encouraged by the members of the adult community. I think their individualism, drive, and outside-the-box thinking will pave the way for future success.

I can say with some level of certainty that I believe the best days are not behind us, but ahead of us. Sex is sex, but the adult entertainment industry and its very colorful and fascinating members will continue to find ways to make that most basic of biological functions into a paying, and profitable, business.

Footnotes

[1] Schulz, M. (2005, April 4). Sex in the Stone Age: Pornography in Clay. Spiegel Online International. Retrieved May 29, 2011 from:
http://www.spiegel.de/international/spiegel/0,1518,350042,00.html

[2] Slade, J. W. (2001). Pornography and sexual representation: Volume 1. Greenwood Press: Westport, Connecticut.

[3] Franklin, B. (1745). Advice to a young man on the choice of a mistress. Retrieved June 1, 2011 from: http://www.swarthmore.edu/SocSci/bdorsey1/41docs/51-fra.html.

[4] Franklin, B. (1745). Advice to a young man on the choice of a mistress. Retrieved June 1, 2011 from: http://www.swarthmore.edu/SocSci/bdorsey1/41docs/51-fra.html.

[5] Chansanchai, A. (2008, February 13). Sex toys: The ultimate in hardware? MSNBC.com. Retrieved May 24, 2011 from:
http://www.msnbc.msn.com/id/23128830/ns/technology_and_science-tech_and_gadgets/t/sex-toys-ultimate-hardware.

[6] Lynn, R. (2004, September 24). Ins and outs of teledildonics. Wired.com. Retrieved May 23, 2011 from: http://www.wired.com/culture/lifestyle/commentary/sexdrive/2004/09/65064

[7] Pornography industry is larger than the revenues of the top technology. (2010, January 1). Cy.Talk News Blog. Retrieved May 25, 2011 from: http://blog.cytalk.com/2010/01/web-porn-revenue.

[8] Pornography industry is larger than the revenues of the top technology. (2010, January 1). Cy.Talk News Blog. Retrieved May 25, 2011 from: http://blog.cytalk.com/2010/01/web-porn-revenue.

[9] Pornography. (2010). U.S. Legal. Retrieved May 24, 2011 from:
http://internetlaw.uslegal.com/pornography.

[10] Pornography. (2010). U.S. Legal. Retrieved May 24, 2011 from:
http://internetlaw.uslegal.com/pornography.

[11] Miller, M. (2005, July 4). The (Porn) Player. Forbes.com. Retrieved July 14, 2011 from:
http://www.forbes.com/free_forbes/2005/0704/124.html.

[12] U.S. Hardcore Pornography Titles Released. Grab Stats. Retrieved from:
http://www.grabstats.com/statmain.asp?StatID=175.

[13] U.S. Adult Video Sales and Rental Units. Grab Stats. Retrieved from:
http://www.grabstats.com/statmain.asp?StatID=174.

[14] 1996-97 Adult Video Rentals and Sales in Local Video Stores Break All Previous Records. Retrieved from: http://www.thefreelibrary.com/1996-97+Adult+Video+Rentals+And+Sales+in+Local+Video+Stores+Break+All...-a019999641.

[15] Pornography, Obscenity and the Law. (n.d.) Retrieved from: http://civil-rights.lawyers.com/Pornography-Obscenity-and-the-Law.html.

[16] Reed-Ward, P. (2009, January 25). Obscenity case begs question: Whose standard? Retrieved from: http://www.post-gazette.com/pg/09025/944328-52.stm.

[17] Richtel, M. (2008, June 24). What's Obscene? Google could have an answer. NY Times. Retrieved from: http://www.nytimes.com/2008/06/24/technology/24obscene.html

[18] http://www.newscientist.com/article/dn16680-porn-in-the-usa-conservatives-are-biggest-consumers

[19] Hsu, S.S. (2010, July 17). U.S. District judge drops porn charges against video producer John A. Stagliano. The Washington Post. Retrieved August 2, 2011 from: http://www.washingtonpost.com/wp-dyn/content/article/2010/07/16/AR2010071605750.html

[20] Rainwater, L. (1974). Social problems and public policy: Deviance and Liberty, p. 143.

[21] Tatalovich, R & Daynes, B.W. (1998). Moral controversies in American politics: Cases in social regulatory policy, 2nd ed.

[22] Linz, D., Donnerstein, E., Penrod, S. (1987, October). The findings and recommendations of the Attorney General's Commission on Pornography: Do the psychological "facts" fit the political fury? American Psychologist, 42 (10), 946-953.

[23] Slade, J.W. (2001). Pornography and sexual representation: A reference guide. Volume 1.

[24] Slade, J.W. (2001). Pornography and sexual representation: A reference guide. Volume 1.

[25] Hsu, S.S. (2010, July 17). U.S. District judge drops porn charges against video producer John A. Stagliano. The Washington Post. Retrieved August 2, 2011 from: http://www.washingtonpost.com/wp-dyn/content/article/2010/07/16/AR2010071605750.html

[26] Abowitz, R. (2010, July 12). The Trial of John Stagliano. Reason.com. Retrieved August 5, 2011 from: http://reason.com/archives/2010/07/12/the-trial-of-john-stagliano/1.

[27] Obama's porn king at Justice. (2009, March 18). The Washington Times. Retrieved from: http://www.washingtontimes.com/news/2009/mar/18/obamas-porn-king-at-justice.

[28] Aune, S.P. (2010, June 26). Porn Domain Names Inch Closer to Reality. TechnoBuffalo. Retrieved from: http://www.technobuffalo.com/internet/porn-domain-names-inch-closer-to-reality.

[29] Hachman, M. (2011, March 17). Update: Adult Industry Protests .xxx domain. Retrieved from: http://www.pcmag.com/article2/0,2817,2382185,00.asp.

[30] Hachman, M. (2011, March 17). Update: Adult Industry Protests .xxx domain. Retrieved from: http://www.pcmag.com/article2/0,2817,2382185,00.asp.

[31] Karlinsky, N. (2010, February 11). Porn in the Digital Age: Why Pay? Retrieved from: http://abcnews.go.com/Nightline/porn-industry-struggles-free-content-piracy/story?id=9795710.

[32] Chiang, O.J. (2009, August 5). The challenge of user-generated porn. *Forbes.com*. Retrieved from: http://www.forbes.com/2009/08/04/digital-playground-video-technology-e-gang-09-ali-joone.html.

[33] Swartz, J. (2010, March 2). Free porn on 'tube sites' puts a big dent in industry. USA Today. Retrieved from: http://www.usatoday.com/tech/news/2010-03-02-porn02_ST_N.htm.

[34] Swartz, J. (2010, March 2). Free porn on 'tube sites' puts a big dent in industry. USA Today. Retrieved from: http://www.usatoday.com/tech/news/2010-03-02-porn02_ST_N.htm.

[35] Tynan, D. (2008, December 21). Thank you porn! 12 ways the sex trade has changed the web. PC Word. Retrieved from: http://www.pcworld.com/article/155745-3/thank_you_porn_12_ways_the_sex_trade_has_changed_the_web.html.

[36] Global mobile statistics 2012: All quality mobile marketing research. Retrieved from: http://mobithinking.com/mobile-marketing-tools/latest-mobile-stats.

[37] Reardon, M. (2007, February 26). Red-light district on a tiny mobile screen. CNet. Retrieved from: http://news.cnet.com/Red-light-district-on-a-tiny-mobile-screen/2100-1039_3-6161930.html.

[38] Pappas, S. (2010, October 11). New technologies let pornography producers stay on top. TechNews Daily. Retrieved from: http://www.technewsdaily.com/1329-technology-pornography-online-sex.html.

[39] Caplan, J. (2008, June 18). The iPhone's next frontier: porn. Time Business. Retrieved from: http://www.time.com/time/business/article/0,8599,1815933,00.html.

[40] Berman, J. (2012, February 7). Adult Entertainment Industry awaits glasses-free 3D. Consumer Electronics Daily. Retrieved from: http://consumerelectronicsdaily.com/Content/Porn-companies-stil-split-on-3D.aspx.

[41] Kurzweil, R. (2001, March 7). The Law of Accelerating Returns. Retrieved from: http://www.kurzweilai.net/the-law-of-accelerating-returns.

www.ingramcontent.com/pod-product-compliance
Lightning Source LLC
Chambersburg PA
CBHW031921190326
41519CB00007B/367